PRAISE FOR *DON'T BLAME MOTHER:*

"A valuable book."
—Los Angeles Examiner

"Eye-opening."
—Boston Globe

"*Don't Blame Mother* is intelligent, well-written, and vigorous. As an experienced clinician, Caplan alternates between careful listening, offers of insight, education, and encouragement."
—Journal of Women & Therapy

"Essential reading for every woman who has ever felt the love and pain of difficult interactions with her mother. Written with equal sensitivity and respect toward both mothers and daughters, this refreshingly hopeful book presents a major innovative contribution to our understanding of women's relationships within the family in the context of today's society."
—Rachel Josefowitz Siegel, M.S.W.,
co-editor of *Women Changing Therapy*

"I would recommend this book to every man who has a mother he has ever slighted or contemptuously dismissed. Paula Caplan's book made me do an emotional double-take to face the...fact that I truly loved my mother, and for good reason."
—Jeffrey Moussaieff Masson, author of *The Assault on Truth*

Don't Blame Mother

Mending the Mother–Daughter Relationship

Paula J. Caplan, Ph.D.

For Nancy
In sisterhood —
Paula J. Caplan

PERENNIAL LIBRARY

Harper & Row, Publishers, New York
Grand Rapids, Philadelphia, St. Louis, San Francisco
London, Singapore, Sydney, Tokyo, Toronto

Portions of this book were taken or adapted from Paula J. Caplan, *Between Women: Lowering the Barriers* (Toronto: Personal Library, 1981).

Material from *The Prince of Tides* by Pat Conroy is reprinted with the permission of Houghton Mifflin Company. Copyright © 1986.

A hardcover edition of this book was published in 1989 by Harper & Row, Publishers.

First PERENNIAL LIBRARY edition published 1990.

The Library of Congress has catalogued the hardcover edition as follows:

Caplan, Paula J.
　　Don't blame mother: mending the mother-daughter relationship/Paula J. Caplan.—1st ed.
　　　　p.　cm.
　　Bibliography: p.
　　Includes index.
　　ISBN 0-06-016102-7
　　1. Mothers and daughters.　2. Women—Psychology.　3. Motherhood—Psychological aspects.　4. Intergenerational relations. I. Title.
HQ755.85.C355　1989
306.8'743—dc19　　　　　　　　　　　　　　　　　　88-45890

ISBN 0-06-091697-4 (pbk.)
90 91 92 93 94 FG 10 9 8 7 6 5 4 3 2 1

For my parents,
Theda Ann Karchmer Caplan and Jerome Arnold Caplan,
and my children,
Jeremy Benjamin Caplan and Emily Julia Caplan,
with all my love

❦ Contents

🍓 *Acknowledgments*

A BOOK LIKE THIS cannot be written in isolation. I was blessed to be able to write it from within a rich web of relationships.

I want to thank my agent, Connie Clausen, and her assistant, Guy Kettelhack, for setting me on the road to writing this book, and my editor, Janet Goldstein, for her brilliant, thoughtful, and painstaking work in helping me learn how to write this kind of book. Thanks also to Guy for keeping my spirits up when the going got rough.

My gratitude goes to many other people who have helped in various ways—to the memory of my maternal grandmother, Esther Shana Milner Karchmer, and to my paternal grandmother, Gertrude Dorothy Gorbach Caplan, for their love, their stories, and their inspiration; to my children—Jeremy and Emily, my parents—Tac and Jerry, and David Friendly, for their love, support, patience, and involvement in many ways in the writing and editing process; to Rachel Friendly for her sweetness and moral support; to Graham Berman, Catherine Gildiner, Rachel Josefowitz Siegel, and Betty Jane Turner for carefully reading and sensitively commenting on the entire final draft; to Susan Gilbert Carrell, Jennifer Chambers, Debbie Friendly, Lily Friendly, Margaret Grant, Donna Sharon, and Wendy Whitfield for reading and commenting on sections of the book; to Joan Mayer Caplan, Phyllis Chesler, Gilda Freeman, Harold Friendly, Marilyn Friendly, Maureen Gans, Amy Hanen, Maria Matias, Kathryn Morgan, Frances Newman, Heather-jane Robertson, Jan Silverman, and Janet Surrey for

🍎 *Acknowledgments*

providing warmth, suggestions, and helpful information; to my secretary, Julie Fung, for her kindness and her help with the typing and administrative work; to Chris Devon, Frieda Forman, Peggy Bristow, and the library staff at the Ontario Institute for Studies in Education, for help with the references; to Carola Barczak and Daria Love for teaching me how to keep up my stamina; to Janet Stickney for allowing me to use the title of her wonderful *Don't Blame Mother* conference as the title of this book; and to the students in my courses on "Mothers" and my other women's studies courses, as well as the many other friends, patients, and former strangers who allowed me to interview them or who wrote to tell me their stories for this work. I also want to thank my family and friends for their patience in the face of my limited availability while I was involved in this project.

Since I failed to know my mother, I was denied the gift of knowing the other women who would cross my path.

—Pat Conroy, *The Prince of Tides*

1 ❧ Getting Started

How are we to be the mothers we want our daughters to
have, if we are still sorting out who our own mothers are
and what they mean to us?
　　　　　　　　　　　　　　　—Letty Cottin Pogrebin

[In the story of mothers and daughters] the plot is not
entirely of our own making. We may be free to unravel the
tale, but we have not been free to create the social relations
upon which it is based.
　　　　　　　　　　　　　　　　　—Marcia Westkott

YOU'RE READING A BOOK called *Don't Blame Mother*, so
chances are, no matter how sad, upset, or angry you are at your
mother, you'd rather improve your relationship with her than
simply stay upset. This book is an offering to you, to let you know
what has helped other mothers and daughters resolve their difficulties.

If you're busy blaming your mother or wishing you could "divorce" her, you are caught in a psychological prison. You can't
get free, and you can't really grow up. There are practical problems. For example, you dread family parties: Your mother might
not like what you're wearing. Or she might love what you're wearing and say to everyone, "Doesn't my daughter look gorgeous?!"
—and you'd be mortified.

That kind of practical problem is a symptom of the fact that
mother-blame limits your freedom: You can't be an adult who
freely considers all of life's possibilities. You restrict yourself to
certain activities, interests, and friends in order to prove how
different from Mother you are. You can't look honestly at who *you*
are, because you might discover ways that you are like her! Frantic to avoid what you consider her failures, you overreact, throw-
ing out the good with the bad: You grow tough because you think

she's sentimental, or you become a doormat because she wasn't warm enough. All that reaction *against* her, that desperate drive to prove your difference, restricts and damages your relationships with the other people you love—your mate, your children, your other relatives, and your friends. You offer them only a part of your true self, a caricature.

ANGEL-IN-THE-HOUSE OR WICKED WITCH?

If you feel sadness, irritation, anger, or even outright fury toward your mother, I suggest that you stop right now and let yourself experience it. Look at it. Cry. Scream. Hit pillows. Make a list of the five worst things she's ever done to you. Then consider this: The biggest reason daughters are upset and angry with their mothers is that they have been *taught* to be so.

Most women sincerely but mistakenly believe that anguish in their relationships with their mothers is inevitable because their mothers are so limited, so dependent, or so terrible. Largely unaware that our culture's polarized mother-images create barriers between mothers and daughters, we have held each other responsible.

Mothers are either idealized or blamed for everything that goes wrong. Both mother and daughter learn to think of women in general, and mothers in particular, as angels or witches or some of each. Our normal, human needs, feelings, and wishes are distorted in ways that erode our relationships by making us expect too much of each other and by making us exaggerate the bad or mistake the neutral and positive for negative. As many mothers and daughters admit, one minute they can overflow with love and admiration for each other, thinking of each other as positively perfect, and the next minute they can be overwhelmed with rage and contempt.

The polarized images have long and complicated histories. In part, in our predominantly Anglo-American culture, for instance, the idealized ones stem from our heritage from the Victorian era, when the mother was supposed to be the "Angel in the House" who soothed husband's and children's tired feet and fevered brows, spoke sweetly and gently, and considered meeting their needs her life's mission.

The "Wicked Witch" mother-images familiar to most of us come partly from fairy tales about horrid women. Although they're rarely called mothers, they are often stepmothers or characters who harm children while filling mother-type roles, like the witch in "Hansel and Gretel" who lures the children with food, or the horrid stepmother who appears in motherly guise and offers (poisoned) nourishment to Snow White.

Both extremes cause trouble: How *can* you have a relationship with a perfect being who's way up on a pedestal, but who would *want* to get closer to a person you believe caused all your problems? Even without these images, other problems in mother-daughter relationships would still exist—such as problems of communication, of sibling rivalry, of real individual psychological problems. But each of the two images is supported by a number of trouble-making myths or beliefs; for example, if we believe the "Perfect Mother myth" that a mother meets *all* her children's needs, we feel cheated and angry when our mother doesn't measure up, and if we believe the "Bad Mother myth" that it's wrong for a mother to stay closely connected with her adult daughter, we fear and resent our mother's offers of help or advice. These myths create *avoidable* problems that make dealing with the *inevitable* ones much harder.

The angel-witch, Perfect Mother-Bad Mother myths that alienate mothers and daughters from each other are rooted in a powerful tradition of mother-blame that pervades our whole culture. Most mothers are insecure about their performance as mothers and desperately need the approval of other women, including their own daughters. Yet, tragically, as daughters we are taught to belittle the work of mothering and to blame our mothers for almost everything that goes wrong in our lives. We all too easily point out our mothers' failings, without ever examining how much our negative view was shaped and intensified by the myths that lead to mother-blame.

As daughters and mothers, we have for generations been trapped in a dark web we did not spin. But once we are aware of the myth-threads that form the web, as we tell our mothers' stories and our own, we can begin to sort them out and pick apart the web. Daughters have to go beyond both kinds of images, taking away the masks of motherhood, as they try to see who their mothers really are.

At some level we all know how hard it is to be a mother, and most of us sense how hard our mothers have *tried* to do right by us, even if they didn't always succeed. Understanding societal barriers to good mother-daughter relationships frees you to see your mother's good *and* bad points in all their complexity and subtlety, rather than as examples of anti-mother stereotypes— guilt-inducing mother, demanding mother, needy mother, over- whelming and judgmental mother, cold and remote mother. When you look at your list of the worst things your mother has done to you, after you've read *Don't Blame Mother*, you'll probably understand more about why she treated you the way she did, and as a result you'll feel differently about both her and yourself.

Relationships based on myths and stereotypes rather than on clear visions of one another have no chance of improving. But when you look at your mother realistically, you begin to break down barriers and reduce the energy you both waste on anguish about each other.

This book is based on my experiences as a therapist, on my research and the research of other people, on women's responses to my earlier writing about mothers and the mother-daughter relationship, and on my university course on "Mothers."

I have not systematically explored the effects of race, religion, class, age, or sexual orientation, or such factors as whether the daughter is an only daughter or an only child, or has or does not have children of her own. The women described in this book vary in all of these ways—and more. But the focus here is on the com- monalities in mother-daughter experiences, because in so many respects we women are treated alike, regardless of our differences and membership in other groups.

As you read true stories from my own life and from those of my friends, family members, students, workshop participants, and patients, I hope you will come to see that you are not the world's worst daughter, nor is your mother the world's worst mother—and, conversely, that *you* are not the world's worst mother, nor do you have the world's worst daughter. The stories and examples should also help you decide how to put to work the principles and research presented in this book, so that you can plan what to say the next time your mother calls or the next time you feel a fight with your daughter coming on.

THE EMPEROR'S NEW CLOTHES:
SEEING THROUGH MOTHER-BLAME

Mother-blame used to come easily to me, and it continues to come easily to most therapists, because that is how generations of therapists have been trained. I spent years seeing therapy patients before I realized how common mother-blame is and how much damage it does. Mother-blame is as rampant today as it was when I began my graduate training in 1969. In fact, it was and is so common that for years I hardly noticed it.

When I worked in the U.S. and Canada with psychiatric patients of all ages in a general hospital, with delinquent teenagers who were mental hospital inpatients, with children who had school problems, and with families whose members had a variety of problems, I heard my colleagues lay at mothers' feet the responsibility for most of the patients' problems. If anyone in the family was depressed, aggressive, or otherwise emotionally disturbed, the mother was likely to be blamed: "She's overprotective," "She makes her kids so nervous," and so on. If the mother herself was the patient, she was blamed for her own problems—"She's a masochist" or "She comes on so strong—no wonder her husband hits her!"

In many of these settings, we therapists often saw patients together and then, in case conferences, heard each other describe them and attempt to identify the causes of their depression, anxiety, violent behavior, or other problems. Most of what I actually *saw* most mothers do ranged from pretty good to terrific; but my colleagues usually described their actions in negative ways. I tended to leave case conferences feeling vaguely ashamed but not knowing why. One day, I realized that it was because, as a woman —and even more, as a mother—I was a member of the group that my colleagues seemed to think caused all the world's psychological problems.

I felt like the child in the fairy tale who knew the emperor was naked while everyone else praised his elaborate clothing. A most distressing characteristic of mother-blaming among mental health professionals is how few of them seem to be aware they do it. Even when therapists are alerted to mother-blaming attitudes and comments, they usually deny that they themselves could do such a thing.

After I became conscious of the clash between what I saw with my own eyes and what my colleagues said they saw, I began in each case conference to ask a simple question: "In addition to the mother's influence, what are the *various* factors that *could* have contributed to this person's (or couple's or family's) problems?" When I asked my question, my colleagues said I was "soft on mothers" and "overidentified" with them. And their case presentations continued to be focused not on *whether* the mother had caused the problem but on *how* she had done so.

In spite of these responses, I was inspired to continue my questioning by the growing literature on mothers. At last, it seemed, mothers were deemed a subject worthy of study. Such studies were a mixed bag, however. Only a few books—Adrienne Rich's *Of Woman Born*, Judith Arcana's *Our Mothers' Daughters*, and parts of Phyllis Chesler's *Women and Madness* and *With Child* —offered positive views of mothers.

Most writers continued primarily to find fault with mothers and describe the ways they ruined their children's lives. Some writers (such as Nancy Chodorow, Luise Eichenbaum, and Susie Orbach) began well, saying that all women have a rough time in our society; but mother-blaming is still present in essential threads of their writing, when they explain how mothers can't let go of their children, keep their daughters too dependent on them, are never satisfied, profoundly disappoint us, and burden us with unbearable guilt. For instance, in their book *Understanding Women: A Psychoanalytic Approach*, Eichenbaum and Orbach tell us:

A daughter hides the little-girl part of herself because she has picked up a painful and powerful message from mother that tells her she should not have expectations of being looked after emotionally, or of having her desires met, either by mother or by anyone else. Mother encourages her daughter to look to a man to be emotionally involved with; she teaches her daughter to direct her energies toward men and to someday depend on a man. But at the same time there is another message. As she lets her daughter know she must look to men, mother simultaneously transmits a message of disappointment and frustration. She conveys that her daughter must not expect a man to really help or understand her. Mothers often let their daughters know both overtly and covertly that men are disappointments. They may convey disdain and contempt for them. Mother's messages about men are thus more than a little ambivalent.

Eichenbaum and Orbach unfortunately offer no explanation of *why* a mother may fail to be nurturant, why she may feel she has to warn her female child not to expect much from this world in general or from men in particular; nor do they ask why the father doesn't provide much nurturance in a family in which the mother "fails" to do so.

In the enormously popular book *My Mother/My Self*, Nancy Friday presented such a pessimistic view of mothers and the mother-daughter relationship that many women found themselves more hopeless after reading it than before—and thought that meant something was wrong with their mothers and with them, rather than with the book.

Despite this continued focus on mothers' limitations, I noticed the beneficial effects of all the loving, empowering things that mothers were doing—they rocked babies, cooked nourishing meals, soothed hurt feelings. These things were hardly mentioned by anyone. For all the inspiration of books by Rich, Chesler, and Arcana, little or nothing changed among mainstream psychotherapists. From my own experience, I saw that simply voicing objections to mother-blame had no positive results. I needed to document systematically the scapegoating of mothers by mental health professionals. In Chapter 3, I shall describe some of the documentation that I gathered, but I was not surprised when our study revealed that mother-blame had not abated, even in the face of the modern wave of the women's movement.

To document the problem and its effects on mother-daughter relationships was one thing; to figure out what to do about it was another. Rich, Chesler, and Arcana had begun to describe what it feels like to be a mother and to be a daughter, and Jean Baker Miller—in her classic *Toward a New Psychology of Women*—had clearly described the nature of the subordination of women in general. But still missing was some idea of where or how to begin to mend the rifts between daughters and their mothers.

For the most part, this is still unexplored terrain. In fact, almost no *systematic* research has been conducted on woman-woman relationships of any kind; the funding for such research has simply not been available. Despite a recent spate of books about women's friendships and a few current academic studies, the focus of nearly all psychological research until recently has been on male-male relationships (competition, achievement in the workplace, aggression, etc.) or male-female relationships—in other words, on any relationship that included at least one male.

Knowing this is important, because it means that almost everything the so-called experts say about mother-daughter relationships has come *not* from research but from individuals' speculations. Of course, some such speculations are based on sensitive clinical observation and on a balanced, compassionate, and realistic view of women. But it is hard to avoid the influence of stereotypes when we try to look at the realities of mothers and daughters, and Ph.D. and M.D. degrees do not immunize us against those biases. It is time to cut a path through the myths and toward the truth. We owe it to ourselves, our mothers, our daughters, and other women to accord mother-daughter relationships their due, to declare that they are worthy of our time, our effort, and our respect.

MOTHERS AND OTHER STRANGERS

If we can temporarily think of our mothers as if they were strangers, we can more easily put them and their treatment of us into perspective; even when we become very angry at strangers, we can see them in a new light more readily, since we have no long, shared history, we may have no common future, and certainly we do not have the intimacy and complexity that characterizes our relationships with our mothers.

Recently, I became impatient because an iron I had left in a repair shop still wasn't ready six weeks and many telephone inquiries later. At last, I called and told the store manager that I needed to pick it up even if it wasn't ready. She spoke curtly to me and slammed down the telephone. Dreading an unpleasant encounter, I went to the shop the next day and found, to my surprise, that not only was the iron repaired and ready but also the manager was pleasant. I then recalled something I had heard years ago: The manager, a woman probably in her sixties, keeps the shop running so that her ninety-year-old father can keep working. I realized that she must have a terrible time keeping him happy by running the business, while also trying to hold on to some clientele in the face of her father's slowness (but excellent repair work). When I remembered this, my irritation with her vanished. My perspective changed.

Much of the work of mending the mother-daughter relationship involves placing mother-daughter problems in similar perspective, by looking at the forces that shaped our mothers and by looking at the pressures our culture puts on mothers and daughters to have a particular kind of relationship. We owe it to our mothers and to ourselves to think of our relationships with the same compassion as we do our business relationships with the neighborhood fix-it store manager. Furthermore, our feelings about our mothers have profound effects on our relationships with our daughters and with women in general. Those of us who believe we are supportive of women but deeply resent our own mothers are probably not as wholeheartedly benevolent toward women in general as we think we are. The better the connections we have with our mothers, the better our connections with other women tend to be.

As they think through their problems with their mothers, most daughters find that their mothers have seemed *worse* than they really are because the motherhood myths have badly distorted their view. Some daughters, however, have a very different experience and find that their own view of themselves changes even more than does their view of their mothers. As one woman told me:

> Although my mother really did some bad things to me, I now realize that it was not *my* fault. She hardly paid any attention to me when I was a child, and I thought I was to blame. When I was about thirty, she told me for the first time that my father had been so jealous of her love for me when I was a baby, that she felt she had to downplay our closeness. I'm still upset that she buckled under his childish jealousy, but I no longer believe that I was—or am—unlovable.

Some mothers are so difficult or hurtful that changing them is beyond anyone's power; but even in those cases, a daughter's understanding of the motherhood myths can strengthen her own self-esteem. I saw this happen gradually during the past two years to an eight-year-old daughter of divorced parents.

The child, whom I'll call Ginger, needed to believe—as most

children do—that her mother was perfect. Sadly, her mother was an unusually brittle, chilly woman who had been seriously disturbed from early childhood and still has trouble in close relationships. The mother told me:

> The year my husband and I split up, Ginger was in first grade. A few times, she called me from school in the morning and begged me to let her come home for lunch. But I wasn't going to let her manipulate me. So I just took to putting my answering machine on first thing in the morning.

Since Ginger was six, she has struggled to understand why her mother doesn't show that she is a loving person. Ginger concluded that she herself must be undeserving of love: "Mom doesn't seem to love me, so I must be a bad child. In fact, I know I am," she told me at age seven. But during the next year, as she spent more time in other children's homes and saw how their mothers treated both them and her, Ginger began to see that the problem is her mother's, not her own. Recently, she told me:

> It's been really hard to see that my mother is mean to me and even lies to me, because mothers aren't supposed to do that, you know? But each time she's mean, I think about how many times she's been like that before. At least now that I know that she treats everyone that way, I don't feel so much like a rotten kid any more.

If eight-year-old Ginger can gain this insight, adult daughters can do as much.

Some of you may be so angry at your mother that you can hardly speak to her. Some of you may feel overwhelmed or intimidated by her. Still others may simply feel remote or detached from her. Not *all* mothers and daughters have trouble, but nearly all have trouble sometimes. And although mother-daughter relationships are no worse than mother-son, father-son, or father-daughter ones are, several unique features characterize those between mothers and daughters.

Because mother-daughter relationships tend to be very close, they combine the potential for much joy as well as much pain. The joy comes because most women have been taught to develop their interpersonal sensitivity and skills, so mother and daughter have a good chance of making their relationship flower beautifully, once they see how to do it. Although they frequently have problems, mothers and daughters usually find ways to show that they care about each other and share some interests, values, or even jokes. In general, women are more willing than men to work on relationships, so when mother and daughter clash, they are likely to try to work out a solution *in order to improve the relationship* rather than to focus on winning the battle.

Part of the special pain between mother and daughter comes about because they feel that anger and alienation are not supposed to be part of the mother-daughter relationship. According to our cultural ideals, a mother is always gentle and loving—and so is her daughter. But precisely because of women's skill at understanding other people's emotions, many mothers and daughters can both wound and heal, both hurt and delight each other better than anyone else can.

LEARNING THE STORIES

In more than twenty years of studying and practicing psychology, I have found that most mothers and daughters mistakenly believe that their problems with each other are mostly the result of their own, individual craziness, or each other's, or both. Those beliefs help neither one of them. In fact, most mother-daughter relationships improve once the women understand that they have both been duped (daughter into mother-blaming, mother into self-hate) and have been divided against each other by the myths.

When someone asks, "What causes the trouble between you and your mother?" most of us are ready with an explanation. We have our stories to tell—stories about her, and stories about our relationship with her. But some stories are closer to the truth than others. We need to get as close as we can to knowing the real story about our mothers and ourselves. An old friend told me:

> All my life I had thought that Momma loved my sister more than me. I never questioned it, never asked about it, just believed it. When I turned 21, Momma had a party for me, and I started talking about my childhood. As I said for the first time in my life the words, "Of course, Momma always loved Beth best," I wondered for the first time whether or not it was true. Saying it out loud was such a definite thing to do. I suddenly felt a responsibility to Momma, to find out whether it was true before I kept on believing it myself.

When we tell the story of our relationship with each other, a mother and a daughter teach each other parts of the truth: "Oh, is *that* how you felt then—scared?! I thought you hated me!" When we strip our stories of the myths and then tell them again, we begin to mend our rifts as we learn what we have in common and as we experience the joy of discovering both great and tiny jewels of facts and feelings we hadn't known before.

CHANGES

Although some fortunate mothers and daughters can talk openly to each other about the problems between them, many women are daunted by the thought of doing so, or of *trying* to do so *again*. But mother-daughter problems *can* be worked on successfully, and it needn't require years of expensive psychotherapy. It is striking to see how often, as soon as a daughter is educated about our mother-blaming culture, she takes off rapidly from there.

Sometimes, naturally, it takes longer. At the end of the one-semester course I teach on "Mothers," the students write about how their feelings about and relationships with their mothers have changed during the course. The following are typical comments: In September, a woman described her mother as "cold," "distant," and "in pain" and said, in regard to her mother, she wished that "it could have been different between me and my mother, so I wouldn't have had to struggle so hard by myself in the past"; in December she wrote that her perspective had been broadened: "I have hope for further changes in myself, and I'd like to meet with other women concerning these issues. This is new for me and it feels good."

Another woman wrote, "I have more respect for my mother than when we began this course, and I feel closer to her. . . . I am more tolerant of the things about my mother that bother me. . . . I no longer feel I am competing with my mother—but have more of a sense that we are both on the same team."

These changes did *not* require the daughters to suppress their feelings of anger or frustration and put on a smiling facade. Once some myth-based guilt, anger, and anguish are gone, the remaining feelings are easier to accept, to understand, and to work on. This is especially true when mothers and daughters feel they are on the same team, working out problems together, rather than on opposite sides of an insurmountable brick wall or of a decades-long, full-scale war.

Sharing, Listening, and Learning

Not all mothers are saints, nor are all daughters automatically wrong for thinking their mothers made mistakes. Mothers are human; they do make mistakes, and sometimes the way our mothers brought us up wasn't very good. Few mothers, though, are complete monsters. However, we easily believe they are monsters if we don't know how else to think about them—and that is where talking to other women comes in.

Most women *want* to talk about their mothers and, for some, about their roles as mothers. I have found that nearly all women are filled with a mixture of anger, guilt, fear, and uncertainty about many aspects of their relationships with their mothers and/or daughters.

Through my patients and students I have learned that it is often easier to take a clear look at someone else's dilemma than at our own, stale anguish. Without a fresh look, simple and obvious ways to talk to each other or to think about how we interact just don't come to mind. The daughter continues to blame her mother and fear her disapproval, and the mother continues to blame herself and agonize about the distance or conflict between herself and her daughter. Thus, both of them feel guilty. Each becomes entrenched in her own agony about their relationship and finds it harder and harder to understand the other's point of view and to think of constructive ways they can be together.

Two activities have been especially helpful in my work with women. The first is simply to hear other women describe painful and infuriating feelings or situations similar to their own. The second is to describe their own experiences as mothers. Every time a woman has told how angry she has been at her mother, something she was sure that only *she* had ever felt with such intensity, she has found that many of the women listening have felt the same—and done the same "horrible" things because of it.

One woman, for instance, described a wild temper tantrum that she threw when she was in third grade and her mother brought *store-bought* cupcakes to the school Halloween party.

Hearing what other women have to say helps daughters feel less crazy and mean. This releases energy they have been using to cover up what they regarded as their craziness or viciousness; they become freer to find better ways to deal with their mothers. If we think our problems are unusual, we doubt we'll find solutions; once we know that other people have been in the same boat, we can help to teach each other.

In my classes and workshops, I ask the participants to listen to other women's complaints about their mothers in new ways. Rather than feeding each other's mother-blame, they learn first to acknowledge the daughter's frustration and then to ask whether she might be misinterpreting or mislabeling the mother's motives and behavior. For example, when a woman describes her mother as overprotective, the participants ask whether it *might* be more accurate to describe her as loving and nurturant. The new, less angry labels don't always fit, but it is amazing how often they do. When women see how apt the new labels are, they realize how deeply the culture has ingrained in us the lesson, "When something is wrong, just blame mother."

Through descriptions of their frustrations *as mothers*, women can provide each other with insights into their mothers' situations. For instance, in one discussion group several women talked about how they enjoyed their careers but felt torn apart daily when they dropped their clinging toddlers off at the daycare center. This discussion inspired a few women in the group to ask their own mothers how they had coped during those years.

Another woman talked movingly about her feelings when the hospital nurse told her that her newborn was jaundiced and would have to be placed under special lights that would make him very listless. She was ashamed both of her terror about what the jaundice might signify and of her powerlessness to help her baby. Watching him under the lights, she found that the only way she could maintain some semblance of calm was to take dozens of photographs of him. She believed that her worries were overblown and her helplessness shameful, and she felt guilty about her ability to distance herself through taking pictures. Although she was simply doing her best to cope, she felt simultaneously pathologically attached and pathologically detached. Her story helped other women in the group to gain a new perspective on what had seemed to them to be *their* mothers' detached behavior. Instead of seeing their mothers' detachment as a sign that their mothers didn't care about them, they began to consider what else might have been behind such seeming lack of concern. They began to wonder about the bigger picture.

THE GOALS OF THIS BOOK

The goals of this book are simple:

- To reduce the pain felt by both daughters and mothers in their relationships with each other
- To help daughters and mothers to feel better about themselves, by understanding the nature of the barriers between them
- To give daughters and mothers a wider range of choices about how to conduct their lives by freeing them from the myths that limit their vision of their options and by teaching them new techniques and practical skills
- To heighten both daughters' and mothers' awareness of how they have been kept apart by the ways they've been taught to think about each other

To keep track of how you think and feel about your mother, keep paper and pen nearby as you read the following chapters. Jot down *anything* that comes to mind that might help in the unmasking process—things you realize you don't know about your mother and want to find out; a word or phrase that rings a bell for you, even if you're not yet sure why; stories that match your experience *and* stories that seem totally different from yours; questions that come to your mind. If you don't find the answers here, chances are you'll want to find them with other people or in other books, such as those in the bibliography.

Some of you will find that as soon as you read about a particular problem or issue, you will know how it applies to you and your mother, and you'll throw down the book in mid-chapter to put it into practice. Others will want to read the whole book, think about the issues, talk to other people, and do further reading before even *considering* taking any action. Many readers will be in the second group because, after a lifetime of being socialized into mother-blame, even a full chapter's worth of antidotes will be only a beginning. And if you gave up hope years ago, you'll have to work to get your engine revved up again.

Even daughters whose mothers have died have a great deal to gain from imagining, as vividly as possible, what they would say to their mothers if they could, and what they think their mothers might answer. In such cases, talking to your mother's close friends or other family members can be helpful, since one or more of them are bound to have a somewhat different perspective on her, and other information about her, than you have.

Daughter's Move, Mother's Move

Initiating changes in your relationship with your mother, or in the way you think about her (if she has died or if you decide not to discuss these issues with her directly), may be mostly up to you. For that reason, this book is largely addressed to daughters, although mothers may find it useful as well. Knowing what has shaped her daughter's view of her can be very helpful to a mother who wants to understand the way her daughter treats her. Because mother-blame is a much more deeply ingrained practice than daughter-blame, daughters are more likely to be aware of feeling angry at their mothers than vice versa; so a daughter may need to do more work, more peeling away of layers of blame and myths, than a mother. But a mother who reads this book will probably understand more about her own mother (and about *their* relationship), and this can shed light on her relationship with her daughter.

Usually, when a daughter is angry at or alienated from her mother, the mother is also suffering, for mothers tend to be excellent sensors of discomfort and emotional distance. Despite their pain, though, most mothers of adult women come from generations deeply indoctrinated in the belief that mothers haven't the right to ask for much (even though some of them founded the modern women's movement); their daughters are more likely to feel comfortable analyzing and questioning the roles that mothers are shaped by our culture to play and our perceptions of our own mothers. This is not to say that the taboos about questioning motherhood have disappeared. The night I finished writing my first major effort about mothers, I woke in terror, feeling that I had blasphemed and that in some way I would be punished—not because of what I had said (because my view of mothers was generally sympathetic) but just for *looking* at mothers.

Our mothers generally feel this taboo even more: For them, even more than for most of us, society expected, first, that they would become mothers and second, that they would try, without asking why or wherefore, to fit the self-sacrificing, uncomplaining pattern that was the motherhood mold. When their children reject or criticize them, most of our mothers feel that they have no right to complain, that the failure must have been their own—for mothers themselves have internalized mother-blame. To take the risk, when their daughters are grown, of hauling old wounds into the light for examination or reexamination is too frightening—unless and until they know that they will not be attacked just for doing so. Furthermore, mothers know that members of one generation have difficulty understanding the members of another. A mother is skeptical that her daughter could understand how hard growing up during the Depression was or just how badly an unwed mother was treated thirty years ago. Comments like, "But Mom, the Depression ended decades ago! You're rich now!" quickly seal a mother's lips. Mothers need to know that their daughters are moving off the team that points an accusing finger and onto *their* mutually respectful and supportive team—not blindly or totally but thoughtfully.

Most women really care about forming close relationships and working out anything that interrupts that closeness. For most mothers and daughters, no matter how furious at each other we get, we don't want to stay angry after the immediate release or empowerment of anger is over. We'd rather reestablish the closeness. We are sad and wistful when a bond is broken.

I hope to provide some tools for repairing that bond. By understanding how the myths hinder their rapprochement—for it's hard in different ways to reapproach an angel or a witch—mothers and daughters will be prepared to reevaluate the history of problems between them, retell their shared story in a more truthful way, and begin their next chapter with a clearer vision of both the bridges and the gaps between them.

2 ❧ *Such Love, Such Rage*

"MY RELATIONSHIP WITH my mother is so emotionally resonant—my feelings about her echo throughout my lifetime," a thirty-year-old graduate student told me, and for most adult daughters that rings true. We find ourselves thinking about our mothers in the middle of the night, first thing in the morning, in the midst of a crowd, while arguing with or hugging our daughters.

What are we thinking? We are longing for closeness with our mother; we are hating her for her power to make us feel infantile, ridiculous, and inadequate; we are chewing over what we said to each other last Thanksgiving in a horrible argument; we are trying for the thousandth time to think of just the right way to talk to her about a subject that we never seem to address calmly together.

All of this effort reveals our deep conflicts about our mothers. But it also shows us how much *we really care.* Although we may often think our best bet would be to move to the opposite end of the earth, in fact our struggles signal to us that we need to find less anguished ways to interact with our mothers. Deep down, most daughters don't really want to stay totally away from their mothers; what they want is to have an easier, more enjoyable time together. Elaine, a 44-year-old woman, felt such a need. She told me that she had spent years resenting her mother—and didn't like herself for feeling that way:

> My mother had some wonderful characteristics: she was warm, loving, bright, and witty. So, I *wanted* to enjoy my time with her, and I wanted

to be a loving person when we were together. But my mother's negative features loomed so large in my view, and so infuriated me, *I couldn't be the kind of loving woman I like to be.* I hated myself when I was with her —I hated my criticalness, my withdrawal, my anger. So I ended up hating her *and* me.

Dealing with this dilemma and growing beyond some of our anger requires first that we explore some of our most upsetting feelings about our mothers, as we do in this chapter; then, that we look at how and why we get stuck in these emotional ruts (Chapters 3, 4, and 5), and finally, that we consider how to make productive changes (Chapters 6 through 9). There *is* a way out of the mother-daughter stalemate. And finding that way is profoundly important, because in order to accept ourselves fully we need to learn to understand more about our mothers and to accept—if not always to forgive—them.

You may not find in this chapter all of the upsetting feelings you have about your mother, but as you read about some of the most common negative feelings daughters have about their mothers, you will probably find some that apply to you. Keep in mind that, although recognizing and exploring these feelings can be painful, they are essential steps toward mending mother-daughter relationships. The more you understand about your negative feelings, the better prepared you will be to start making positive changes.

AMBIVALENCE ABOUT MOTHERS

Mother Wonderful, Mother Horrible

Most mother-daughter relationships involve a great deal of ambivalence. In the most loving of mother-daughter relationships, the difficult times can be excruciating. They are excruciating partly because we know or we can imagine how wonderful they could be—the rough times are more painful by contrast. My relationship with my mother is basically very good, and she's a wonderful woman, but that does not mean that we do not have our painful clashes and periods of alienation from each other. Just ask me—and just ask her. Even in more troubled mother-daughter relationships, the situation is rarely *all* bad; both mother and daughter usually think wistfully of good times they shared in the past and long for better times in the future.

Most women are very disconcerted when asked if they love their mothers: "Of course I do—she's my mother!" Not to love your mother seems unthinkable at best, inhuman at worst. Ask the average woman to describe her relationship with her mother, however, and the qualifications start to pile up: "Well, she's never really understood me. . . . She's always comparing me to other people, and somehow I never measure up. . . . She still treats me like a little kid." Resentments build: "I'm not on the phone two minutes with her before she starts trying to run my life. . . . I don't think there's *one* man I've gone out with that she's approved of!" Now, suddenly, rage: "It's no wonder I'm so screwed up! She's passed all of *her* neuroses on to *me*. Oh, I know she thinks she did the best she could, but if only she had [choose one]: (1) paid more attention to me; (2) paid less attention to me; (3) encouraged me more; (4) not pushed me so hard."

Why is it that in the space of a moment or two, we move from "Of course I love my mother!" to blaming her for everything wrong in our lives? The very word *mother* elicits a wealth of conflicting, ambivalent feelings—protectiveness, a desire for her approval, need for her love versus rage at the terrible damage we feel she's done to us, however unwittingly. We feel justified in blaming her. After all, who had greater control over our lives when we were most vulnerable? Where did we learn our first "rules" about the world, about life, if not from her? The experts tell us that the first three (or five, or six) years of life are the most important in our lives, the time when our basic personalities are formed, so we think it's obvious that the woman who influenced those three (or five, or six) years the most is responsible for much of what has gone wrong since then. How powerless we were! We don't even *remember* what our mothers may have taught us at this crucial time, how they may have planted the seeds of our neuroses. Once we are adults, when we *think* about it, rationally, we know it's not exactly her fault—but we still *feel*, somehow, "If only she had. . . ."

Women have ridden this exhausting merry-go-round for generations, to our own and our mothers' immense pain and misfortune. The love and fun we've shared (fed by the cultural idealization of mothers) combines with our anger and disappointment (fed by the cultural denunciation of mothers) and results in profound ambivalence. We know how best to please *and* to wound each other.

Coping by Blocking

Living with such powerfully loving and intensely painful feelings at the same time often seems impossible. Sometimes we try to cope by focusing on only one feeling at a time and blocking out the rest. About ten years ago, I was asked to speak about mother-daughter relationships to a group of young mothers. When I asked them to tell me about their mothers, nearly all of the women expressed love, gratitude, and admiration for them, even though some of their attitudes were rather patronizing. They denied having conflicts or problems with their own mothers. But when I asked about how they were raising their own children, nearly all of them spoke with strong feelings—of fear, of awe, of hope—about their difficulties.

Now, it is remotely possible—but unlikely—that a roomful of women had perfect mothers and yet were encountering many difficulties in raising their own daughters and sons. It is much more likely that these women were suppressing their negative feelings. They had just met me and, in the presence of a stranger, it is not nice to say nasty things about your mother.

Blocking out negative feelings is one way that daughters deal with their ambivalence, especially publicly. But privately, or given the least encouragement, daughters often do a complete reversal, ventilating their worst feelings about mother, so that their positive feelings are overwhelmed. For example, in her study of mothers, Zenith Henkin Gross found that the adult women she interviewed "drew . . . shockingly rejecting portraits of their mothers." Workshops and seminars on mothers and daughters not uncommonly degenerate into orgies of mother-trashing as soon as the first critical comment is made: when the socially created and culturally fueled mother-blaming bandwagon pulls up, women rush to hop on. A well-known essayist described to me her experience at a workshop on mothers and daughters:

> After a lecture on common mother-daughter problems, we broke up into small groups. In my group, we talked briefly about how limited our

mothers' lives were, how they felt they had no choice but to get married and have children. There seemed to be a lot of heartfelt sympathy for our mothers. But then, one very angry woman said, "*My* mother drives me wild! She thinks it's her job to tell me how to run my life." For the next hour, none of the women had a good word to say about their mothers.

Living with powerfully ambivalent feelings about our mothers is very hard. We feel insincere when we pretend our mothers are all-good, and we feel vicious when we focus exclusively on their faults. And yet, the Perfect-Mother-Bad-Mother myths push us from one extreme to another.

Some ambivalence is present in any close relationship, but in mother-daughter ones it often seems more intense. Part of that intensity comes from a good feature of the mother-daughter interaction: both members of this relationship are female, and girls and women are far more likely than men and boys to learn to be emotionally expressive and sensitive to the feelings of others. (As a general rule, males are more likely to suppress, ignore, or deny many of their feelings.) So both mother and daughter are immersed in the realm of feelings and more likely to be aware of a variety of strong feelings on both sides.

In one of the rare research studies of woman-woman relationships, psychologists Lorette Woolsey and Laura-Lynne McBain documented this ambivalence through direct questions and observations. They found that relationships between women are emotionally richer than those between men but that the former include the potential for both strongly positive and strongly negative emotions.

The dramatically polarized mother-images of Angel and Witch, described in Chapter 1, fuel daughters' ambivalence about their mothers. The Perfect Mother myths are a source of pressure on us not just to love but to *adore* our mothers. The Bad Mother myths transform our irritation and disappointment with mother into fury and a sense of betrayal. Because the one feeling our culture prohibits women from expressing openly is anger, both mother and daughter suppress negative feelings, creating a pressure-cooker atmosphere and, ultimately, explosions of rage.

These intensely ambivalent feelings generally surface on the first day of a graduate school class I teach on "Mothers," when I conduct the following exercise: I ask the students to (anonymously) (1) write down the first three things they think of when I say the word *mother;* (2) take a little time to expand on those three things or to write anything else that comes to mind about their mothers; and (3) complete the sentence, "In regard to my mother, I wish that. . . ."

One woman wrote that her first three thoughts about her mother were "warm," "friendly," and "colorful." But immediately afterward she wrote: "My mother's influence on me has been one of strict guidance. I always felt as if she were hovering over my shoulder, watching my every move." She wished that her mother "had had more children so that her focus would not have been so singularly on me. Perhaps then, more of the good qualities of our relationship could have emerged and less of the petty squabbling would have taken place."

Another woman also began with positive images—the first three that came to her mind were "warm," "large," and "giving." But that woman's next words about her mother were that she had "made me hopeful, but guilty; not provided a role model and had low self-esteem." She wished that her mother "could feel stronger in herself; I wish I didn't get so triggered by her insecurity."

A woman who found her mother "opinionated," "loving," and "sad" went on to write that she felt very close to her mother, despite feeling harshly criticized by her. And one whose first images of her mother were "cold," "distant," and "in pain," also said she was "courageous," "intelligent," and "generous."

A healthy range of ambivalence in a close relationship *is* normal; we usually see and respond to the other person's good and bad points. But the pressure on women to be perfect mothers and perfectly accepting daughters can make them uncomfortable with what is really normal ambivalence.

DESPAIR AND BETRAYAL

The polarization of mother-images also leads to two other feelings that adult daughters commonly have about their mothers: their despair of ever pleasing them and their sense of betrayal about their mothers' failure to nurture them enough. These feelings originate in the expectations that mothers should produce perfect daughters and *be* perfect themselves. During those times when you think your mother is perfect (or *she's* thinking she *should* be perfect), you may feel that you can never satisfy her, from your choice of clothes to your decision about whether or not to have children. Somehow she seems to do everything right—to *be* right—and you can never catch up. Conversely, since she's supposed to be perfect, you're likely to feel betrayed by her when she's unable to meet your needs, instead of regarding her as an average, imperfect human being. At such times, you usually feel disappointment or even rage, followed by guilt about those feelings. The mother who is on the receiving end of this despair and sense of betrayal feels understandably helpless, for she cannot be an ordinary person; in her daughter's eyes, her strengths put her on a pedestal and make her seem to have unmeetable standards, but the limitations on her ability to help her daughter are construed as dramatically letting her daughter down.

My friend Ellen and her mother, Sue, had an experience that elicited these feelings. When Ellen and her husband split up, she took her three teenaged children and moved back to her hometown. Ellen's parents had lived there since before she was born, and they were loving and supportive while she learned to cope with single parenting and being a divorced woman in a city that retained its small-town attitudes. Toward the end of the year, she fell in love with someone new. When he asked her to take a week's vacation with him, Ellen talked to her mother about the invitation and said she considered her kids (aged 15, 16, and 17) old enough to stay on their own. She chided Ellen, saying, "But it's just terrible for you to travel with this man. My friends will be shocked. How *can* you do this to me?" Ellen was floored. She had been so sure that her mother would be happy for her. Sue also said, "Since you're determined to go on this trip, I don't think you should leave the kids alone. Please let them stay with me."

While Ellen was away, her kids repeatedly broke the curfew their grandparents set, which drove Sue crazy with worry. Finally, she told them they were old enough to take care of themselves but that she was too old to put up with their nonsense. She sent them back to Ellen's house for the last half of the week. When Ellen came home, Sue yelled at her, "Don't *ever* ask me to take care of those kids again. I just can't take it!" Ellen felt betrayed: her mother had *asked* to have the kids stay with her but then had turned on Ellen as though Ellen had *imposed* it on her. At such times, she despaired of re-establishing the loving relationship that she had had as a child with her mother.

So many daughters recognize this all-too-familiar trap, this feeling of having been betrayed by their mothers but of wanting to be closer to them. They wonder if greater closeness is possible and worth the trouble or if they should just give up. If they are *not* going to give up, they feel stuck—they just don't know how to begin; they feel they have tried everything. Despairing, they wonder, "Why attempt again the approaches that seem to have failed miserably for years?"

ANGER

Our cultural idealization of mothers makes our anger at mother almost inevitable; if you expect someone to be perfect, sooner or later you'll criticize them for having *any* faults. A young patient had this liberating insight:

> Mom needed so much for me to think she was a perfect mother—and I bought it: I really believed she was like the mothers on 'Family Ties' and 'The Cosby Show.' You can imagine how furious I was any time that image cracked! If I hadn't felt that she *ought* to be perfect, my fury about her imperfection wouldn't have been so boundless.

Energy spent in angry blaming of our mothers (and ourselves as both daughters and mothers) blocks our growth. One of the world's biggest sources of misdirected emotional energy is tied up in millions of women's rage at their mothers. Major works of art could be created, social problems solved, and identity crises resolved if the force in this obsessive mother-blaming were more productively channeled. But the rechanneling is blocked by the powerful messages we get from professionals and from each other, telling us that our worst problems stem from our mothers—simultaneously, at some level, we've learned that a good mother is a perfect mother. No wonder we get angry at them.

The Uses of Anger

Anger is a secondary emotion. We don't go from feeling nothing to feeling angry. Anger is usually the feeling we have when we don't like having an earlier feeling. For example, someone ignores us and we feel hurt and, because we don't like the hurt feeling, we get angry at the person who caused it. Similarly, we become angry at bureaucrats because they make us feel powerless; impotence is an uncomfortable feeling to have. Suppressing, denying, or ignoring anger doesn't make either the anger or the primary feelings go away, but expressing *only* the anger usually doesn't help much.

Anger *can* help us to overcome our feelings of powerlessness: When we see that we don't deserve to feel powerless (or humiliated or hurt) and that we have the right to object to such treatment, then showing some anger can be empowering. Anger can be a way to say, "I deserve better than this, and I *can* speak up and defend myself. I don't have to wait quietly, hoping I'll be treated better."

In the words of a friend of mine, "I was formerly a very angry and attacking daughter, and I think that to some extent that was how I survived—it kept me sane by separating me from my mother's impossible demands." Her mother's demands may or may not have been impossible; she may have been wrong in thinking of her mother as a witch. But since that was her image of her mother, her anger felt empowering. It was a way of maintaining her integrity, of refusing to attempt to meet unreasonable demands. And once she knew that she could protect herself in this way, she didn't feel as angry at her mother and was better able to accept her.

Accepting one's anger at an exceptionally abusive and/or rejecting mother is justified and can be empowering, making the daughter feel less unworthy: if her mother's unreasonable demands are the problem, then the daughter is not deficient for failing to satisfy them.

Going Beyond the Anger

We have to go beyond just expressing anger, however, because anger usually doesn't change the other person's behavior or prevent a repetition of the original, hurtful events. If I just tell you, for instance, that I'm angry at you because you were rude to me, then like most human beings you will leap to your own defense, often by attacking or criticizing me. That can start an unending cycle of anger. Furthermore, you may not be aware of having done anything rude, so even if you *want* to avoid making me angry in the future, you're not sure how to do that. But if I explain to you the underlying feelings that made me angry—and tell you specifically what provoked those feelings in me—that gives you the power to improve our relationship by changing your behavior. If I tell you, "When I walked in the door, you finished talking to Dad before you said hello to me, and that hurt my feelings, and then I got angry that you had hurt me," then IF you care about me, you know how to prevent my feeling hurt—and then angry—the next time.

No matter how bad she is, seeing mother as a person rather than a demon is helpful. If, after reading all the way through this book, you believe your situation is one of those rare ones, that your mother is profoundly damaged or unusually hurtful, then keeping your interactions with her to a minimum, or waiting to see her until you feel much stronger or clearer about how you want to conduct yourself—even if it takes a long time to get to that point—may be the best route to your well-being. In the meantime you can continue to learn and understand more about your mother, yourself, and the relationship the two of you have. At least you'll know that you did your part and that you're not responsible or at fault. Furthermore, finding out what feelings underlie the anger helps in three ways: (1) A daughter who realizes she's sad, guilty, or afraid of her mother, rather than just angry, no longer thinks of herself as simply an angry person. (2) Identifying these feelings in herself makes the daughter feel less the villain than anger does, since it's more acceptable to feel sad, guilty, or afraid of an idealized mother than to be angry at her. (3) Sadness, guilt, and fear can diminish as we become aware of them.

We also have to go beyond the anger because women tend to feel guilty, much more than men, about being angry, especially at our mothers. Twenty-four-year-old Shauna described the vicious cycle of anger and guilt that is set up:

> After I've gotten mad at my mother, I feel guilty and ashamed of myself. Then I get mad at her *because* she's the reason I feel guilty and ashamed: the guilt is because I don't want to hurt her, and the shame is because she's the one who always said I should learn to control my anger.

So not only can anger lead to guilt, but guilt can also lead to anger. Women are very good at feeling guilty any time they think they've hurt or disappointed anyone, but all the more so with their mothers. After all, daughters know that, outside the family, their mothers get no pay and little respect for motherwork, and chances are they get little or none at home; since daughters are supposed to be sensitive and supportive, we feel, how can we—of all people—let mother down? But guilt is a heavy burden, and when enough of it piles up, daughters either get simply angry or both depressed and angry. Sadly, this anger is usually aimed at mother herself rather than at the social arrangements that caused the daughter's guilt.

Most of us want our mothers' approval; when we don't get it, or don't get it wholeheartedly, we may automatically respond by attacking or blaming them. But this response is destructive to the relationship; it also intensifies our *self*-hate. I am not suggesting that all *anger* should be wiped out; but attacking and blaming are different from healthy expressions of anger or frustration. We'll feel less guilty once we understand *why* we're so angry—both the feelings that underlie the anger and the nature of the mother-blaming that promotes the anger.

Anger and Self-esteem

A common cause of a daughter's anger is what seem to be her mother's assaults on her self-esteem. This is what happened to Elaine—the woman mentioned at the beginning of this chapter whose resentment of her mother prevented her from being the kind of woman she wanted to be. She deeply desired her mother's approval but felt continually criticized by her. This wounded her self-esteem and increased even more her need for her mother's approval. She was all the more devastated, and then infuriated, when the approval didn't seem to be forthcoming.

Nearly all women have trouble with self-esteem, as Linda Tschirhart Sanford and Mary Ellen Donovan have described in their book, *Women and Self-esteem*, and our mothers' approval means a lot to us. When we don't get it—or don't get enough or *believe* we don't get it—we defend ourselves by saying, "Nothing's wrong with *me!* She's just impossible to please." But our poor self-esteem and need for mother's approval locks us into our often-buried anger when she gives us anything less than her total approval. In addition, poor self-esteem makes us exaggerate the slightest criticism from other people; even if mother mostly loves and admires us, we won't see it. Listen to Pamela, a woman in her mid-fifties who had enrolled in law school after raising three children:

> After graduating from law school, my first job was with a huge law firm that had hired very few women. The senior partners were especially tough on us women, and my self-confidence—which had never been terrific but had improved when I did well in law school—just plummeted. One evening, after one of the senior partners had taken me to task for what was really a minor error on my part, I dropped by to see Ma. When I told her my troubles, she said, "I guess you have to expect to be monitored closely, when you're one of the first women to do something."
>
> I hit the ceiling. I had wanted her sympathy, and I thought she was being really hard on me. I flounced out and drove home. When I walked in the door, the phone was ringing, and it was Ma. She didn't know why I was so upset, because her comment was meant to be sympathetic— "It's hard being one of the first women and have people watching you like hawks." I had been so afraid she wouldn't support me that I mistakenly believed she wasn't.

There is a vicious cycle: poor self-esteem intensifies our need for mother's approval while intensifying our belief that she generally *disapproves* of us; we get angry at her, we become hypercritical of her, and our self-respect plummets even more because our interactions are angry and painful. We become less and less the women we really want to be.

FEAR

Three of the major fears a daughter has in relation to her mother are: the fear of losing her love, the fear of her death, and the fear of being like her or repeating her mistakes.

Fear of losing mother's love is related to being unable to please her mother, of being unable to live up to her mother's goals for her. As a 55-year-old secretary named Joan told me, "Fear is that hollow feeling I *still* get in the pit of my stomach when I've displeased my mother. If I don't please her, she might stop loving me."

Women who feel they haven't met their mothers' standards or have let them down in other ways—women who have not yet made some sort of peace with their mothers—develop an intense dread of their mother's death. They sense how guilty they will feel about their unresolved conflicts, their lingering anger at her and their guilt about that anger. Daughters have come to me, frantic with worry, saying,

> I'm terrified to think about the fact that my mother will die someday. I *can't* think about it—when I try to, my heart pounds and I start to cry. It's partly because we're not as close as we used to be, and we argue a lot. I'm not sure why that is or what to do about it, and my fear that we won't *ever* get anything resolved, that we'll still be fighting and alienated when she dies, is so overwhelming that I can't think calmly about how to try to work things out with her.

Advice columnists such as Ann Landers and Abigail Van Buren have frequently printed letters from daughters overcome with remorse after their mothers have died. On her television show, Sally Jessy Raphael recently interviewed adults whose mothers had died as long as twenty years ago and who (including Raphael herself) could still hardly speak about them, partly because of their guilt. Because this dread of our mother's death has such power, few of us can simply write our mothers off, put them out of our minds. Yet this is the positive side of that fear. Fear is an emotional parallel to physical pain. Just as pain is the body's way of telling us something is physically wrong, so fear and apprehension are signals that important emotional work remains undone. If we can recognize this kind of fear, we can realize that we don't have to just sit and dread our mother's death; our fear can propel us in our search for ways to overcome the barriers between our mothers and ourselves in *this* life.

Fear of Repetition

If we weren't deeply affected by a mother-blaming atmosphere, we wouldn't be *afraid* of being compared to our mothers; we could even be proud. Blaming our mothers is destructive to *ourselves*, because *what we believe about our mothers, we often suspect about ourselves*. It's hard to find a woman who does not spend time thinking she acts just like her mother, or thinking she is very different from her mother, or both. In all of those thoughts, her mother is the standard of comparison—so what she believes about her mother matters a great deal. Even women who say they adore their mothers often fear that they have picked up their mothers' bad qualities. Among my women therapy patients and my friends, this is a common worry—in some, an obsession. Here is a typical comment:

> Everyone loved my mother, because she was so sweet and had such a great sense of humor. It's true that she was very kind and generous, and I loved her for that. But her sense of humor was sometimes shockingly bawdy, and that used to embarrass me no end. I love to tell jokes myself, but I never tell any joke that's the least bit off-color, because I'm so afraid I'll seem as crude as she did. It's as though I can't figure out how to tell a sexy joke without sounding exactly like her.

If we regard our mothers as masochistic, rejecting, critical, demanding, guilt-inducing, or just embarrassing, then we usually begin to suspect that we are, too. Most daughters try hard to avoid repeating what they consider the specific mistakes that their mothers made with them, and many daughters are determined to dress differently, to choose friends differently, to have different values from those their mothers have. At the same time, we often have an almost superstitious belief that we simply *cannot* avoid that repetition. We secretly fear that we are exactly like our mothers in all the ways that we dislike.

Since we tend to believe that we are like our mothers, deprecation of them usually leads us also to self-deprecation. Hatred not only hurts the person who is hated; it is destructive also to the person who hates. Ultimately, hatred and blame keep us tied to the target of those feelings. They lead to our preoccupation with the target, who is always on our minds. Our behavior is controlled by the need to get revenge on them, to "show" them, to react against them, to ostracize them, or to prove them wrong. At one of my lectures, a woman said:

> I used to feel that everything my mother did reflected on me. I was embarrassed by her looks, the way she dressed, the way she talked, and I hated her for it. But then I also hated myself for hating her. I wasn't proud of letting my mother's appearance bother me so much.

To a disturbing degree, we don't want to be like our mothers. Why *should* we want to be like them, we might ask, since so much of what they do is ignored or devalued? Isn't that like wanting to be a welfare recipient or a kid in the slow reading group? But in our mothers' eyes, our wish to be different from them seems one more sign that no one values the way they've spent their lives.

In her interviews with a large number of women, Lucy Rose Fischer found only one daughter who "described a positive similarity to her mother." Daughters often *believe* that they want to avoid taking on their mothers' individual, personal characteristics. But a little probing usually shows that what daughters really want to avoid is anything connected with women's devalued and limited position: her mother's weight doesn't fit the slender feminine mold; she gets no respect outside the home; she is intimidated by her husband; she has no skills that are appreciated in the public world.

SADNESS, NUMBNESS, AND ALIENATION

Sadness is the predominant feeling many adult daughters have about their mothers. For some, the sadness comes from mother's failure to match the idealized mother image. As one woman said, "I still can't stop wishing she will love and protect me completely and tell me—as she did when I was a child—that everything I do is wonderful. I really feel that I have lost something."

When I encouraged this woman to think back over her childhood, she recalled some occasions on which her mother had not been completely loving and supportive; after all, her mother, too, is just a human being. So this daughter's sadness came not so much from changes in her mother as from the contrast between reality and her distorted memories. And those distortions came from the idealized side of mother-images.

For other daughters, the sadness about their mothers comes from their sense of the emotional distance between them. Since most women are raised to care a great deal about close relationships, when anything goes wrong they are acutely aware of a sense of loss. Something that's usually there is missing, and that something is the closeness; what the daughter feels is sadness or alienation. After one of my lectures about mothers and daughters, a woman told me this story:

> As you spoke today I realized that my mother and I grew apart when I got promoted to an executive job in the department store where I had

worked for eight years. Until then, my mother always told me how proud she was that I was a buyer for the women's clothing department. But once I got my promotion, she started falling silent whenever I was around. And just today I understood that that is because, in her eyes, my executive job puts me in the same world as my father. As long as I was a women's clothes buyer, I did work she knew something about. But my father is a business executive, so now Dad and I have something in common, and Mom feels left out.

Perhaps this mother and daughter were driven apart by the daughter's promotion because high-powered paid employment and difficult, unpaid household work are not equally valued. Or perhaps this mother felt left out or was very competitive. Whatever drove them apart, the result was that they felt alienated and sad because they were unable to share their experiences.

For some daughters, the sadness comes from sorrow over the closeness they lost during their rebellious years. A little adolescent rebellion is commonly believed to be healthy, enabling the growing offspring to separate from the parents. For sons, a fair amount of rebelliousness is often encouraged, especially when done in the name of breaking away from Mom, who—we often think—represents yards of knotted apron strings. For daughters, rebellion is harder to carry out, partly because it's not in keeping with the accepted feminine role and partly because—in the idealized version of mother-daughter images—daughters are supposed to want to stay very close to their mothers. So daughters' rebellion is likely to be more painful, more in danger of being misinterpreted as betrayal of their mothers, than is sons' rebellion. And so daughters are more inclined to believe their rebellious times were indeed a betrayal.

Perhaps even more worrying than ambivalence, anger, guilt, despair, fear, and sadness about mother is the emotional numbness or the sense of alienation that some daughters feel in relation to their mothers. Sometimes, numbness and alienation set in when other feelings become too overpowering. One can only endure so much anger, guilt, and despair before emotionally shutting down for awhile. A well-known politician whose visits with her mother begin well, then become tense and upsetting, and end with feelings of alienation, has said that her mother likes the *idea* of her visiting but not the reality. She thought she should just let her mother meet her at the airport, then get the next plane back.

When a sense of numbness or alienation predominates, a daughter's first question to herself should be whether that is masking a surfeit of other, underlying feelings. If the answer is yes, then she can begin to think about each of those feelings, using the framework and the methods that are suggested in the rest of this book. The block against feelings can be removed, although it should be removed with care, so that the onrush of bottled-up feelings isn't too frightening or overwhelming; after all, the intensity of those feelings in the first place was so great that they had to be suppressed. As a woman who attended one of my workshops explained a few weeks later:

> I realized that the feeling of deadness I had about my mother was a safe cover-up, to protect me from my strong feelings of powerlessness to change the misery that's in her life because she never went beyond grade four in school and is afraid to go back to school. And then I was knocked out by how much sadness and rage I felt. I felt sad for her, and I felt enraged because nothing I could do seemed to help. She sits at home all day, watching TV and feeling useless, but she's clearly just too frightened to go back to school and get enough upgrading to get a job. Even my offer to go with her didn't make any difference.
>
> It was a good thing I had talked to other women in similar positions at the workshop, because after my initial burst of sorrow and rage, I felt the old numbness setting in. I found that I started thinking of ways to avoid seeing Mom. But then I remembered what other daughters had said about *their* feelings of powerlessness when they couldn't save their mothers, and how our group had decided that even if we can't save them, it doesn't help us or our mothers for us to run away. It's a struggle to acknowledge how helpless we are to change our mothers, but only when we've done that can we stay close to them and offer what *will* help them, which is our continuing love and support. My mother needs my love and support, even if she can't use it to do what I wish she could.

Occasionally, a daughter goes emotionally numb to protect herself from a truly unlovable, vicious, or very sick mother, or from a mother who has been toughened up by a very different culture. Creating a wall may be the only way the daughter can stop blaming herself and stop feeling unlovable because of her mother's treatment of her. It may also stem the tide of guilt that she feels for not loving her mother. A young adult woman described her experience this way:

> My mother has always been a very unhappy woman. Her family immigrated to this country when she was twelve—a terrible age to make such

a big adjustment—and she never did feel at home in America. When I hit adolescence and started doing all the typical adolescent things like talking on the telephone for hours or worrying about what clothes were "in," she turned on me and tore me down at every turn. She'd accusingly say things like, "In my country, girls didn't worry about such *superficial* things. We took life seriously and worked hard." I knew she was afraid that as I got more what she considered "American," I was growing farther and farther away from her, and I felt bad about that. But I just couldn't take her really vicious criticism and humiliation of me. She made me feel totally worthless, even though at some level I knew I was just normal. The only way I could cope was by tuning her out completely. As soon as she'd start to speak, I'd think about something else. For all practical purposes, she vanished from my emotional life. I stopped counting on her for any warmth or approval. I stopped feeling anything for her. I didn't want to hate her, so feeling nothing was the only option I had.

Because the Perfect Mother images exist, daughters feel guilty for not regarding their mothers as perfect; but if they don't, a whole culture out there is ready to pounce, to encourage them to see her as a miserable failure. No matter what a mother has done to her daughter, the chances are that sometime she did something good, so that her daughter feels guilty about branding her as a failure. In addition, no matter how bad a mother is, her daughter usually senses that either within or outside the family, people identify her with her mother. So if she is going to regard mother as thoroughly horrible, what does that make her? A society that encouraged us to see our mothers simply as people would diminish the need to go emotionally limp.

PENT-UP LOVE

We are used to believing that pent-up *hostility* is dangerous; but the real tragedy for daughters is pent-up *love*. When mother-blaming attitudes overshadow our view of our mothers, it is far too easy to believe they deserve only our scorn and blame; but bottling up our loving feelings makes us feel inhuman, mechanical, cold. We feel better about ourselves when we are free to show love, warmth, and respect. So the release of pent-up love and respect for our mothers brings the added gift of love and respect for ourselves. Furthermore, as many experienced therapists agree, digging around in our past in order to find the cause of current problems has only limited value. What works much better—and is more empowering (perhaps the most important aim of therapy) —is to focus on what we can do now and how we can go beyond mother-blaming. Ruth's story illustrates this process. Like most adolescents, Ruth had serious self-doubts. At first, she was relieved to believe that her mother was deficient, not she herself:

> I believe that prior to blaming my mother for not loving me enough or for disappointing me in various ways, I blamed myself for being unlovable and the cause of her failure as a mother.

For Ruth, mother-blaming was one step away from self-hate and self-blame. As an adult, Ruth realized that neither she nor her mother was so terrible. Just recently, she reports, raising her own daughter has made her appreciate her mother more, and she is pleased about that.

Sue and Ellen, the mother and daughter described earlier, found a way to go beyond their stalemate (about Ellen's trip with her boyfriend) to release some of their pent-up love. Ellen felt both despair and anger at her mother, because nothing she did seemed to meet her mother's standards: her divorce was an embarrassment to her mother, but so was her new relationship. Leaving her teenagers alone for a week was not acceptable to Sue, nor was leaving them *with her*. Ellen also felt betrayed, as though her mother did not love her enough—for if her mother did, she would have been thrilled at Ellen's chance to travel with her new man.

Ellen could have simply blamed and chided her mother for being unreasonable, but doing *only* that would have meant ignoring her own wish to be more loving with her mother. Wisely, Ellen thought to ask Sue why she was so upset.

Sue explained that she was terrified that her friends would disapprove of Ellen's traveling with a man to whom she was not married and would consider it a mark of Sue's failure as a mother. She already knew that many of her friends considered her a failure because Ellen "hadn't managed to keep her marriage together." Talking to her, Ellen learned that *that* was why Sue could not rejoice in Ellen's vacation plans. She had wanted to help Ellen but also felt embarrassed and worried; when the children misbehaved she was overwhelmed and unable to cope. Furthermore,

Sue was afraid that Ellen was vulnerable, having so recently left a difficult marriage, and would have her hopes for a romantic, globe-trotting adventure dashed by a less glorious reality. Sue had adored Ellen's husband and treated him like a son, so Ellen's divorce involved a loss of a relationship for Sue, too. Understandably, Sue held back from getting her own hopes up about this new man.

As Sue and Ellen talked, Sue managed—at least for the moment—to stop feeling she should be Supergrandma. She described how taking care of Ellen's children, though well-intended, had proven to be more than she could handle. As she talked, she realized that her failure wasn't Ellen's fault, and Ellen realized that her mother was neither perfect nor totally unreasonable but an ordinary person. Sue was relieved to hear that her daughter wasn't horrified by her inability to handle the teenagers—after all, who could sympathize with the frustration of that task more than Ellen? Together, Ellen and Sue saw that they had both been controlled by the unreasonable expectations that if Sue were a Good Mother she would immediately and wholeheartedly approve of everything Ellen did and would manage to meet the needs of Ellen and her children with grace and ease. Most of all, their improved mutual understanding lowered the barrier between them and replaced it with a bridge.

IT NEEDN'T BE SO HARD

Mothers and daughters have not always been plagued by enormous anguish in their relationships with each other. In her article "The Female World of Love and Ritual: Relations Between Women in Nineteenth-Century America," historian Carroll Smith-Rosenberg notes that in the eighteenth and nineteenth centuries, women relatives "assumed an emotional centrality in each others' lives," "hostility and criticism of other women were discouraged," and "Women, who had little status or power in the larger world of male concerns, possessed status and power in the lives and worlds of other women." Writing specifically about mother-daughter relationships during the past two centuries, Smith-Rosenberg gives a moving description of great intimacy and shared sympathy and joy; expressions of hostility were rare,

Smith-Rosenberg believes, not because they were suppressed but because such feelings were actually uncommon.

Guilt and agony have not always characterized mother-daughter relationships in the past, so perhaps they need not characterize our relationships today. And if cultural and social changes have magnified mother-daughter problems, understanding the nature of those changes can take us a long way toward overcoming our difficulties.

In order to see our mothers as they really are, and really have been, we have to understand the very fabric of mother-blaming, to think about a variety of its manifestations, to learn how it works so that we can catch ourselves doing it. Chapter 3 begins this exploration.

3 ❦ *Mother-Blaming*

> If you really want to know why this child is a mess, just look at its mother!
> — frequent, informal assessment by both real and armchair psychologists

> MOTHER-IN-LAW IN TRUNK
> — seen on hundreds of car bumper-stickers

START WITH THIS fact: in our society it is acceptable to blame Mom. Then add the Perfect Mother and Bad Mother images, which lead us to blame Mom for not being perfect when she doesn't live up to our idealized image and, when she does something not so terrific, to blame her for being horrible rather than only human. This set of practices plagues mother-daughter relationships.

Most women are stuck in the mother-blaming mold. Journalist Zenith Henkin Gross studied 121 women who described in depth their view of their own mothers' mothering performance; only eight women—slightly more than six percent—saw their mothers as admirable models to be emulated. This percentage is shockingly low in view of the intense social pressure placed on girls to be "little mothers": their most salient model is not regarded as a worthy one.

Mother-blaming is like air pollution. I live in a large city with moderate pollution I rarely notice—until I get out into the fresh country air, when I suddenly recall how good it feels to breathe really well. My students and patients swear that getting away from mother-blaming helps them breathe more freely.

The essential foundation for improving our mother-daughter relationships is a thorough understanding of mother-blaming, for only when we see how easy blaming mother is will we have a chance of doing otherwise. Only when we see the pollution can we clear the air.

We need to explore the fabric of our prejudices with care. We daughters can't expect to forget the irritating or infuriating things our mothers do and just focus on the wonderful ones. But we need to realize that our culture encourages us to focus *only* on our *mothers' faults* and to let their good points slip our minds. Blaming our mothers is so easy that we rarely stop to consider whether anyone else might be to blame, or even that no one is to blame. For us mothers, understanding how mother-blaming operates can lighten our load. After all, untapped energy is bound up not only in the daughter's mother-blaming but also in the mother's self-blame and self-hate.

The less a group is valued and respected, the easier it is to target its members as scapegoats. The undervaluing of mothers is revealed not just through anecdotes but also by hard facts. According to the U.S. Department of Labor, the skill level needed to be a homemaker, childcare attendant, or nursery school teacher is rated at 878 on a scale of 1 to 887, where 1 is the highest skill level! On this scale, the rating for a dog trainer is 228. Apparently, the skill raters have never tried taking care of children! (With daycare now receiving more attention than in our mothers' child-rearing days, these ratings ought to increase.)

This undervaluing is largely a product of our times. Before the technological revolution mothers did most of their work at home. Their children could see them "in the garden, in the yard, tending chickens, cleaning, laundering, cooking, preparing food, mending, sewing, hauling water and firewood—all obviously hard work," explains sociologist Jessie Bernard. Now, however, mothers spend much of their time and energy trying to meet their children's emotional, psychological, and learning needs; they have nothing concrete, visible, and immediate to show for it—no woven shawls, no fresh eggs. Mothers now are often thought to spend most of their time doing nothing, or nothing of consequence.

How easily did our mothers' work become invisible! How easily did our mothers face the accusations of husbands who assumed women had nothing to do all day! "Why isn't dinner on the table? Why isn't the house in order? Why aren't the kids in bed?" Men wanted their needs met and discounted the fact that mothers were chauffeuring the children to and from school and activities, taking them to doctors' appointments, entertaining them and their friends, refereeing siblings' and neighbor children's conflicts, empathizing with the children about their minor and major life tragedies, and trying to give and receive a little support from other women who were also trying to be terrific mothers and terrified they weren't.

For women raising children today, the undervaluing of our mothering work has become more complex. Those of us with paid employment *may* feel valued in our work environments but often wind up feeling unappreciated for the enormous weight of our double load. Mothering tasks, after all, are still believed to require little or no skill or effort. And hand in hand with mother-blaming goes a taboo against father-blaming.

My friend Mary is a busy psychologist, and her husband Steve is a surgeon. When Mary tired of making all of the travel plans for family vacations, she informed Steve that, for the next December holiday, she would leave all plans for their annual family ski trip to him. He made no plans. When she told him how disappointed she was, their six-year-old son said angrily, *"Don't* get mad at Daddy. He is a surgeon and he works very hard. He's so busy and important that he has to have a nurse *and* an assistant. He doesn't have *time* to make travel plans." And another son added, "That's right. And Daddy's so important that he even has a dictaphone. *You* don't have a dictaphone!" Many people hear such stories and just laugh, not recognizing how much the devaluation and blame can hurt.

Mother-work is not only undervalued but often unnoticed. Even an assembly-line worker in a boring factory receives a regular paycheck, which carries with it the message, "Someone values the work that you do." In contrast, not only are mothers not paid but also most of their boring or difficult work is unnoticed or made light of. What mother has had her children or husband say, "That was a great week's worth of dusting you did! Thanks!"?

You may feel that *your* mother doesn't go unnoticed. In fact, many women tell me that their mothers are "very strong women," as though that means that they are appreciated. That may be true in some cases, but if you think of your mother as strong, be careful: that image is often another way to brand mothers negatively—"Oh, don't worry about my mother. She comes on like a Mack truck!" (As we shall see in Chapter 5, perceiving a mother as powerful often means perceiving her as dangerous *because of* that power.) When we unthinkingly describe mother as strong, we often focus on her power to make us put our dirty clothes in the hamper or make us feel guilty; we don't recognize that she has no power outside the home. Quite possibly, she receives no respect or appreciation even in the home, only mockery and fear.

People whose eyes tear up when they talk about "motherhood" or when they talk *about* their own mothers often treat their mothers with disdain when they are face-to-face. Paradoxically, motherhood *in principle* and *in general* is described in glowing, all-important terms—so that mothers feel ashamed to complain about their low status *in fact* and *individually*.

During the 1950s, an era now infamous for the popularity of the image of happy-little-wife-at-home, author Philip Wylie pulled together every demeaning image of mothers and gave them ugly, vicious form. In his *Generation of Vipers*, his loathing of mothers vibrates with intensity, and although this book is painful to read, we need to know that it was popular when mothers were raising the children who are now in their thirties and forties:

> . . . megaloid momworship has got completely out of hand. Our land, subjectively mapped, would have more silver cords and apron strings crisscrossing it than railroads and telephone wires. Mom is everywhere and everything and damned near everybody, and from her depends all the rest of the U.S. Disguised as good old mom, dear old mom, sweet old mom, your loving mom, and so on. . . .
> . . . nobody among [American sages]—no great man or brave—from the first day of the first congressional meeting to the present ever stood in our halls of state and pronounced the one indubitably most-needed American verity: "Gentlemen, mom is a jerk."
> . . . [Mom used to be so busy with childraising and housework] that she was rarely a problem to her family or to her equally busy friends, and never one to herself. Usually, until very recently, mom folded up and died of hard work somewhere in the middle of her life.
> . . . Nowadays, with nothing to do, and all the tens of thousands of men . . . to maintain her, every clattering prickamette in the republic survives for an incredible number of years, to stamp and jibber in the midst of man, a noisy neuter by natural default or a scientific gelding sustained by science, all tongue and teat and razzmatazz.

Wylie's words continue to be widely quoted, used as justification for mother-trashing, used to make men feel ashamed of loving their mothers and of refusing to revile them, used to make women feel that motherlove is sick, since who in their right mind could love the kind of creature Wylie so vividly described? Even people who never read Wylie's actual work are familiar with the essential features of his mother-images.

Wylie coined the term *momism*, which became widely used to refer scathingly and fearfully to mothers' allegedly excessive domination, reflecting Wylie's own attitude toward mothers. To this day, mother-blaming perpetuates "momism" in a different sense, one that parallels other "isms": sexism, racism, ageism, classism. Perhaps it is time to use the word *momism* to label mother-blame and mother-hate explicitly and succinctly as a form of prejudice as virulent as the other "isms" are acknowledged to be.

In subsequent years, mother-hating books like *How To Be a Jewish Mother* and *Portnoy's Complaint* appeared. How well I remember reading *Portnoy's Complaint* and then, when discussing it with friends, realizing that I was supposed to say I thought it was funny and rang true, although clearly a *little bit* exaggerated (most mothers don't actually wield a large *knife* over their children's heads to make them eat!). Anyone who said that the author of *Portnoy* had cruelly defamed mothers, and Jewish mothers in particular, was accused of having no sense of humor, of not being a good sport. Thankfully, by the late 1960s and early 1970s, expressing anti-Black sentiments publicly was becoming *declassé* (although racism itself persisted and persists, of course); but it remained acceptable to say venomous things about Blacks as long as they were Black *mothers* or about Jewish mothers, Italian mothers, Catholic mothers, funny old grannies, or mothers-in-law. So racist statements about Blacks or other people of color were on their way out, as were anti-Semitic comments, but only when they were about groups (sex unspecified) or about males. This pattern continues today. Jokes about mothers and mothers-in-law, as noted earlier, are far more common than jokes about fathers and fathers-in-law. And it is a terrible thing to be a mother and know that you are expected to find them funny, that you are not supposed to be deeply hurt by them, that to be hurt is to be overly sensitive—or ridiculous.

Once we're aware that mother-blaming comes easily and that it distorts our view, we can begin to catch ourselves doing it. A friend who knew that I was writing this book explained,

> I couldn't sleep last night. I kept thinking about my 85-year-old mother. She's in a nursing home, and she's very ill and may not live much longer. Every time my sister and I talk on the telephone, we moan and groan, saying, "Do you know what she said to me today!? She asked me why I'd had my hair cut so short! Do you believe it? Why doesn't she leave us alone?!"
>
> I kept thinking about the things she says to me that make me crazy, and about the things I wanted her to do that she'd never done. Then, I thought about your book, and I sat up in bed and asked myself why I always focus on the ways she has failed or upset me. Why do I never think about the good things she's done for me? And I started remembering how, after my husband and I split up, she came and stayed with the children and me and helped to take care of us. I thought of all the things she had done over the years to make my life easier or to make me laugh.

This woman has begun to see the mother-blaming mold in which her experience has been shaped, and she understands that this threw her mother's love and humor into shadow while turning the spotlight on her mother's weak points. Whether or not she suspects it, she may be using mother-blame to avoid her fear of her mother's impending death.

MOTHER-BLAMING ALL AROUND

If you are a daughter, don't think that it's only you—or other daughters—whose view of mothers is distorted. Mother-blaming is interwoven throughout our daily lives. At every level of conversation and discussion, in every conceivable arena, mothers are ignored, demeaned, and scapegoated—in jokes (often unfunny), on bumper stickers, on television and at the movies, in works by popular authors, in our own families, in the research literature, in the courts, and in psychotherapists' offices.

Our everyday language reflects this pattern: try to think of terms that are as demeaning to fathers as everyday terms like "son of a bitch." Even for expressions that are not profane, such as "mama's boy," the parallel "daddy's girl" is not really equivalent. "Mama's boy" calls up images of a smothering, overprotective mother whose "boy" seems psychologically sick, or at least unmanly and ridiculous, through his association with her. A "daddy's girl," on the other hand, is the lucky, feminine daughter who has been singled out by the high-status parent. At worst, she might be thought of as overly reliant on her "feminine wiles."

Mockery of mothers is a staple of feature films. In the popular movie *Dirty Dancing*, hilarious laughter greets the stand-up comic who says, "I finally met a girl exactly like my mother—dresses like her, acts like her. So I brought her home . . . my father doesn't like her."

Toronto social worker Ruth Goodman told me the following story: At the Toronto Festival of Festivals a filmmaker was asked why his film included so much violence. He replied, "If you knew my mother, you'd understand." The audience snickered. This glib response allowed him to disown responsibility for his actions by switching the focus to his mother. Ironically, the only sins of the mother in the movie were that she had corny wallpaper and liked Muzak, whereas the father was a very disturbing person.

When my book *The Myth of Women's Masochism* was published in 1985, I did a great deal of speaking in the United States and Canada. I had carefully avoided mother-blaming, but many readers managed to work it in anyway; strikingly often, one or more women approached me after my lecture and said something like this: "I read your book and really understood what you said, and now I agree with you that women are not masochists, they do not like to suffer. Except one: my mother." Apparently, untold numbers of otherwise thoughtful women believe that *their* mother is the world's only living masochist, the worst of the sickos.

The most poignant instances of mother-blaming within the family are those in which the mother blames herself for whatever goes wrong. Mothers of misbehaving kids blame themselves for "not setting enough limits" if they are slightly less rigid disciplinarians than average, and if they are slightly more rigid, they blame themselves for "coming down too hard" on the child. Mothers whose children get many colds are far more likely to berate themselves for failing to dress them warmly enough (even when they haven't failed to do so) than to blame the pediatrician for not suggesting that the coughs and runny noses could be caused by food allergies or that colds are hard to prevent when kids spend all day in groups. Hearing ourselves and other mothers blamed from all sides, we naturally learn to do it ourselves.

I am still surprised when I hear successful, well-educated women putting themselves down as mothers, even when they might not be totally responsible for all of their children's suffering. One very successful woman was a frequent face on the lecture circuit. Upon learning that one of her daughters was bulimic, she stopped her media tour and rushed home to nurse her daughter back to health—which she succeeded in doing! But she concluded that she was to blame for her daughter's bulimia; she believed that she had neglected her daughter's emotional needs for years because she had been preoccupied with her own career and had hungrily fed on her daughter's admiration for her work.

Although the typical *father* is preoccupied with his work and wants his children's respect and approval, such fathers are not blamed for their children's problems. Furthermore, the lecturer was divorced from her daughter's father, so what preceded or followed the divorce, perhaps even something in the father's treatment of the daughter, just *might* have contributed to the bulimia. So might a host of other factors. *But the mother never mentioned any of this in her lecture.*

Hearing this successful woman publicly offer up her "guilt" as proof of mothers' failures and their culpability was tragic—and frightening. Not only was she doing an injustice to herself, but also she was reinforcing the blaming of other mothers and their self-blame.

Even when we're not faulting ourselves, other family members often do it for us. Essayist Nancy Mairs said that when her sixteen-year-old daughter Anne went to Central America as a volunteer worker, Mairs' parents-in-law chided her for allowing Anne to go:

> [George's parents] never mentioned the matter to him. I was at first hurt, angry, feeling picked on; later I came to understand that I was the natural target of their misgivings. George couldn't be counted on to know what girls should or shouldn't do, or to communicate his knowledge if he did. But I could. I was Anne's mother.

Mother-blaming among laypeople is well-nourished by the words of mental health researchers and practitioners, whom our culture considers to be experts on human behavior. *Because* we consider them experts, we often forget that their theories and their research are influenced by the same tendency to scapegoat mothers that pervades the whole society.

MOTHER-BLAMING AMONG THE EXPERTS

If Researchers Say It, It Must Be True

In Chapter 1, I mentioned my study of mother-blaming by mental health professionals. My documentation came from their own writings in scholarly journals, and the results show that they generally make little or no attempt to hide their mother-blaming; apparently they feel no need to conceal it.

My student Ian Hall-McCorquodale and I read 125 articles published in nine different major mental health journals in 1970, 1976, and 1982. Some articles were single case studies, and some were reports of research on large numbers of people with emotional problems. We categorized each article according to 63 different types of mother-blaming. These ranged from "number of words used to describe mother" and "number of words used to describe father" to the repetition of earlier mother-blaming claims without questioning whether they apply in the current case. We found that, regardless of the author's sex or occupation as psychoanalyst, psychiatrist, psychologist, or social worker, mental health professionals were overwhelmingly indulging in mother-blaming. In the 125 articles, mothers were blamed for 72 different kinds of problems in their offspring, ranging from bedwetting to schizophrenia, from inability to deal with color blindness to aggressive behavior, from learning problems to "homicidal transsexualism."

Two articles reporting our findings were published in 1985, and the responses were gratifying. In a typical letter, one woman wrote, "My husband and I are both practicing psychiatrists, and I have been trying to convince him for years that mothers get blamed for everything. Now I have documented proof!" Her letter illustrated an important point: most therapists, like this woman's husband, are not even aware of how much mother-blaming they and others do. The rare negative responses we received were all from people who were worried that reducing mother-blame meant increasing father-blame, though we never advocated the latter. The alarm about the *possibility* that father-blaming *might* increase *somewhat* starkly contrasted with most therapists' comfort with mother-blaming.

The biases in research and theory are not new. They predate the time when our mothers were raising us. One 65-year-old mother of three told me that she remembers learning in a university course that the severe emotional disorder called infantile autism was caused by cold mothers who rejected their infants (which was later found to be untrue). She says: "Every time I felt a little tired or distracted when I picked up one of my babies, I was sure I was going to drive her into an autistic state!"

One parallel contemporary example is making it mothers' responsibility to provide the technical help for their children who have learning disabilities. I spent years working with such children and writing about their problems. Even though *by definition* learning difficulties are not caused by motivational problems or lack of exposure to learning, I often heard mothers held totally responsible for dealing with their children's disabilities. As one mother told me:

> I read all the books about how to teach your child to read, and I *tried* to use them to teach Jessica. But we just haven't gotten anywhere. At the end of every tutoring session, she and I both feel like failures. The teacher says I should keep working with Jessica, but I don't know what else to do.

As sociologists Dorothy Smith and Alison Griffith have found in their research, school systems depend heavily on mothers to help them accomplish the work they are supposed to do. This is true not only for children who have problems but right down to the expectation that kindergarten and first-grade students will come to school already knowing their ABCs because their mothers have taught them.

CHILD ABUSE: A CASE IN POINT

One of the most sobering examples of mother-blaming interpretations of research is in the area of child abuse. Conducting good research about child abuse is difficult because abuse tends to be hidden, especially among wealthier, better-educated people.

For this reason, research on the question *"Who* abuses children?" has given us a skewed picture of the truth. Many so-called authorities on child abuse claim that mothers are more likely than fathers to abuse their children. This comes as a surprise to people who think of mothers in idealized terms as the "Angel in the House." But it fits the darker cultural stereotype about mothers: that they are "Wicked Witches," unable or unwilling to control their unlimited rages.

Researchers who make these claims rarely ask how much time each parent spends with the children. In general, mothers spend far more time than fathers with children, and many of the fathers in studies of abuse have left their families or are rarely home. So for each hour spent with the children, the mothers actually abuse them far *less* than the fathers do. But many "experts" continue to believe that mothers are more likely than fathers to commit child abuse—and this belief is a serious distortion.

This distortion affects every mother, because nearly everyone who has taken care of children has sometimes felt so frustrated, exhausted, and helpless that they have used some physical punishment or abused our children outright (then felt horribly guilty for doing so). Although child abuse is wrong and damaging to children, my own work in this area has shown that the misinterpretation of research findings takes the focus off important issues that contribute to the abuse, like mothers' lack of support, their sometimes desperate circumstances, and so on. It feeds the fear that mothers are indeed dangerous, especially compared to fathers, and it can create a self-fulfilling prophecy: when a woman truly believes that she is a horrible mother, her self-esteem plunges and her sense of isolation grows, increasing the likelihood that she *will* be abusive.

Some researchers, who say that child welfare workers should use their findings to identify abusive parents, also focus on mothers. A recent press release from a major university conveyed the impression that only mothers abuse their children. Although the release was headlined, "Study of Family Interaction Leads to New Understanding of Abusive *Parents*" [my italics], the entire section reporting the study's results describes only mothers. According to the release, researchers produced a profile of abusive "parents," but in fact they studied only mothers—one hundred of them! Then, reporting their results, they described various kinds of abusive mothers—harsh/intrusive, covert/hostile, and emotionally detached ones:

> "Harsh/intrusive" mothers are excessively harsh and constantly badger their child to behave. . . .
> A "covert/hostile" mother shows no positive feelings towards her child. She makes blatant attacks on the child's self-worth and denies him affection or attention. . . .
> An "emotionally detached" mother has very little involvement with her child. She appears depressed and uninterested in the child's activities.

Thus, the blame is placed on the mental illness or just plain nastiness of individual mothers, as though fathers are never abusive, as though more complex family and social factors play no role in leading to abuse.

Often, a researcher's mother-blaming work is used by someone else as a source of information, with the second party unquestioningly taking on the researcher's mother-blaming attitude. In a pamphlet published by a highly respected nurses' association, case workers were told that child sexual abuse is characterized by the following: the mother is aware of the abuse, may see it as a relief for herself, organizes time for her husband and daughter to be alone, may have refused to sleep with her husband, and will not risk exposing the abuse.

This list is unforgivable, in view of what is really known about father-daughter incest. As Dr. Kathleen Coulbourn Faller of the University of Michigan School of Social Work has shown in her paper based on more than three hundred cases of sexual abuse, the mother usually does *not* know that it is happening. When she does know, she usually brings it into the open and takes steps to ensure that it stops; when she doesn't report it, she is often afraid of her husband's threats to harm her and their daughter further if she tells or because she has been taught that a good woman's first task is to keep the family together (and perhaps even to obey her husband no matter what). And, of course, the discovery of abuse often *does* destroy the two-parent family.

Some daughters who try to inform their mothers about the abuse do so in such vague or unclear ways—because they feel afraid or guilty—that mother doesn't understand; and since sexual abuse is unthinkable for most people, often the mother genuinely never realizes what her daughter is trying to tell her. (This may be all the more true if the abuser is the mother's *own father*.) As one highly educated, loving mother said, "Before I found out that my ex-husband was abusing my daughter, if you had asked me, I would have said, 'He's selfish and ruthless and sneaky—but sexual abuse? *That* he would *never* do.' "

In the nurses' association pamphlet, the "indicators" were unduly focused on mothers. They did not include, for example, the well-documented sneakiness of the fathers who perpetrate incest. In general, these men are like alcoholics in the lengths to which they will go to deny and conceal the incest. And, of course, a mother who does *not* "organize time" for father and daughter to be alone risks being called possessive and smothering.

Even in extreme cases of mother-blaming for abuse, however, there is hope.

> One incest survivor, a woman in her twenties, disclosed at her survivors' group meeting that an adult male neighbor sexually abused her when she was a very young child. She said that when she told her mother about it at the time, her mother had never said a word, never reacted at all. She had always felt that her mother had betrayed her and failed to support her because of this. Her group leader urged her to talk to her mother about it, and the woman gathered up her courage and did so. Her mother's response was, "When you told me I was so afraid that I would say or do the wrong thing, something that would be bad for you, that I tried not to react at all. So I went to the psychiatrist to ask *him* what I should do, and he said that for your sake, the best thing I could do would be never to mention it again."

Naturally, the daughter had spent years blaming her mother; it's what we all are taught to do.

Mother-Blaming Among Therapists

Psychotherapists had begun acquiring an aura of authority by the time our mothers were raising us, and that aura very much persists right now. In popular books and articles and on television and radio talk shows, mental health professionals communicate to the public at large the mother-blaming messages they learn in their training. Psychotherapists had even more influence in our mothers' childraising days, because in the 1930s, 1940s, and 1950s the public tended even more than now to defer to psychiatrists.

Some fair and sensitive psychotherapists have been enormously supportive and helpful to distraught mothers and daughters. But all too many—knowingly or unwittingly—have intensively promoted mother-blaming in their capacity as therapists, both in our mothers' childrearing years and in our own adult years, and this has often been even more devastating to mothers than mother-blaming research. A psychotherapy patient reveals her most intimate feelings and her most shameful secrets to her therapist. Her therapist learns things about her that no one else has ever known. She goes to the therapist seeking help both to feel better and to learn more of the truth about herself and her life. This gives the therapist enormous power over her. Because the training for most therapists involves so much mother-blame and woman-blame, only the unusual ones help the patient to go beyond mother-blame and self-blame. Traditional therapists tend to believe sincerely that mother-blaming fits reality, and they regard themselves as helping their patients to accept this reality. Thus, women are primed to accept the therapist's descriptions of them and their mothers—or themselves *as* mothers—as manipulative, overprotective, intrusive, cold, rejecting, and so on. Let us look at some examples of therapists' demeaning descriptions of mothers.

Since the 1960s, therapists' attitudes toward mothers have been widely influenced by Margaret Mahler's work on the importance of the child's psychological "separation and individuation" from its mother. (Although Mahler did important work on profoundly disturbed children, her writings have been widely applied in mother-blaming ways.) Mahler advised therapists to watch carefully when a mother entered the room used for observing the family's dynamics. They were to take note of whether she carried the child "like a part of herself"—which would then brand the mother as being unable to separate from the child—or "like an inanimate object"—which would label her as the cold-and-rejecting type. Imagine being a mother observed by a therapist who used such a pigeonholing scheme, in which each pigeonhole is a different form of bad mothering! Even more painful to imagine are the kinds of messages such a therapist would convey to the mother about her relationship with her child.

The names of Mahler and some of her like-minded colleagues never became known to most laypeople, but many theories that share the same mother-blaming foundation have become familiar as presumed truths. In one currently fashionable type of psycho-therapy, the wives of alcoholics, drug addicts, compulsive gamblers and womanizers are said to make life hard for their children, because they support their husbands' addictions and compulsions. Proponents of these theories use the term "co-dependent" to describe the wife/mother, and they say she "needs" or "likes" her husband's problems to continue: "She loves playing the holier-than-thou game with him" or "She gets her jollies from seeing how abject and disgusting he is when he is drunk."

In fact, however, if you ask these women how they would feel if you could magically take away their husbands' problem behaviors, they sigh with relief at the thought. Men who try to stop their addictive behavior find it physically and/or psychologically difficult, and all too many take out their frustrations on their families, including subjecting their wives and their children to severe beatings or verbal abuse. When the wives bemoan this worsened behavior, many therapists say, "Aha! She doesn't *want* him to stop drinking!" They ignore the fact that the wives wish the men would stop both the drinking *and* the abuse.

Other recovering men are humiliated to face the wives who knew them when they were drunks, so they want to leave them. No wonder some women are frightened by the prospect of their husbands' recovery—but this is a far cry from wanting the compulsion to continue. The irony is that mothers who *leave* such husbands are blamed for breaking up the family and depriving the children of their father, but women who *stay* are given the demeaning, pathologizing term "co-dependent" and are accused of "loving too much" and failing to save the children from their father's addictive behavior.

You don't have to be a mental health professional to absorb the cultural propensity for blaming mother for father's alcoholism. Television star Suzanne Somers has described the anger that she and her siblings felt toward their mother because of their father's drinking. Sensing the danger in confronting their abusive, alcoholic father but trying to find a way out, they directed their disappointment and rage toward Mom. The happy ending to Somers' story is that their father is sober, and she and her siblings appreciate their mother's strength and love, which enabled them to overcome the bad times.

As I have mentioned, when the patient is not the mother's

husband but rather her child, mother-blaming knows no bounds. A friend described for me her experience in 1987 as the target of psychiatrists' mother-blaming, in a situation in which she already felt helpless and frightened because her child was sick. The mother, whom I'll call Caroline, took care of her ten-year-old daughter, Laurel, who had what seemed to be a stomach virus, including nausea and vomiting. For weeks after the vomiting stopped, Laurel was extremely tired and listless, and she said she could not eat anything without feeling nauseated. Caroline used every gentle technique she could think of to induce her to eat a little, but the listlessness and nausea persisted. The family doctor ordered numerous, expensive medical tests, which revealed no physical problem; so the doctor sent Caroline and Laurel to the state university's hospital, a three-hour drive away.

The university's regular medical staff found no physical cause for Laurel's problems and transferred her to the psychiatric ward. The psychiatric staff instructed Caroline to leave Laurel there for three weeks and have no contact with her during that time. When Laurel wept from loneliness, the psychiatrists concluded that her problem was that "her relationship with her mother is too close, symbiotic." At the end of the three weeks, they shipped her home, still physically ill and depressed. Both Caroline and Laurel were now psychiatrically labeled, and Caroline felt guilty and ashamed. Months later, on the advice of a friend, Caroline gave Laurel a little of a commercially available medication that soothes the digestive tract. Laurel's nausea vanished, she began to eat normally, and as she became well-nourished, her depression disappeared.

Of course, there are many, many variations on this limited set of examples. For instance, in my own investigation of mother-blaming, I found an article in which the authors' stated purpose was to study whether children of male prisoners-of-war suffered because of their fathers' experiences. They described these fathers as filled with various feelings of distress and emotionally distant from their families. The authors found that these children indeed had a high incidence of emotional problems; however, they said that the fault was their mothers'! They presented their reasoning clearly: the women were upset at seeing their husbands' anguish, and this interfered with their ability to mother their children properly! These children are now fully grown, but mother-blaming in similar situations hasn't abated, as Aphrodite Matsakis documents in her new book about Vietnam veterans' wives, who are blamed for the ill effects their husbands' psychiatric symptoms have on their families.

Therapists often make explicit, crude attempts to alienate daughters from their mothers. Fraydele Oysher, mother of comedian and mimic Marilyn Michaels, told an interviewer that Marilyn doesn't call her mother very often: "It began," says Ms. Oysher, "when she started seeing a psychiatrist. She said her psychiatrist told her she had to be her own person. So now she's the psychiatrist's person." Fraydele Oysher clearly has a kind of insight that is rarely displayed by the so-called "professionals." She saw not only the psychiatrist's dangerous tampering with Marilyn's feelings about her mother but also the insidious way in which he simply shifted her from dependence on (or quite possibly her warm involvement with) her mother to dependence on him.

Usually, women who are able to go beyond mother-blaming do so on their own or with the help of other people, not their therapists. A forty-year-old professional woman told me that her therapist had helped her to get angry at her mother but not to go beyond that:

> My mother was intimidated by my father, and she did use me to stand up to him, from the time I was four years old. She and I both knew that I had the guts to say things to him that she didn't dare say. And it wasn't fair to put me in that position. My therapist helped me feel my anger about that, but then he just left me there, furious at my mother for being so manipulative.

What changed this woman's view was her own later experience, not her work with her therapist:

> Only after I became a mother myself did I put her "manipulations" in perspective. First of all, I realized that, yes, she had been somewhat manipulative, but *mostly* she had been a terrific mother. And all my therapist wanted me to do was talk about the bad side of her. Having my own children and seeing how hard it was to work toward that impossible image of the perfect mother made me appreciate how much she had done for me. Instead of just being stuck thinking of her as getting me to stand up to Dad, other memories started to come back to me: the time she volunteered to drive two hours to pick up the Girl Scout cookies for four hundred Scouts to sell—and then at 2:30 in the morning, as we

continued stacking them all through the house, said, "Well, the night is young! And we've only got the mint ones left to do!" She had a wonderful sense of humor and was totally supportive of me and of everything I did. And in the course of my therapy that had slipped my mind.

When we consider such numerous and varied examples of mother-blaming by therapists, that such things can really happen may seem surprising. We must understand that they do occur and to have some idea about why they do.

THERAPISTS AREN'T HELD ACCOUNTABLE

We don't tend to question the opinions of high-status people very energetically; for that one powerful reason, therapists get away with unjustifiably increasing women's alienation from their mothers. Also, therapists are rarely held accountable for their claims. At a conference on mothers and daughters, a woman therapist showed a videotape of an interview with a mother, a father, and their young adult daughter. The therapist and the audience joined in groaning, laughing mockery of the mother for "not participating" when the father and daughter were interacting and for "sitting there, looking left out and pitiful." But in fact the daughter might be considered a classic "daddy's girl" who showed an unhealthy adoration of her father, a Real Man who went out into the Real World and made a living! The father treated his daughter like a pampered doll. Neither one of them wanted any part of the mother, apparently because the mother knew their faults, and they needed to keep up their charade of adored, adoring, perfect father and adored, adoring, perfect daughter. The therapist didn't seem to realize that the mother was the only member of that family whom no one held in high esteem. The father was respected because he was male and the financial provider for the family. The daughter was valued because she was young, attractive, and prepared to worship her father unquestioningly. But the mother was "only" a housewife. When an audience member objected to the mother-blaming interpretations, the therapist ignored her comments.

Another revelation of therapists' poor accountability for what they practice and preach appeared when I was conducting a research project in 1987. In the course of that research, a group that included psychology students Maureen Gans, Cindy Brooks, Ilana Sunshine, Wendy Whitfield, and I mailed requests for about fifty papers about psychotherapy that had been presented at the 1987 American Psychiatric Association convention. We asked for those papers because we anticipated that we could learn something from them about how psychiatrists are currently treating their therapy patients and, we hoped, how they talk to patients about their mothers. We received only two papers—four percent of what we had requested. As a psychologist, I have requested in the neighborhood of one thousand convention papers from other psychologists, who are generally regarded as lower-status than psychiatrists; it is very rare that nothing is sent in reply.

Our experience taught us that the latest thinking of psychiatrists—the highest-status, highest-paid therapists—is largely unavailable to professional or public scrutiny, unless you are able to attend psychiatric or related conventions. Until people opposed to automatic mother-blaming start to attend such conventions in droves, and to make their objections known, this lack of accountability will continue to provide protective cover for psychiatrists' practices.

Mothers in Court

In the justice system, mothers are often rendered completely powerless. Phyllis Chesler has documented the way that, since well before our mothers' day, judges have been ordering the unwarranted removal of child custody from mothers who range from acceptable to wonderful. Good mothers have been denied custody of their children both because they *have* paying jobs ("they care more about their careers than about their children") and because they *don't* have paying jobs ("they don't love their kids enough to contribute to their financial support"), both because they *are* living with a man ("they are promiscuous") and because they are *not* living with a man ("they are isolated or cannot provide a stable, healthy, heterosexual childrearing environment").

Today, and even more so in our mothers' childrearing days, judges rarely consider a man's sexual or physical abuse of his children, or of his wife in front of their children, to be legitimate grounds for refusing him custody of his children. So mothers who are abused or who watch their husbands abuse their children feel understandably helpless.

Therapists commonly bring their mother-blaming into the courtroom when they appear as "expert witnesses" in custody battles. In these cases, the justice system and the mental health system provide a double whammy of mother-blaming. Many mothers who have thought that psychiatric assessment would help them get custody of their children, especially if the father was violent, irresponsible, or emotionally disturbed, have been sorely disappointed to find that they themselves were pathologized, whereas the husband—despite his problems—was praised simply for "caring enough about his children" to sue for custody.

We used child abuse to illustrate therapists' mother-blaming; it also illustrates the way mental health workers and the legal system band together to blame mothers. For hundreds of years, children's reports of sexual abuse were ignored or suppressed. Some of the most powerful reasons for this emerged from the fact that adult men are the most common perpetrators of child sexual abuse. Reports of such abuse have been suppressed because of people's refusal to believe that adult men could do such things, the reluctance to challenge fathers' rights and authority within their family, the failure to consider a child's need for protection from assault and betrayal as important, the labeling of mothers' testimony as "hysterical" compared to the "trustworthy" words of the assaulters, and a general suppression of anything related to sex.

Within the past ten years or so, mostly because of the strength of the women's movement, hundreds of thousands of adult women who had been victims of incest have come forward and told their stories—in therapy groups, where they went to try to heal their old, aching emotional scars; in family gatherings, where they bravely confronted the men after learning that they were now abusing members of the newest generation; in books and articles that they wrote to try to heal themselves as well as to let other women know they were not alone; and even in court, where they went to prevent the abusers from hurting more children. For a while, since these survivors were now adults and could command a little more respect than when they were being victimized, people listened and believed them. Not always, but sometimes.

During the past couple of years, however, there has been a dangerous shift. The reports of now-adult victims are treated as though they have little or nothing to do with current reports of sexual abuse. Disrespect for mothers' and children's reports has resurfaced, and now the fashion is to say that mothers coach their children to claim falsely that the mothers' ex-husbands have abused them. What is said to be the mothers' motive? That they are vicious, manipulative ex-wives out to take revenge on their husbands. Such things have happened occasionally, and when they have, the unjustly accused has received a great deal of publicity. To be one of those men must indeed be awful. But, unfortunately, some innocent people are falsely accused under every law, and we don't hear clamoring to strike down laws designed to punish thieves or murderers. In fact, most reports of sexual abuse of children are true.

Father-daughter sexual abuse puts mothers in a Catch-22 situation, then: a mother who does *not* report the abuse is said to be complicit, or even to have consciously or unconsciously instigated the abuse, and a mother who *does* report it is said to be vicious, man-hating, lying, or hysterical.

I have been shocked to learn how much the anti-woman backlash is promoted by lawyers. In 1986, a group of family lawyers asked me to speak to them about how, as their leader's invitation went, "women get shafted by our legal system." I soon saw clearly that the lawyers (one woman and about twenty men) had no interest in hearing about women's mistreatment in the justice system. They wanted to talk about scheming, vengeful ex-wives who construct false reports of sexual abuse to keep their ex-husbands away from the children.

Experienced and fair-minded therapists such as Dr. Peter Jaffe, Director of the London, Ontario, Family Court Clinic, present a more accurate picture. Dr. Jaffe explains that he has seen more than five hundred cases involving custody and access disputes in the past six years; only two involved false allegations of sexual abuse, and in both of those cases the mothers genuinely believed that abuse had occurred.

Sadly, too few people care about the facts. In a recent, typical case a social worker who had extensively assessed a family was asked whether the father had sexually abused his nine-year-old daughter. The worker concluded: "It wasn't clear whether or not he had sexually abused her, because this was brought up in the context of a custody dispute, so the mother's bitterness toward her ex-husband was her motivation." When he was reminded that there was no custody dispute (during the seven years since the parents' divorce, the mother had always had custody of the child and the question of custody had not been mentioned even after sexual abuse was reported), he backtracked only slightly. The primary issue—the sexual abuse of a little girl—was lost because of the social worker's insistent mother-blaming.

Skepticism about mothers prevents proper attention being given to abused children all over North America, even when the husband and wife still live together. The attorney for a southern state's Department of Social Services claims that some mothers really are responsible for their husbands' sexual abuse of their daughters. His evidence for this? "A woman went back to get her Ph.D. and got a part-time job, leaving her husband and daughter alone together." One woman called me after seeing me on a television program. She had recently learned that her husband was sexually abusing their young daughter, and she had gone to her local hospital's sexual abuse clinic for help. The only recommendation the sexual abuse team made, even after she told them that her young daughter had said, "Daddy puts his thing in my pee-pee, and it hurts a lot," was for the mother to take medication because they thought she might be manic-depressive. Period.

Such stories are hard to believe, but they are not uncommon. Why would members of a team whose purpose is to stop child abuse be so insensitive? One reason is that, despite their heightened awareness of abuse, most of them were trained in traditional, mother-blaming programs; they and their supervisors are often skeptical of sexual abuse reports. Furthermore, even members of abuse teams are not immune to social pressure coming from the anti-woman groups who claim that sexually abused children and their mothers fabricate their stories.

With such "experts" constructing false, negative pictures of mothers, no wonder mother-blaming becomes second nature to so many people. Not only is mother-blaming untrue; it also creates unproductive, misdirected anger toward mothers.

MOTHER-BLAME SERVES A PURPOSE

Mother-blaming is a cornerstone of the current structure of our society, because it perpetuates the unequal distribution of power between men and women. It does this through various routes. First, it keeps women down, ashamed, frightened; we are the judged, not the judges. Second, it drains women's energies into both the work of mothering and the fear of doing it inadequately or badly; this leaves us less energy for working toward greater sharing of power between women and men.

Why should men object to women's—or mothers'—power? Much could be said about that, but I want to focus on two parts of the answer: fear and envy.

(1) Men are afraid that if women were freed from shame, anxiety, and fear, they would indeed be capable of wielding enormous power. That frightens many people, especially men who don't want to share the kinds of power they have. Women do pack the potential for great *emotional* power, because they have been encouraged to stay in touch with a range of feelings and not to shy away from expressing them. Many men, having learned to be either uninterested in or frankly uncomfortable about emotions, fear their unfamiliar strength. In this respect, their fear is of the unknown.

Furthermore, many men fear the kind of power that their mothers had over them when they were young. Now, as adult members of the dominant sex who believe it is unmasculine to be controlled by someone else, losing power reminds them of their relatively powerless days of childhood. Back then, mother was likely to have had day-to-day control over them, and so now they must avoid mother's power in order to prove their manliness. Because mothers can make little children feel both so good and so bad, they seem very powerful to children of both sexes. But men feel more pressure than women to show that they have grown beyond the influence of mothers: such independence makes them feel both adult and masculine.

Although being loved, especially by our mothers, can empower us—by giving us support, self-confidence, and strength—many men are so afraid of being "engulfed" by love that they don't learn about its positive qualities. Then, the greatest love of all—their mother's love—comes to seem dangerous.

If just one mother seems too powerful, how much more threatening is a group of mothers! No one feels threatened when women work in groups as men's auxiliaries or as advocates or helpers of the poor, the ill, the disabled, or anyone except themselves and other women. Men who consider women's emotional power a threat are led to contemplate the economic, social, and political power that women wield when we get together.

In any society, the forces that maintain the status quo are usually stronger than the forces that push for change. Supporters of mother-blame belong to the former group. Those who aim to keep mothers in their place use *anything* that mothers do as "evidence" that they deserve blame; the Perfect Mother myths and the Bad Mother myths are excellent "evidence" (see Chapters 4 and 5). After all, if we stopped blaming our mothers for all our problems, we would see that in order to combat many of our social problems, we would need to make some major changes in our society (e.g., pay equity, respect and pension for housewives), *and* we women would find it easier to band together to press for those changes. So, even when we are tempted to praise or appreciate our mothers, supporters of the status quo find ways to keep us stuck in mother-blaming.

(2) *Men fear mothers' power because womb envy is alive and well, though often disguised.* Partly as an antidote to Sigmund Freud's claim that all women have penis envy, men are said to have womb envy. Many people have laughed at this idea, but as men become more open about their feelings, many are acknowledging their envy of women's capacity to give birth and to breast-feed. Men's eagerness to participate in the childbirth process, to write books about their participation, and to videotape it attest to that fact as well.

The magic and power associated with these functions are substantial in themselves; they are also associated with the emotional power that adheres to women. "Womb envy" is not just literal, then; it is not just a wish to be able to become pregnant and nurse an infant, but it also symbolizes men's envy of women's freedom to be nurturant and to express a range of feelings. Many so-called New Men write long treatises about the pain of being called "effeminate" or "wimpy" when they show their tender, expressive side. Most of North America is not yet ready for expressive men. So most men continue to suppress their feelings, to have trouble knowing *how* to express them when they want to, and to wish that they were as free to do this as women are.

Because of their fear and envy of women's power, many men have exaggerated mothers' bad behavior and mislabeled the positive as negative. They have said that up is down, plus is minus, mothers are bad. It is time for us to notice that up is up, plus is plus, and mothers are often good.

Internalizing Mother-Blame

Who among us has managed to escape the social pressure to blame our mothers for whatever went wrong? The pressure is so pervasive that, eventually, most of us internalize the attitude and the techniques. We initiate mother-blaming ourselves, without waiting for pressure from outside, and then are reinforced by others for doing so. We can really get and keep each other going. A fifty-year-old friend told me recently:

> I just got back from a dinner with three women I've known decades— and we spent the whole meal going after our mothers. I tell you, we ripped them apart. When I got home, I felt very unsettled, and as I thought about what we had done, I realized to my horror that we had just joined the big mother-hating conspiracy! And all of us are mothers ourselves! Our fathers got off scot-free.

These women acted like most people in our culture: they allowed even the most vicious or unfair mother-blaming remarks to pass unquestioned. Chances are, they had been egged on in the past when criticizing their mothers, and so they carried on as before.

Blaming our mothers gives us temporary relief from self-examination and self-doubt. As one of my students put it, ". . . I simply found reasons to blame my mother for every wrong that befell me. In this way, I would not have to look at what was happening between my mother and myself."

Painful though it is to be angry at our mothers, it is less threatening than acknowledging that we need to take a good, hard look at ourselves. But in the long run, being angry is a destructive way to cope: when someone dies, the process of mourning is harder if we had mixed or angry feelings toward the deceased than if we had a basically good relationship. Once they are dead, it is too late to make amends; our guilt can never be truly assuaged. As long as we take the trouble to hate, we are connected. Guilt, blame, and hatred are powerful glues, binding us to the object of those feelings; but little good comes from them. Furthermore, most women get no pleasure from having negative feelings: they are not productive, we have been taught that nice people (especially women) don't have them, and they release chemicals in our bodies that make us continue to feel bad.

Conflict can be either constructive or destructive. An argument can be a sincere effort by two people to thrash out differences about which they have strong feelings or fears, or it can be a chance to release hostility or wield power in destructive, demeaning ways. When we think about a problem, we can try to understand its causes, or we can simply assign *fault*. The difference is between knowing who's responsible and laying blame. Blaming is a way of saying, "It's not my fault. It's all *hers*." Assigning blame may make you feel temporarily better because it helps you believe that you are the good person of the pair; but if you have any interest in a continuing relationship with the blamed one, or in changing yourself, you'll need to do something else. No one reacts well to being blamed—so if you insist on blaming your mother, you can probably forget about improving your relationship with her. Blame is a conversation-stopper; it obstructs the pursuit of insight. It promotes estrangement and anger rather than mutual love and respect for our own and our mothers' autonomy.

IT DOESN'T HAVE TO HAPPEN

In the face of all of this mother-blaming, we are heartened to know that it's not inevitable. Gloria Joseph wrote in *Common Differences: Conflict in Black and White Feminist Perspectives*:

> Black daughters learn at an early age that their mothers are not personally responsible for not being able, through their individual efforts, to make basic changes in their lives or the lives of their children. This recognition enables daughters in later life to be more appreciative, understanding, and forgiving of their mothers when they are unable to fulfill and meet the daughter's expectations and needs for material and emotional comforts.

Although black women and other women of color have to cope with the additional burdens that racism places on mothers' shoulders, all mothers in our culture care for their children in an environment in which the work of mothering is devalued and demeaned. The following story is about my mother's struggle against a self-described expert's efforts to demean both my grandmother and her relationship with my mother.

Fighting Back: Daring to Love Your Mother

As we saw earlier, daughters who have problems are often urged to cut themselves off from the alleged source of their problems—their mothers. Friends, relatives, advice-givers in the media, and therapists freely dispense this advice, and it can be tempting to follow a recommendation that is offered as the way out of all our troubles. But ignoring such advice *is* possible. A psychiatrist made such a recommendation years ago to my mother, Tac, who had consulted him for reasons unrelated to her mother.

When Tac was in her late thirties, she resented the repeated offers of her mother, Esther, to do her grocery or butcher shopping for her. "With the therapist's urging," she says, "I interpreted this as an attempt by my mother to control me. I told her, 'You're making me feel like I don't know anything, like I can't choose decent food for my family.' "

Her psychiatrist advised her to refuse to see her mother for six months, in order to "break away from her need to control you." In the late 1960s—perhaps even more than today—a psychiatrist's word was considered golden. But my mother found the strength to reject his advice, because, she recently told me:

> My mother was very friendly and warm and fun-loving, and basically I did feel very good about her and *wanted* to feel good about her. I had a good relationship with her, and there were lots of times we did have a good time together.

In light of that, my mother was certain that not seeing her mother for six months was, at least, serious overkill. It involved both an undue emphasis on the problems and a failure to acknowledge the strengths of their mother-daughter relationship.

My mother was able to resist the therapist's directive because, as she grew older, her previously low self-confidence improved. She felt better about herself and trusted her own perspective. She realized that if I put [my mother] down, I felt momentarily better, but it really wasn't working. I felt better about myself when I took some positive action.

These changes enabled Tac to think for the first time about whether her mother's motives might include anything other than those she considered to be direct insults to her.

As she thought about her mother's life—and then asked Esther about it—she realized that the grocery offers had nothing to do with her mother's lack of faith in her. Instead, her mother had been brought up to believe that a woman's value lay primarily in providing for others. Esther did not have a paying job, her children were grown, and except when she cooked for her family and cared for her grandchildren, she felt useless. Shopping for her daughter was her desperate attempt, within her familiar framework, to convince herself that she was still a needed, and therefore a worthwhile, person.

As Tac came to this understanding, totally *without* her psychiatrist's help, she underwent a transformation from a resentful child lacking in self-confidence to a compassionate adult in a more egalitarian relationship with her mother. And this happened none too soon, for shortly afterward, Esther was found to have cancer and died within six months. When she was in the hospital, she and Tac talked about how happy they were that Tac had ignored her therapist's advice and had started the process of understanding her mother.

My mother told me that this experience showed her how understanding our separateness and difference from mother can reduce the need to blame and pull away from her; it can instead decrease the estrangement and increase the love and respect on both sides. As Tac no longer resented her mother, Esther no longer felt that the one bit of help she was able to offer was scorned. Each realized that she was loved and appreciated by the other.

How many years of mother-daughter estrangement could have been avoided, how many chasms bridged if, instead of simply blaming them, daughters had known to ask *why* their mothers did what seemed to be intrusive, insensitive, or uncaring?

When we stem the tide of our own mother-blaming, some of our anger at our mothers abates; our insecurity and self-hate subside as we realize that our close relationships to our mothers are not always cause for alarm and may even be cause for pleasure and pride.

Mother-blaming is so pervasive that it's almost a wonder that women choose to become mothers and that daughters ever speak to their mothers. If someone offered you a job, saying, "If *anything* goes wrong, even sixty or seventy years from now, you will be blamed," you'd tell them to forget it. But that is what motherhood is. Millions of mothers throughout the world feed, bathe, heal, and talk to their children every day, filled with anxiety, guilt, and fear. They know that if anything goes wrong, they will be held almost totally responsible.

In the next two chapters, we shall see how the general attitude of mother-blaming harms mother-daughter relationships through the Perfect Mother myths (Chapter 4) and the Bad Mother myths (Chapter 5), which impede our views of who our mothers (and our daughters) really are. Then, in the last chapters, we'll see how we can go beyond mother-blaming and the myths and begin to mend our relationships with our mothers.

4 ❦ Mother–Daughter Barriers: The Perfect Mother Myths

TO UNDERSTAND WHAT has happened between our mothers and ourselves, to tell our true mother-daughter stories, we have to see clearly how our inner needs and fears have interacted with society's needs and fears.

As daughters, we need to feel like decent, acceptable people; some of that feeling comes from acceptance by our mothers and society in general, and some from our sense of integrity and honesty. (Although we also need to feel accepted by our fathers, my focus is on the mother-daughter issues, and we are less likely to blame fathers for our low self-esteem.) We also need to have close, loving relationships with our mothers. We fear rejection by our mothers and by society; since mother often does society's bidding, we hope that if we can learn to please her we can please society at large. When we have to choose between pleasing mother and pleasing society, we are caught between the enormous control she has over our daily lives and the message from our culture that mother's opinion isn't very important or worthwhile. (And a great source of irony is that often the mother whom we believe to be society's minion is in quiet or vocal rebellion against social pressures.)

What are society's needs? They include the need for women—both mothers and daughters—to fit the traditional feminine stereotype; the need for mothers to accept the chore of training their daughters to fit that stereotype; and the need to keep mothers and daughters divided against each other and so anguished about their relationship that they don't notice that societal expectations are the problem. Instead, they blame themselves and each other. Myths about mothers serve these functions. Although myths, by definition, are not real, the barriers they create between mothers and daughters certainly are.

At least nine major myths help keep mother-blaming alive and strong. Listing the myths is an important beginning, for the process of solving a problem begins with giving it a name. We shall see how each myth produces mother-daughter barriers—in the form of the kinds of painful feelings described in Chapter 2— and what we can do about it. This chapter is about the Perfect Mother Myths, and the next is about the Bad Mother Myths.

Each myth rests near either the Angel or the Witch pole of mother-images that were described in Chapter 1; in the daughter's eyes, the Perfect Mother myths make all mothers' good efforts seem inadequate because they're imperfect, and the Bad Mother myths highlight mothers' failings and even make some of their strengths or neutral points seem harmful.

As we daughters realize that we may have mislabeled and misinterpreted our mothers' motives and behavior, we can learn how the myths have led us to do that. In addition, when we keep the myths clearly in mind, we can see how they shaped our mothers' behavior as well as our own; we stop feeling that our mothers have hurt, rejected, or confused us willfully.

Mothers are familiar with the Perfect Mother myths; even before their children notice, they see where they fall short and fear their children's disappointment. Mothers are as frightened of matching the Bad Mother myths as of failing to match the Perfect Mother ones; in both cases, they fear their offspring's (and other people's) rejection and scorn.

You'll notice the absence of a set of Reasonably Good Mother myths (despite a few mental health professionals' attempts to speculate about the "good enough mother"). A mother is not allowed to make many good efforts but be humanly flawed; she has to be perfect, because so much is at stake—the physical and mental health of her children, for which she is assumed to be totally responsible.

The myths discussed in these chapters may not be the only ones that support mother-blaming, and you may think of others. But these nine will be familiar because we have been raised

among them; many were even more powerful during our mothers'
childrearing years.

The four Perfect Mother myths I've identified establish standards that no mother can meet:

- The Measure of a Good Mother is a "Perfect" Daughter
- Mothers Are Endless Founts of Nurturance
- Mothers Naturally Know How To Raise Children
- Mothers Don't Get Angry

MYTH ONE: THE MEASURE OF A GOOD MOTHER IS A "PERFECT" DAUGHTER

Daughters feel anger for many reasons: because they see their mothers
pressuring them to conform to society's expectations of girls and
women, or because they find their mothers paying too little attention to
those expectations and offering scant emotional support to daughters
attempting to conform. Mothers grow angry at daughters either because
daughters don't fulfill their expectations or because their daughters expect too much of them.

—Susan Koppelman

Every culture has molds into which it wants each new generation to fit. In our culture, the responsibility for that molding is
mainly delegated to families, which in practice usually means
that mothers are the ones to mold their children into the cultural
pattern. For most of us, our mother, more than anyone else, said:
"Do this." "Don't do that." "Brush your teeth." "Pick up your
toys." "Don't talk to strangers."

As daughters, we heard many additional "Dos" and "Don'ts"
that our brothers escaped: "Cross your legs." "Smile." "Be nice."
Girls are thought to be *naturally* tidy and restrained, but when a
daughter doesn't act that way her *mother* is blamed for not *teaching* her well enough. We might well ask, "Why does something
that comes naturally have to be taught?" We shall see this pattern
repeatedly as we examine the myths of mother-blame: in a culture that subordinates women, glaring contradictions can persist,
as long as they help keep women down by restricting or demeaning us. In this case, women's behavior is restricted by our diligent
efforts to be tidy and restrained, in order to seem *naturally* feminine. All women are demeaned when anyone believes that a

daughter's untidiness or lack of restraint is the fault of a woman —her mother.

Society has perched on our mothers' shoulders, whispering, "If you want us to think you are a good mother, you'll teach your daughter to be sweet and to cross her legs." (For mothers today, the message is more likely to end with the words, "you'll teach your daughter to get an education, develop herself, *and* be sweet and cross her legs.")

Many young daughters sense that the "feminine" pattern they are following at mother's direction is the very thing that often makes mother unhappy, and they feel that she is betraying them by urging them into the patterns that are the source of her own misery. Claudette told me she hated sweeping the kitchen floor and cleaning the bathrooms when she was a child:

> It was partly because they are crummy jobs, but it was also because my mother was constantly complaining about how exhausted she was from cleaning our house. I didn't see why she made me do the things she hated. It didn't seem fair.

The frightening flip side of the myth that a "perfect" daughter is the sign of a good mother is that a "bad" (or atypical) daughter is the sign of a "bad" mother. This social equation causes mothers and daughters a great deal of unnecessary anguish. Every mother wants to be considered a good mother. But not every mother thinks that her daughter should have to follow the traditional feminine model, nor does every daughter take to such a pre-scribed role, especially if her *mother* seems unhappy in that role. Should a mother, then, carry out society's orders in order to se-cure her reputation as a good mother, or should she act in her daughter's best interests? How can a mother choose between her daughter's welfare and her own need for approval? And what are her daughter's best interests—to develop her full potential and risk being a "misfit"?

When daughters describe to me their wish to please their mothers, their tension is often palpable. Some haven't even understood why so much was at stake in relation to following mother's rules. But they have sensed that society's opinion of their mother's achievement as a mother depended on the daugh-ter's display of the right kinds of behavior. No matter how much we might revile the narrowness of our mothers' lives, which of us wants to bear the guilty burden of being the public signboard of her failure?

Furthermore, since the only good mother is a perfect mother, no amount of rule-following seems enough. No daughter ever feels she's done everything that society—through her mother—wants her to do, since it's impossible always to be nurturing, self-denying, sweet, and slim and to achieve all the other hallmarks of good daughterhood. No wonder so many daughters feel unable to please their mothers.

As daughters, we assume that the urgency in mother's rule-making comes from her individual, critical, controlling nature; we don't often recognize that the rules come from a fundamental cultural belief, and mother is just its transmitter—or some rules come from mother's attempt to protect her daughter from the forms of violence against and harassment of women that are so common. What the daughter thinks she sees is a neurotic, up-tight, or even heartless woman who has generated a host of pre-scriptions in order to torment her.

In my work with women, I often find that a daughter's belief that her mother uncompromisingly disapproves of her actually is a misinterpretation of her mother's role as rule enforcer. Sadly, then, instead of daughter and mother getting together, seeing that the source of their problem is the set of impossible cultural standards for mothers and daughters, and then trying to change that culture, mother gets trapped into trying to produce a perfect specimen of a daughter (for *both* their sakes), and daughter hates mother for being so unreasonable. A huge wedge is driven between them. A 92-year-old woman named Betty told me that she was worried about her daughter's failing, forty-year marriage. She said:

> I told her I knew her husband has a terrible temper and lashes out at her for no good reason. But I said that my husband was the same way, and a woman has to learn to overlook that. But I felt bad for doing that, because overlooking my husband's temper never helped me, and I knew it wouldn't do my daughter any good either.

One particularly tricky set of rules involves the ones that growing girls are supposed to learn about emotional control. We are assumed to be extremely emotional by nature (certainly more so than growing boys), but we are carefully taught that our emotions must not interfere with other people's comfort. By the time we reach young womanhood, we are supposed to be emotional enough to meet men's and children's needs for love and support without "burdening" them with our feelings. Women are assumed to keep their feelings under control only with great difficulty—although a woman who *is* emotionally reserved is in danger of being called cold and unfeminine. Thus, women are expected to remain in touch with our feelings only for the purpose of helping our men and our children.

Mother and daughter each sometimes find it disconcerting for the other to be warm and expressive, because we're not quite sure whether that's OK. If we get too comfortable allowing our feelings free rein when we are with each other, then won't that make it easier to slip up and be "inappropriately" or "intrusively" expressive when we go back to our men and our children? Furthermore, some men regard a close mother-daughter relationship as a threat to their wife's allegiance to them.

Mother as Enforcer; Daddy as Darling

The daughter tends to resent her mother as most people resent the imposers of rules, but even more so because there are more rules for daughters than for sons. She also resents her mother for being so tough on her—after all, Daddy isn't. (The familiar warning by mother, "Wait till your father gets home," is rarely translated into actual punishment by father for the behavior that leads to mother's anger. Fathers' physical or sexual abuse of their daughters is usually quite separate from these types of warnings by mother.) Daddy's greater leniency is usually a side effect of his generally lesser involvement in childrearing than his wife's. But all the daughter knows is that Daddy treats her better. (Of course he does—when you don't have the major responsibility for someone's behavior, you can afford to be more lax about discipline!) A thirty-year-old woman recently told me in an interview:

> Until last year, I always thought my father loved me more than my mother did. The reason I thought that was that he never punished me when I was growing up. In fact, when Mom announced punishments for me, he always persuaded her to make them more lenient.
> But last year, when my kids were four and six years old, I suddenly realized that the same thing is happening in my own family now: my

husband tells me I'm really great with the kids, but that's just his way of staying out of the nitty-gritty of parenting. *I* have to be the heavy, I'm always the one who disciplines the kids, and then once the punishment is over, my husband sweeps in and takes them out for ice cream. Naturally, they think he's terrific, and I'm the one they're scared of. You can bet that I appreciate my mother a lot more, now that I see how I ended up preferring my father over her!

Do We EVER Stop Fearing Mother's Disapproval?

The highly competent and polished host of a radio phone-in show told me about her most recent visit with her mother. She had flown from California to Florida, where her mother lives, and as she walked off the plane, her mother told her that the color of her dress was all wrong for her:

> Here I am, 48 years old, and I still *care* so much about what she thinks! I receive compliments all the time on my good fashion sense, but not from her. And one note of criticism from her is enough to undermine all the self-confidence about my appearance that it's taken me years to build up.

We are so vulnerable to what our mothers think of us; when they seem to have reservations about us we are devastated, whether we are children, teenagers, young adults, or middle-aged or even old women. Our mother's power to make us feel inadequate often makes us angry—we may even hate her for it. Once, in reality, she had enormous power over us, could lock us in our rooms or, by withdrawing her love from us, ensure that we received little love at all from anyone. When you're six years old, it's harder to run out of the house to look for a friend or relative who'll say they like your clothes, even if your mother doesn't. Even as adults we can't just run away and never see or call our mothers again—and most of us *don't want to*. What most of us want is not to banish our mothers from our lives but to end both their power to make us feel bad and our guilt over *our* power to make *them* feel like failures.

Now that we are adults, we can see that our mothers were not so much the rule makers as the rule enforcers, and that many of the rules they enforced were rules that constrained their own lives, too. One of my students, who is in her late twenties and specializes in counseling mothers and daughters, says she knew when she was a child that her mother felt trapped in her house-wife-mother role:

> My mother had been forced to quit school after the eighth grade, since attending ninth grade would have meant going to a school in another town. Her mother had told her that it was a lot more trouble to raise a daughter than a son, and she was pretty much pushed into a kind of arranged marriage to the only member of their church who was of marriageable age. Then the kids started coming—eight of us, and oh, did she feel trapped.

While my student knew deep inside that her mother felt trapped, she still grew up resenting her mother for her stifling upbringing. Only when she began to think about how limited her mother's options were did she begin to see her in a different light:

> Both my uncle and my father used to scream at her for putting us girls in jeans rather than dresses. *She* didn't think we should have to wear dresses, though, except to church, so that was one rule of femininity we often got to break. But she had to make us follow a lot of rules, because the only thing she had was being a mother, and she couldn't stand to have my father and my uncle always telling her she was a failure.

Daughters should understand that mother herself worries that she will be judged by her daughter's success—which partly depends on her appearance or behavior. Daughter understandably resents the fact that her mother's acceptance by society seems to depend so much on her. From childhood we have sensed our mothers' fear that any misstep on our part could reveal her shortcomings as a mother. Once we know that the source of that feeling is society's withholding of approval from so-called "inadequate mothers," we easily see that *our* dress doesn't signal *her* failure as a mother but that she is understandably afraid that someone will think so.

Each Other's Judges

Part of growing up female has meant that daughters, like mothers, are expected to take on the role of guardians of society's (largely man-made) rules. In other words, it is not just mothers who do the monitoring; daughters catch on early to society's expectations and begin to monitor their mothers' behavior as well.

In this way, mother and daughter come to fear each other as their harshest judges.

A growing daughter who catches her mother failing to fulfill any social expectations often feels betrayed ("Why don't *you* bake cookies for our class parties?") or superior to her mother ("Since *you* don't know how to sew, *I* do all the buttons and hems for this family!"), neither of which endears her to her mother.

Furthermore, as a mother limits her daughter's exuberance, assertiveness, and aggressiveness, she unwittingly conveys the message, "This aspect of you is not good, and therefore I do not accept, love, or cherish it," thereby lowering the daughter's self-esteem. When mother makes daughter feel bad about herself, she drives a wedge of resentment between them.

The problem is cyclical. Many mothers are especially anxious to keep their daughters from breaking the rules because the mothers recall how unhappy they were when they, as children, were punished for doing so. Forty-eight-year-old Ashley described to me in a therapy session the effect an incident in her childhood had on her treatment of her daughter:

> When I was twelve years old, a teacher caught me climbing a tree. In a disgusted voice, she chided me, "Don't you know the boys can look straight up your dress when you climb?" I wasn't sure *why* that was so horrid, but I felt totally ashamed. She made me feel like a slut.
>
> When my daughter, Janice, started sixth grade, and started developing physically, I became very tense. I wanted to protect her from sexual insinuations like the one my teacher had aimed at me. What really upset me, though, was that the only way I seemed to be able to do this was by sounding like my teacher myself. To my horror, I found myself saying things to Janice like, "Don't talk so loud" as though she were committing a major crime rather than just doing something unfeminine. But I was doing it to try to protect her from other people's disapproval. The tragedy was that, in so doing, I made her the butt of *my* disapproval, and that probably hurt her more than harshness from strangers would have done.

In such situations, the daughter usually senses her mother's fear and anxiety, and she surely feels her mother's disapproval. Since we tend to stay away from people whom we make anxious or who disapprove of us, the wistful distance between mother and daughter grows. No mother purposely inflicts such anxiety or harshness on her daughter, but few daughters can help feeling hurt when their mothers have those feelings. These childhood hurts can stay deep and sore throughout our lives if we never go back and hear from our mothers why they behaved as they did.

MYTH TWO: MOTHERS ARE ENDLESS FOUNTS OF NURTURANCE

Woman needs to give. She cannot help herself. . . . This flow of life is not intended only for her children but also for her mate. . . . [Woman's primal driving force is] love and the service of those she loves.
—Irene Claremont de Castillejo

. . . that reflexive maternal guilt . . . emerges at the infant's first wail: "I'm sorry. I'm sorry. I'm sorry I pushed you from this warm womb into the arms of strangers, me among them. I'm sorry I can't keep you perfectly full, perfectly dry, perfectly free from gas and fear, perfectly, perfectly happy."

—Nancy Mairs

Myth Two is the myth that women are born nurturers, capable of giving of ourselves endlessly. Being a warm, generous person is not a bad thing; the "endless" part is what causes the trouble between mother and daughter.

The Cinderella story may be the most familiar example of this womanly ideal. Cinderella represents goodness because of her unhappiness, suffering, deprivation, and toiling for others, in contrast to her stepsisters' selfishness. Cinderella's lesson to us is that a woman's selflessness, suffering, and passivity earn her a fairy godmother and a prince.

The story of Snow White and the Seven Dwarfs is also about this role. To become ripe and ready for marriage, Snow White must take care of seven little men. The fact that the dwarfs are both little and male prepares her to nurture both children and husband. She does this—as most of our mothers did—alone and isolated.

Through the centuries, women have been expected to fill a nurturant role. In a book called *Letters to Mothers*, the popular nineteenth-century author Lydia Howard Sigourney suggested how mothers should raise their daughters:

Inspire her with a desire to make all around her, comfortable and happy. Instruct her in the rudiments of that science, whose results are so beautiful. Teach her, that not selfish gratification, but the good of a household, the improvement of even the humblest dependent, is the business of her sex . . . especially, if you visit the aged, or go on errands of mercy to the sick and poor, let her be your companion. Allow her to sit by the side of the sufferer, and learn those nursing services which afford relief to pain.

This was our grandmothers' and our mothers' heritage. Books mothers read while raising daughters now in their twenties and thirties offered similar advice. As recently as 1973, at the height of the women's movement, in a popular advice book called *Mothers and Daughters* author Edith Neisser asked, "How much help should a girl be?" and gave an answer that Sigourney might have written more than a century earlier: "One mother claims that the best laborsaving device known is a daughter between the ages of nine and twelve. . . ." Neisser tried to make the daughter's tasks sound intellectually challenging:

> Junior housekeepers deserve to be assigned some of the creative as well as the menial jobs. The nine-year-old who dreams up a fresh, if somewhat bizarre, variation on the recurrent custard pudding is serving the cause of the family's well-being as faithfully as does the girl who scrubs the pans, and she has the reward that comes with innovation, as well.

Contemporary personality theorists have also reinforced the myth. For example, Jungian theorist Irene Claremont de Castillejo writes that the basic feminine attitude involves an attitude of "acceptance" and that women need to give *in order not to feel empty*. And most recently, Toni Grant makes a similar claim in her book *Being a Woman*.

Fortunately, some contemporary writers are calling attention to the nature and danger of this myth. Psychologist Harriet Goldhor Lerner writes: "Women have been taught that they must be non-threatening help-mates and ego-builders to men, lest men feel castrated and emasculated." And in *The Mermaid and The Minotaur*, Dorothy Dinnerstein explains that woman is "seen as . . . the being so peculiarly needed to confirm other people's worth, power, significance that if she fails to render them this service she is a monster, anomalous and useless." Underlining this danger to women, feminist theorist Sheila Rowbotham says that, as girls grow up, they learn to feel they are truly women only when they are self-denying: "Self-affirmation can only come through self-abnegation."

Research shows that women live up to the nurturance myth, spending far more time than men in taking care of the younger generation, the older generation, their spouses, their siblings, and their friends. So resilient is the nurturant-woman myth that even when men lose their jobs, they don't tend to take on more household tasks; instead, the women carry on with those chores and also find paid employment.

Because the woman-as-nurturer myth is so deeply ingrained in our notions of female identity, it is hard for us to stop expecting endless giving from both our mothers and ourselves. When we ask ourselves, "Who am I?" a large part of most women's answer is, "A helper, a giver, a nurturer. If not, then I don't know who I am." As one woman told me:

> I was brought up to say "I'm sorry" when someone in a store stepped on *my* foot. And I felt very feminine and womanly because I was able to do this. So asserting myself, or seeing my mother assert herself, was very disconcerting. It meant something was not right with the world—and certainly not with us.

Where Lies the Harm?

Our mothers' failings and imperfections are often magnified because we expect so much from mothers. We expect less from our fathers, because being masculine doesn't require being nurturant. Some scientists even claim that women are born nurturers but men are not. (Ironically, many people believe that fathers are capable of *loving* children just as much as mothers, but then they say that *mothers* are naturally better at the routine, boring, or difficult parenting tasks like diaper-changing, food preparation, arranging of doctors' appointments, or teaching of the facts of life.) We don't give mothers much credit for what they do for us, but we condemn them as withholding and unnatural when they don't *completely* meet our needs. As theorist Mary O'Brien has said, "If you're *not* a good mother, you're deviant. If you *are* a good mother it's because you can't help it."

Because of the differing expectations, we tend to feel our fathers are terrific when they are even a little bit nurturant. However when our mothers don't quite give us all that we want, we feel that they have let us down. This simple, double standard is so common that we don't even notice it. "Since motherliness means being all-giving," we think, "mother *could* have met all my emotional needs." Yet who among us can give unceasingly? And who should have to? In fact, considering the many ways that women, and especially mothers, are unfairly treated, most mothers are remarkable to give as much as they do.

I remember what a major expedition grocery shopping was when my son was a toddler and my daughter was an infant, as I tried to meet their emotional needs while juggling the parcels. It seemed like a major crisis, because the following dilemma went through my head each time:

> I can't carry the groceries *and* Emily *and* hold Jeremy's hand while he clambers up the stairs. Now, if I leave Emily in her infant seat in the car while I take Jeremy and the groceries upstairs, even if I lock the car so she won't be kidnapped, she might feel abandoned. But if I leave Jeremy in his seatbelt while I take the baby and the groceries upstairs, then Jeremy might feel abandoned, *and* he's old enough that he just might be able to unlock the car door and run away before I get back.

Not until years later did I realize that that is an insane way to have to live, that it was natural and healthy for me to wish their father would do the grocery shopping, and that I wasn't selfish and inadequate for finding the total responsibility for everyday life with children so difficult.

The nurturance myth causes other mother-daughter troubles: nurturing involves making the other person's life better—and women's power to do that is so limited. Our mothers can talk and listen and offer us love and emotional support, but they cannot on their own prevent much of the damage done to us by the unjust treatment of girls and women by our society's institutions or by individuals—even, often, by mother's own husband. Unfortunately, instead of recognizing the culture's responsibility for those limits (and trying to change it), we act as though our mothers had no such limits, and so we blame them for "their" limitations. For our part, as daughters, we can't undo or make amends for the many sources of sorrow in our mothers' lives. Because of this, mother and daughter often face each other wanting to do more to heal each other's wounds but feeling frustrated and ashamed because they cannot. And sometimes, they express their frustration and shame in the form of anger at each other.

The Deepest Wounds; The Sharpest Pains

I believe that the myth of women's endless nurturance, more than any other, may be the source of the deepest, sorest wounds and sharpest pains that daughters feel in relation to their mothers. Why? To open ourselves up, to pour out our hearts makes us vulnerable. Will the recipient of our outpouring both really listen to us and accept what she or he thereby learns about us? If both these happy things occur, we are strengthened; if either or both do not, we are stabbed in a vulnerable spot.

In general, when we open up to our fathers, we do so with some caution, not expecting their full understanding and support. So when we are imperfectly understood, our tenderest places are less likely to have been exposed, and the hurt is less deep, less blood is shed. But since we expect full understanding from our mothers, we're more likely to lay ourselves wide open to them— the risk is great, but if we fully show our real selves and *she does* accept us, what bliss, what security that provides! And when she does not fully accept, what devastation. A woman in her late thirties told this story:

> When I was about 35, I was visiting my parents, and my father came in to wake me up. I had just been having a terrifying nightmare, and as I floated up out of sleep I told Dad about it. When I had finished, he just said, "Well, it's time to get up." I was a little hurt, but mostly I just felt that next time I wouldn't even try to tell him how I felt. I also remember thinking that he loved a lot of things about me and that he loved me in a different way from Mom. I knew that Mom would probably have been more sympathetic about my nightmare.
>
> There have been times, though, when I tried to tell Mom about something that mattered a lot to me, and usually she was pretty receptive. But when she wasn't, I felt that she had seen the deepest core of my being and didn't find me lovable. What despair I felt then!

Turning to Daughter

The myth of endless nurturance can also feed a mother's resentment of her daughter: just as everyone expects nurturance from girls and women in general, so a mother expects such nurturance and support from her daughter. A mother is supposed to train her daughter to be a nurturer, in accordance with the nurturance myth. She believes the myth that a perfect daughter is the measure of a good mother: what more tempting place to begin than by training her daughter to take care of her mother, her closest companion? Such training may seem like the right thing to do. A daughter who takes good care of her mother will be well prepared to fit the ideal: a woman who can nurture her husband and sons. If she begins to feel in infancy or early childhood that such behavior is an obligation, then so much the better for society, for the girl will feel that it "comes naturally." She may even feel uncomfortable or unnatural behaving otherwise.

Leah, a 43-year-old divorced mother of two, told me in an interview that, after working at her nine-to-five job, picking up her kids at daycare, cooking their dinner, and then spending an hour of "quality time" with them, she was ready to collapse:

> I have a bad back, and the pain gets worse when I've been on my feet all day. At night, my lovely seven-year-old daughter sometimes asks if I want a back rub. I always feel a little guilty, because *I'm* supposed to be taking care of *her*—but I am glad she's learning to be good to others, and she does like helping me.

That is a nice story, but when I asked Leah if her nine-year-old son ever rubs her back, she replied that he loves to play with his friends, and she doesn't feel she has the right to interrupt that playtime. In spite of the changes the women's movement has made, the difference in comfort levels between having a daughter and a son help out remains very common.

Some mothers of infants seek nurturance in wishing the baby would behave well, not cry, let her get a good night's sleep, smile at her, and be cuddly. Some mothers need this nurturing because of their unusually lonely, deprived, or upsetting early lives; they hope that, at last, they will get some affection, some peace, or both. For other mothers, the wish for nurturance from the daughter comes from the usual difficulties most women in our culture face—the responsibility and isolation of motherhood, the various forms of sexist treatment to which women are subjected, and so on. Any of these experiences can leave women feeling intensified needs for love and support.

When the baby girl or young daughter does *not* do what is expected, a mother who doesn't get or can't accept support from other people may feel like a failure and develop a lasting resentment of her daughter. Maggie's infant daughter was extremely colicky, had sleep problems, and wasn't cuddly "the way you hope your baby will be." Maggie's mother was chipper, but not warm or supportive; her father was extremely formal, distant, and preoccupied with his business. Maggie considers herself a deprived child, who lost what shreds of parental affection she had when her younger twin sisters were born. "Their birth destroyed my life," she claims. Feeling deprived, she has always lacked confidence in her ability to give love to others.

Maggie never wanted a baby, and now she had one who not only required a lot of giving from her but seemed to offer no affection in return. Her daughter Sara's failure to be close and cuddly was devastating, Maggie says. Even now, eight years later, although Sara has shown that she *can* be warm and loving, Maggie treats her coldly and irritably.

We find forgiving our mothers particularly difficult when their failure to nurture us as much as we want is because their nurturance of our brothers, our fathers, their fathers and brothers, their male bosses—any male—takes priority. As I shall discuss in Chapter 5, most of us have been trained to regard men as the prime needers of our care: "Men are such children. He's lost when I'm not there for dinner. He can't open a can of beans. He has such trouble dealing with his feelings, unless I help him." All such common remarks reflect women's learned belief that men need our help more than women and girls, since the latter more likely *can* open cans of beans and *can* deal with their feelings. But blaming mother for her learned sexism is no more fair or helpful than blaming her for being less than totally giving. Putting her sexism into action is doing what she was taught was the right thing to do.

Once daughters become aware of having different expectations for nurturance from our mothers and our fathers, our anger at our mothers usually diminishes. We should not demean our fathers' nurturance (and some of our fathers are deeply loving and nurturant) but rather show equal appreciation for what our mothers do for us. When mother gives only ninety percent, we may perceive it as eighty percent or as ten percent or as nothing, because it was not all that we wanted. Then we create an unnecessary rift between our mothers and ourselves; furthermore, in this way we shut ourselves off from the good that our mothers do have to offer.

Because of the double standard, we often focus on *what* our mothers have failed to do, without considering *why* they might have failed. All families have their own challenges. Sometimes mothers fail to meet their daughters' needs because other family members need them, too. Or mother may be a single mother, an immigrant mother or a mother of color coping with the consequences of racism; she may be a disabled mother, a mother on welfare, a mother who is physically ill or depressed or anxious, a mother juggling paid work and housework, a mother with a depressed, alcoholic, or abusive partner, or a mother with many children or with a young, ill, or disabled child. And all mothers sometimes fail simply because we are human. If a mother doesn't play with her children as often as she might, then she should be regarded as not playing with them as often as she might, rather than as miserably failing to meet an impossibly high standard.

MYTH THREE: MOTHERS NATURALLY KNOW HOW TO RAISE CHILDREN

Myth Three is the widely believed notion that mothers instinctively know everything that's necessary for raising physically and emotionally healthy children. This myth is closely related to Myth Two, since women's allegedly innate capacity for nurturance is said to be part of our natural fitness for childrearing.

According to the myth, the hormones coursing through a mother's body during labor and delivery cause her to love her newborn immediately and totally, and suddenly she has the million and one bits of information she will need to be an excellent mother. Unfortunately, it isn't true. In her book *Mother Love*, historian Elisabeth Badinter painstakingly documents the evidence that giving birth is not the same as being able to mother, and that one does not lead inevitably to the other. Compelling evidence from psychologists contradicts the claim that mothers bond immediately to their babies and that they must do this for babies to grow up normally. But because mothers have heard that that is what we are *supposed* to do, we believe we have failed if we feel anything else instead. As writer Jain Sherrard has said:

> Women do not have a handy gland called "mother" which is mysteriously activated upon giving birth. Contrary to every myth perpetrated on us throughout history, not all women make good mothers, just as all men don't make good plumbers. That we *can* give birth does not guarantee that we can also mother successfully.

Feeling less than immediate and total love for one's newborn is not uncommon. According to one mother's description,

> Eventually, after 22 hours of labour, this daughter whom I had wanted so desperately . . . was born. I remember looking at her, looking at my husband with the tears in his eyes, and wondering if I *could* love her. He certainly did, but after it was finally all over, I wasn't so sure.

Once a mother gets baby home, her enjoyment of her child is limited by the endless nurturance myth; since the standard is to be naturally happy and serene in motherhood, every time a mother feels fatigued or resentful because of the amount of nurturance her baby needs, she believes she is a failure as a mother. A mother's feelings include rapture, but also panic, fear, rage, and despair. Sometimes the baby's needs seem unmeetable, the meanings of her wails are unclear, or she needs something just when her parents are exhausted or about to leave her for the first time ever. When a woman has these normal feelings, she doesn't feel like a natural mother.

As her child grows up, mother continues to worry; her negative feelings don't disappear, and she never feels she immediately, naturally knows what to do for the child. When she doesn't intuitively know what her *son* needs, mother is less distressed, because after all, he is a member of a different sex. When she is perplexed about what to do for her *daughter*, she is more upset because she feels she has no "excuse."

Roxanne, whose daughter is now fifty years old, was trained as a surgical nurse before she was married. She vividly recalled, as most mothers do even decades later, how new motherhood felt to her:

> Wouldn't you have thought that the combination of being a woman and having been a nurse for eight years before my daughter was born would

have made me the perfect mother? No such luck! When she cried, not only did I feel sorry for her because I didn't know how to help her, but I also felt ashamed because all of this understanding of my baby wasn't coming naturally. I was embarrassed to tell anyone how little I felt I was doing right for my daughter.

When Roxanne's daughter was six weeks old, Roxanne left her with a babysitter for the first time and went to her bridge club. Two members of her club had slightly older infants, so Roxanne hoped they could give her some good advice:

> I described my daughter's late afternoon spells of ceaseless screaming. The other new mothers said their babies didn't do that, and one explained, "When my baby cries, I can always tell whether he's hungry or needs his diaper changed." I was mortified. I felt so inadequate.

Later in the week, Roxanne's mother and mother-in-law came to visit. Although she was grateful for her mother's diagnosis of the baby's crying spells as caused by colic, she was ashamed that she hadn't known that herself. Fortunately, as Roxanne explained:

> Right after my visitors left, one of my bridge club members called to confess that her baby, too, cried every day at five o'clock, and she had no idea what to do. She hadn't wanted to admit that in front of the other women.

Neither Roxanne nor her caller realized that for no woman does all of mothering come naturally. The television sitcoms show that mothers know all the answers and strike the perfect balance between encouraging children's autonomy and setting limits, between loving and letting go. If mothers can be so wise, wonders daughter, why isn't mine? Why does she often say the wrong thing? Why does she make me crazy? As daughters grow up, feeling unhappy or confused or scared, we often blame mother, who was supposed to protect us from pain and teach us how to be happy.

How does this myth create a barrier between mothers and daughters? At the simplest level, a daughter is apt to resent her mother for not doing everything right, not always instinctively knowing what she wants, not always being the perfect mother. After all, how is daughter to know that *her* mother is no worse than others—most mothers try so hard to conceal their weaknesses. And for her part, a mother resents her daughter for having needs her mother can't meet, because that shows she is not a naturally terrific mother.

Precisely because mothering is supposed to come naturally, few mothers tell their children how difficult it can be. This has concerned me for many years—since I first had children—and I have taken some pains to tell my children that I don't always know what's right and don't always know what to do for them. Even so, they are surprised every time I say, "Well, I sure messed that up. I really made the wrong decision there." In a culture in which mothering is generally undervalued, chances are slim that anyone outside mother is going to teach children how much effort and uncertainty are involved in the job. So both daughters and sons grow up thinking mothering is supposed to be easy. We don't see her human struggle, imperfections, and uncertainties; we only see a woman who doesn't measure up to the standard of the naturally selfless, serene, and sage mother. And often, we resent her for that failure.

As adult daughters, when our mothers don't have all the answers, when they can't make things "all better," we either decide they are shamefully deficient or believe they did know what to do but let us down by not doing it *for us.* A daughter called Cyndi described her experience:

> When my kids were three and four years old, my former boss offered to give me back my old job. I was thrilled—but because it was fulltime, it would mean putting my children in daycare. I asked my mother what she thought, and I really desperately wanted her to tell me the right choice to make.
>
> She said, "You'll be happier if you're working, and that would be *good* for the children. But you may miss a lot of important times with them if you're away eight hours a day."
>
> She just presented the pros and cons but wouldn't tell me what to do. I was furious at her. But then I realized that I wasn't mad at my *husband* for refusing to make the decision for me. Because she was my *mother*, I expected her to know the right choice.

MYTH FOUR: MOTHERS (AND "GOOD" DAUGHTERS) DON'T GET ANGRY

Anger presents a special problem in the relationships between mothers and daughters. While anger is a natural part of any close relationship, we all know that anger is unfeminine. In other words, mothers and daughters are not supposed to get angry, and certainly not at each other; if they do, then at least one of them is bad. According to the idealized view, the mother-daughter relationship is a mutually loving, sweet, supportive one with no room for anger. In contrast, showing anger is consistent with the male image, even enhancing it. Father-son hostility is considered healthy competition or masculine aggression, and daughter's anger at father is even more taboo. In a seminar, 52-year-old Mary Ellen acknowledged:

> Looking back, I can see that my husband and I always came down harder on our daughter when she mouthed off at me than on our son when he talked back to my husband. It just seemed so much more inappropriate when *she* acted like that.

The "women don't get angry" message helps to ensure that we women will nurture others: showing anger is not supportive. And as with the other social rules, mother is the one to teach her daughter to suppress her anger. Sometimes she does it as an explicit order: "Don't get mad. Nice girls don't get angry." Sometimes she conveys her message through praise—telling a daughter she is terrific to stay home from a party, without complaining, in order to babysit for her younger brother. Nietzsche wrote that "Praise is more obtrusive than a reproach," and that certainly applies to the mother-daughter relationship: although the mother's praise may make her daughter feel good, it simultaneously irritates her daughter because she earned it by accepting limits on her freedom.

While a daughter may feel like a true woman for not getting angry and for focusing on other people's needs, she will likely resent her mother for taking away her ability to defend and protect herself through anger when necessary. The conflict between maintaining her integrity by expressing justified, self-protective anger and keeping her mother's approval tears the daughter apart.

Precisely because women's anger has been so forbidden, it often becomes the painful center of mother-daughter relationships. Arguing with your mother about clothes and haircuts is a difficult though expected part of mother-daughter interactions; the relationship becomes excruciating when burdened with intense anger that isn't supposed to be there at all. So mother and daughter begin with the pain of hostile feelings between them; then they have to cope with the secondary problem of knowing these are forbidden feelings.

Mother worries that a daughter who doesn't learn to suppress her anger is a sign that mother is a failure and that daughter will not do well in the world. A mother who has spent decades suppressing her own anger will be very unsettled to watch her daughter struggling to control similar feelings; daughter's expression of anger tempts mother to express her own anger. Unfortunately, we want to stay away from someone who elicits our forbidden feelings; we fear they'll bring out the worst in us. A late-middle-aged mother called Judith said in one of my classes:

> For the first year after my daughter separated from her husband, I couldn't stand to be around her, because she was so filled with hostility. I *believed* she had the right to be furious at him, because he'd been unfaithful to her many times, but I just didn't *feel* like being around her. One reason was that I became more irritable with *my* husband every time I saw my daughter. I just got so mad about some of the things men do to women, and that made it harder for me to ignore my husband's lack of warmth toward me.

When, as is inevitable in any relationship, anger arises between mother and daughter, they try to understand why they're not living up to the ideal. Each may blame herself, or they may blame each other. Neither is an attractive alternative, and both are misdirected, for the problem probably doesn't come from within them; it is thrust upon them by society. When we feel we have to suppress any feelings we have about another person, our time together is strained. But strain itself is inconsistent with the popular view of the ideal mother-daughter pair. The daughter in a typical mother-daughter pair who attended one of my public lectures described this experience:

> The first time I came home from college for a visit—at Thanksgiving—both Mother and I expected things to go smoothly. We'd fought like cats and dogs during my last year of high school, but we both blamed that on our sadness about my leaving home. Now that I lived in another state, we both assumed we'd finished our combative stage.
>
> No such luck! We fought horribly on that first visit, and we took turns blaming it all on each other and feeling guilty and blaming ourselves. It was so bad that I didn't attempt another visit home until the

end of the next August, after my summer job ended. She didn't *ask* me to visit any sooner!

As we learn to suppress an emotion, we increasingly feel that if we ever do express it, some disaster will befall us. In the case of women's anger, we not only fear being considered unwomanly if we express that feeling, but we also believe that our anger is so destructive: After all, if our mothers can't accept our anger, we feel, then how dangerous our anger must be!

Earlier in this chapter, I mentioned the mother's and daughter's fears that fully expressing our warm feelings toward each other will make it harder to suppress such feelings in the presence of men, who might consider us "overemotional" or who may be jealous of our closeness to each other. Mother-daughter anger endangers our relationships with men in at least two ways:

1. Many a man can't stand to see an angry woman, even if he's not the butt of her anger, because this clashes with his ideal of femininity.
2. Once mother and daughter get angry, that energy might be turned against men who mistreat them; so, for many men, the presence of a woman who is angry for any reason at all reminds them of how precarious their position would be if that anger were directed at *them*.

Women sense how uncomfortable their anger makes most men (that's one reason women smile so much, even when they don't feel happy), so women who want close relationships with men may feel frightened by anger they feel at their mothers. Thirty-one-year-old Dana felt that way, and in her not-atypical case, she felt two dangers: that her husband would be uncomfortable about her anger at her mother and that her husband and mother would team up against her.

> When my husband and I were engaged, I hated for him to see my mother and me together, but it took me awhile to understand why. I finally realized that, when he was around, she was so anxious for us to get married that she played up to him, agreed with everything he said, had me serve him at the dinner table, and made an even greater show than usual of serving my father in all sorts of ways. I was furious at her for being so subservient, and I've only recently begun to forgive her, because I now understand that she was only doing what she had been taught a good woman should do.

But part of my anger at Mom was because I did *not* want to wait on my husband hand and foot, and when we were engaged he was already expecting me to do that. So there was Mom, doing what George wanted me to do but what I was trying to escape from. It was pretty complicated, because I wanted both Mom and George to love me, but I think I felt they were almost in league with each other against me. And when the three of us were in the same room, I'd get irritated with Mom, and then George would tell me that I shouldn't get so mad at her. Of course, part of the reason he said that was because, in a funny way, she and he were on the same side. If I *had* been able to articulate why I was so damned angry, it would have dashed *his* hopes of having an obedient wife.

To keep a proper perspective, we must realize that hostility between mothers and daughters is often exaggerated. In fact, recent research has shown that in early adolescence the greatest decline in parent-child hostility is in the mother-daughter relationship, and even before the decline, most of their relationships were described as "less positive" rather than frankly negative. Research also shows that teenaged daughters tend to confide "a lot" in their mothers and little or not at all in their fathers. Mother-daughter hostility is often exaggerated because even a little of what is forbidden looms very large.

WHERE DO WE GO FROM HERE?

Recognizing the myths about mothers and daughters, and the many forms they take in our daily culture, is essential to improving our relationships with our mothers. For most women, understanding that our mothers were unwitting vehicles for transporting cultural myths into our hearts and minds is much better and more empowering than believing that our mothers consciously, voluntarily, as individuals untouched by social pressure, chose to impose the myths on us. What mother would willingly teach her daughter such methods of self-destruction? And what woman would want to have to answer to her daughter for having done so? Yet so many mothers have been myth-transmitters. The fact that mothers—most of whom are conscientious about doing right by their children—transmit these myths demonstrates the power of social pressure in a culture that keeps mothers under its heel. (Even when mothers transmit only a fraction of the myths, they are often blamed for transmitting all.)

Seeing how this process works makes it easier for us as mothers and daughters to become allies, to refuse to be divided against each other. When we *see* that the price of society's acceptance of us is our readiness to turn against and blame our mothers, we are less likely to pay the price of that acceptance.

Asking Questions, Seeking Answers

We need to *raise questions*—in our own minds, with our mothers, and with other people.

- Is a mother's success or failure gauged by the way her daughter turns out, rather than by the mother's efforts or by the forces that interfered with those efforts?
- Is a daughter to blame her shortcomings on her mother's inability to meet all her needs?
- Are mothers (or daughters) truly capable of giving of themselves endlessly? And is it right to expect that of anyone?
- Is any woman truly capable of naturally, instinctively doing all it takes to be a perfect mother? And is it fair to expect that of our mothers and ourselves?
- Is women's anger sometimes healthy, and should we expect mothers (and daughters) always to suppress their anger?
- Is it possible to look at what factors that impinge on a daughter's development are overlooked when mother is blamed?
- How do all of the Perfect Mother myths damage mother-daughter relationships? And do those myths do any good at all (because if they do, let's not throw the baby out with the bathwater; for instance, let's encourage mothers and daughters to be nurturant, but stop expecting them to do so unceasingly)?

The long history and power of the myths make them hard to overcome. However, mothers and daughters are encouraged to make the effort when they begin to see what a difference it makes to their relationship. A mother-daughter pair, Lydia and Shelley, who learned how the endless nurturance myth created a barrier between them, jointly wrote me a letter in which they said:

Each of us had felt the other expected too much, but we hadn't realized that we ourselves did, too. Now, when either of us feels the other has let us down, we stop and ask ourselves—and then each other—"Was I expecting your *total* approval again?" And, usually, it's true.

Just asking the question solves most of the problem, because when you put it that way you realize how unrealistic that expectation is. Also, we're both adults now and don't really *need* anyone's total approval. But somehow, being able to say, "I wanted your one hundred percent support" makes it better. For one thing, the other person can tell you she *does* support you wholeheartedly, even if you were too insecure to know that. Or, she can tell you what reservations she has about your lover or dress or job, and you can talk it out. Knowing what the other person is worried about is always better than just feeling she's not giving you her all.

Another example of a mother and daughter whose examination of a myth helped lower a barrier between them involves 37-year-old Stephanie and her mother, Ruth. Stephanie told me about a conversation in which the two of them discussed their fear of anger:

When I told my mother that I was ending my career as fulltime housewife and going to work as a market researcher, she grew very cold toward me. In fact, she seemed to be furious. So, for the first six months of my job, I never talked to her about it. Finally, she asked me how things were going at work, but I was so frightened of her anger that I got tongue-tied. Then she got mad because I wasn't answering her. All I could manage to say at that point was, "I don't think you really want to hear!"

She looked stunned. "Wherever did you get that idea?" she asked. I told her I'd spent the past six months thinking she was angry at me for getting a job and not being home when my kids got home from school. Then, she looked terribly relieved and explained that what I had interpreted as anger at me was really her anger about the time she had wasted by not having a job when my twin brother and I got into high school. Dad hadn't wanted her to work, so she waited until we left for college, and when she finally did start work she had the time of her life. She had always been bitter about the four years she had sat at home, while my brother and I were out at school and extra-curricular activities, and Dad was at work, and she twiddled her thumbs, doing charity work she didn't really enjoy and feeling useless.

As Stephanie and Ruth talked, they realized that Stephanie had felt that having her mother angry at her was thoroughly devastating. Ruth had had no idea either that Stephanie thought she was angry at her (when she was really angry about her own history) or that it mattered so much to Stephanie if she was. Talking about the unacceptability of women's anger in general, and about Stephanie's particular dread of her mother's anger, took away the myth's power.

What the mothers and daughters in these two examples were able to do was to legitimize women's basic humanity. We do this by believing—and helping other people to see—that no one can be a perfect mother, that even the children of terrific mothers can go wrong, that no one can be endlessly nurturant, and that mothers and daughters can have a whole range of feelings, including anger. The women's movement has helped to do some of this educating, partly by showing women the unfairness and impossibility of living up to the traditional feminine stereotypes and partly by showing us that we have many legitimate reasons to be upset and angry. But although many of us now feel less ashamed and apologetic when we are angry or otherwise imperfect, lessening the taboo against women's anger and reducing the requirements for perfection in women in general hasn't necessarily reduced our expectations for mothers or weakened the taboo against anger at or from our mothers. The idealized view of the perfect, unalloyed love we are supposed to have for our mothers, plus injunctions to honor them, combine with genuine appreciation of what they have done for us, and all of this makes us feel horribly guilty about our anger at them. Conversely, the idealized view of how mothers are supposed to act—plus injunctions always to be the perfect, loving, kindly mother—makes mothers feel horribly guilty about what they regard as how they have "failed" us.

Daughters who want to see their mothers more realistically are also helped by contrasting their expectations of their mothers and their expectations of their fathers. Once they attend to this contrast, most daughters quickly recognize that they expect more nurturance and support, more good advice, and less anger from their mothers than from their fathers. Our relationships with our mothers can be improved once both we and they acknowledge the unfairness of that disparity and modify our expectations accordingly. (This double standard of expectations of mothers and fathers is discussed in Chapter 5.)

As if the Perfect Mother myths didn't cause mothers and

daughters enough trouble, there are also the Bad Mother myths, which are the subject of the next chapter and which also need to be understood in order to lower the barriers between mothers and daughters.

5 ❧ *The Bad Mother Myths*

WHERE THE PERFECT Mother myths establish standards every woman will fail to meet, the Bad Mother myths make mothers' ordinary behavior seem worse than it really is. With the help of the Bad Mother myths, we exaggerate our mothers' real faults and transform their neutral or not-so-bad characteristics into monstrosities.

No doubt there are others, but five major Bad Mother myths are:

- Myth Five: Mothers are Inferior to Fathers
- Myth Six: Mothers Need Experts' Advice To Raise Healthy Children
- Myth Seven: Mothers Are Bottomless Pits of Neediness
- Myth Eight: Mother-Daughter Closeness Is Unhealthy
- Myth Nine: Mothers are Dangerous When They're Powerful

MYTH FIVE: MOTHERS ARE INFERIOR TO FATHERS

The myth that mothers are inferior to fathers is probably the most pervasive of all the mother myths. In Chapter 4, we saw how, because of higher expectations for mothers than for fathers, we are quick to criticize our mothers for not being perfect but appreciate our fathers for merely trying. The myth of mothers' inferiority takes many other forms as well. For example, although traditional mother's work—childrearing, housecleaning, cooking, and monitoring the family dynamics—is unpaid and largely unappreciated, the major work of the traditional father is breadwinning, which by definition is paid work. (As mentioned earlier, the respect and honor of her family that are supposed to compensate mother for her lack of pay are rarely forthcoming.)

The myth of mother's inferiority leads to women being far more frequently the target of their husbands' and grown children's violent behavior than men are of their wives' or children's assaults. Furthermore, women victims are assumed to have "brought the violence on themselves," whereas men victims are thought to be undeserving targets who deserve sympathy.

Sexism Starts At Home

The myth of mothers' inferiority leads daughters to think disparagingly of both their mothers and themselves; often, we know, mothers themselves have helped indoctrinate their daughters with the myth. We daughters resent mother because she is the bearer of the bad news about our (and her) supposed inferiority; we don't realize that she never knew she had a choice. No one ever taught *her* to question females' inferiority. Slaves, after all, teach their children to be *obedient* slaves because they want them to survive.

As we saw in Chapter 4, mothers have been pressed to encourage daughters to accept their inferiority, to set "realistically" modest goals, to develop enough humility to avoid scaring off potential husbands. Trying to help daughters survive in a rough world, many mothers schooled their daughters in the myth of female inferiority and taught them to ally themselves with men rather than with their mothers or other women.

When I was a teenager facing a moral dilemma, my mother would discuss it with me and then say, "When your father comes home, ask him. He always knows the right thing to do." My father has always had high moral standards, but so has my mother; unfortunately, *because* of what my mother said, I grew up thinking of him, but not her, in that way.

Flo Kennedy says that the men-are-better myth makes possible what she calls "horizontal hostility":

If you have a sense of your own worthlessness, then somebody else from your class or race or religion is clearly not to be looked up to. This is one of the bases for the pathology of women saying, "I don't get along with women. I get along with men; they're superior, so if I get along with them *I'm* superior; I've left all of my class behind."

Because both mother and daughter are supposed to idolize the husband/father, they can be driven apart if they compete for his attention and overlook each other's value. In this connection, one woman wrote to me, "We all could look smart if we sided with our fathers against our mothers. The parent who invests less effort in the family exposes less of himself to his family to be judged." The typical father spends less time and emotional energy on the family, and his distance leads his children and wife wistfully, longingly, to idealize him—the rational parent, the parent who belongs in the "real," public world outside the home.

Even in families with strong mothers, the myth of female inferiority has been perpetuated, although some substantial psychological contortions have been required. An old friend told me how this happened in her family:

My mother was an amazing woman. She raised four of us kids virtually singlehandedly, and that included knitting all our sweaters herself, doing all the housework and cooking, while starting a mail-order business that eventually did very well. Daddy was at work every night until after dinner and worked half-days on Saturdays. Thanks partly to Mom, I never thought of her as working, but she made it clear that Daddy worked very hard.

When Daddy was due to arrive home every night, she'd get us to wash our faces and settle down. His nightly return home was an event —*because she made it one.* But no one did that for her. When Daddy fell asleep reading the evening paper, *she* made us keep quiet out of respect for how hard he worked. But on the rare occasions when *she* took a nap, he didn't do that for her.

Not until my mother's funeral—when the minister talked about her remarkable strength and energy—did I realize what an unbalanced view of my parents' worth I had.

Women have traditionally been relieved and delighted when their first child is a boy. Their sense of self-worth is likely to be enhanced more by giving birth to a son than to a daughter. Many women—particularly in certain subcultures—know that their husbands will be disappointed if their first child is a girl, who probably won't carry on the patriarchal family name, who won't be such powerful evidence of the father's manhood (Thomas Babe's play, *A Prayer for My Daughter,* includes a dramatic portrayal of this concern). Words like "pride and joy" tend to appear on greeting cards for new baby boys but "small and sweet" on those for baby girls.

A successful businesswoman who was an only child told me the following story. It had never occurred to her that her parents might have preferred a son or valued him more highly than they valued her. When she was in her early twenties, she attended a party with her mother, and the topic of miscarriages arose. One woman told about a friend who had just miscarried, and the businesswoman's mother commented, "Well, I knew a woman who had a *real* tragedy: she lost a baby through miscarriage—and it was a boy!"

The ramifications are especially serious when a mother's disappointment about having a daughter interferes with her ability to care for her child. An infant's world depends so much on her caretakers' treatment of her—and in this culture, "caretaker" primarily means mother. A mother who is disappointed about having a girl is less likely to hold her baby as warmly or as long, to respond as wholeheartedly to her first smile, or to be as patient when she is troublesome as she would if the baby had been a boy. For many mothers, this initial letdown fades as they enjoy their real, live baby girl, but for some it persists forever.

Even today, parents of both sexes often treat their sons differently from their daughters, setting fewer limits on boys' behavior and making fewer demands for them to take care of others. According to Judith Arcana, "[sons'] behavior may deviate from standard, appropriate behavior far more than that of daughters and still be acceptable." When the daughter sees that her mother treats her brother differently, she often believes that her mother loves her less. This gives her yet another reason to feel angry at and betrayed by her mother.

If as a child you were undervalued because of your sex, you may later have realized why you were not wholeheartedly accepted; but by then a great deal of harm had been done. The seeds of poor self-esteem are sown with awesome firmness in the earliest years of life, when a child experiences herself as one who is *not* a source of pride, who is *not* cherished; then, angry about feeling inferior, she often turns her rage against her mother, who was there all the time and did not seem to value her.

The motion picture *Nuts*, in which the character played by Barbra Streisand has been sexually abused by her stepfather, reflects some of the worst harm that can be caused by the male superiority myth. Because of that myth, the mother believed she had to have a man in the family. The film shows that, until the daughter had grown up, the mother was unaware of the abuse, partly because her husband had taken extreme measures to keep it a secret. Furthermore, her first husband had abandoned them, and she was terrified of losing her second. She considered herself worthless because her first husband hadn't wanted her, and she believed her daughter needed a father-figure; in order to persuade her new man to stay with them, she tried desperately to please him and to protect him from all tension and demands. When her daughter started skipping school, becoming promiscuous, and taking drugs, family counseling was suggested. But the stepfather feared that in counseling his secret would be revealed, so he made excuses to avoid it, saying the stepdaughter was the problem, not the family. To avoid angering him, the mother accepted his view.

This film was true-to-life. In families plagued by incest, the father's avoidance of responsibility and his intimidation of both mother and daughter are common. The same is true for fathers who tyrannize their families in other ways. In the course of creating and preserving a traditional nuclear family—that is, to keep an adult male in the home and to protect the father's reputation —the mother's and daughter's psychological and physical safety have often suffered. Sadly, this gives daughter more reason to feel her mother has let her down.

Some of the most serious consequences of the male superiority myth involve mothers and daughters being driven apart by the allegiance either or both of them feels to a man, no matter how much he may be in the wrong. A woman I'll call Maureen had worked diligently to overcome the emotional distance between her widowed mother, Ruth, and herself, and she seemed to be having some success. Then Maureen learned that her brother, Ben, had become a compulsive gambler and was running his family deeply into debt. He didn't want his wife to get a job, so he was the sole breadwinner for himself, his wife, and their three sons.

Maureen went to great lengths to support her sister-in-law's attempts to take her children and leave Ben, but Ruth refused to believe the truth about her son and angrily condemned Maureen's attempts to look out for her nephews. According to Ruth, Maureen —not Ben—was wrong. So great was Ruth's need to safeguard her image of her son that she denied Ben was even capable of serious wrongdoing. So profound was this mother's belief in the superiority of men that, rather than live with the truth, she chose to believe the lies of her son ("He's the only man I have left," she said) and to scorn Maureen's attempts to restore their mother-daughter relationship.

Even when men are clearly inadequate—because of drugs, abusiveness, or extreme emotional withdrawal—mothers and daughters often seek men's approval even while they try to protect each other against the father's abuses of power.

Penis Envy and Penis Pity

In Chapter 3 we saw how mother-blame is validated and reinforced by claims from the scientific world. Sigmund Freud's work was ingenious but not scientifically proven; nevertheless, his theory of "penis envy" has been skillfully used to support the myth of male superiority. According to Freud, all women wish they had a penis and believe that men's genitals make them superior. This idea has become part of everyday culture; at cocktail parties, we talk as though penis envy were a given, as if all women feel it.

Freud said that women hold their mothers responsible for their lack of a penis. In the daughter's eyes, Freud argued, mother is omnipotent; the daughter believes her mother could have endowed her with a penis but chose not to. Freud also suggested that the little girl's embarrassment over her own "inferiority" is connected to her contempt for her mother: "I despise my mother because she is just like me in this deficient way."

Because Freud's influence has been so great, we need to think carefully about penis envy. What Freud calls "penis envy" isn't just about penises: daughters' disappointment over their mothers' failure to give them a penis is less than their disappointment over their mothers' powerlessness compared to father, their mothers' inability to empower them (compared to their brothers), and their mothers' preferential treatment of their brothers. Furthermore, daughters are often sad to see how limited their mothers' lives and choices have been and are alarmed by the poverty of possibility for *their* lives that they see mirrored there. As Kim Chernin wrote in *Reinventing Eve*, "When the daughter at the crossroads rejects her mother and chooses her father instead, it is because she cannot find within the mother-world a way to grow into the full promise of her original female being." For all these reasons, then, we may look down on our mothers and ourselves and look up to our fathers and brothers.

The danger of using the penis as a symbol of the inequities between mother and father, between brother and sister, is that it makes the inequities seem inevitable. Fathers and brothers will continue to have penises, and mothers and sisters will not, so if the penis is the real issue, we may as well believe that males will always be superior and females always deficient. But we need to remember that the penis only *represents* men's greater social, political, and economic power, that that power imbalance is not our mothers' fault, and that it *can* be changed.

Even when we think about penis envy in its literal sense, we need to know that not all girls feel this envy. Many feel what I have called "penis pity." Some people of both sexes think that penises are funny, strange-looking, wobbly, out-of-control, and vulnerable to harm. At the age which Freud said that penis envy appears, when two- to four-year-old girls notice their physical differences from boys, children have important concerns that lead to penis pity—issues of control and self-control, protecting their bodies, and privacy. Little girls at this age may regard themselves as lucky: they needn't try to *control* something that dangles and swings willy-nilly, nor to *protect* something that is externally exposed, sensitive and easily hurt, nor to struggle to *maintain privacy and avoid embarrassment* about visible, easily observable genitalia.

For many little girls penis pity is quite real. According to Simone deBeauvoir in *The Second Sex*, "This tiny bit of flesh hanging between boys' legs is insignificant or even laughable; it is a peculiarity that merges with that of clothes or haircut. . . . It may even happen that the penis is considered to be an anomaly: an outgrowth, something vague that hangs, like wens, breasts, or warts; it can inspire disgust."

How does the concept of penis pity change our vision of the possibilities for the mother-daughter relationship? Believing in penis envy feeds our belief that all daughters resent their mothers for not giving them either penises *or* access to social power, that all women feel contempt for themselves and other women, and that this is natural and unavoidable. But once we realize that penis envy is not inevitable and that little girls may actually feel relieved *not* to have a penis, that justification for resenting our mothers is gone.

As we saw earlier, the myth of mothers' inferiority underlies many of the other mother-myths, and one of those is the notion that without the advice of experts—many of whom are male—mothers cannot raise emotionally healthy children.

MYTH SIX: ONLY THE EXPERTS KNOW HOW TO RAISE CHILDREN

The explosion of advice from childrearing experts during this century has led mothers to believe that the Truth about good childrearing is out there somewhere, if only they can find it and manage to follow it. Mothers read the latest book on childrearing and find that they should be setting firm limits with their eight-year-olds, because young children feel secure only if they know that their impulses won't be given free rein. The next book hot off the press from another expert arrives. Mothers read it and learn that their limits should be very flexible, guidelines for their children's behavior should be set in democratic family councils, and children should play a substantial role in setting the consequences for failing to keep to the guidelines. This expert says that that method is crucial for encouraging the child to develop internal controls and to feel that mother respects the child's ideas.

Mothers think about the apparent disagreement between the two experts and conclude that both make sense. Children probably need some of each. *But* . . . how are they ever going to decide when *their* child needs *how much* of each? The answers to these questions matter desperately, because both the child's current and future happiness and the mother's success as a mother are at stake. Where is the super-expert who will tell them which expert to follow when? Conscientious mothers have made mistakes in trying to follow experts' advice, since no super-expert has been at their elbows to guide them, to say, "Now you're doing too much" and "Now you're not doing enough," and certainly never "Now you're doing it just right!"

The so-called experts carry on unending debates about bottle-feeding versus breastfeeding, feeding on demand versus feeding on a schedule, whether or not to teach your child to read before grade one, whether or not to give immunizations, how best to discipline your child, whether or not having an only child is bad, whether or not to involve the child in a highly structured class-room, and so on. A contemporary of my mother's told me:

> One expert instructed mothers to stay home with their children until they started kindergarten, another said even teenagers need to know mother will be home if they get sick at school, and still another said we should go out to work so that we could feel better about ourselves as people. With the big shots disagreeing with each other, and us mothers feeling hopelessly inadequate, how were we supposed to make our decisions?

On the subject of children's psychological welfare, a great deal has already been discussed in Chapter 2 about the experts' mother-blaming. Even when mother is not directly blamed, she is haunted by the experts' tendency to interpret children's behavior as indicating problems. (Pediatrician Dr. T. Berry Brazelton is a glorious exception, since in his books he takes care to describe how wide is the range of normal behavior.)

Some mothers' experiences with "experts" are especially dev-astating. In one state, a judge awarded custody of a young child with cerebral palsy to her father, telling the mother sternly that she should not have a job, because her child's disability was a warning from God that she should have recognized, and she should stay home with her. On the other hand, some professionals speak disparagingly of mothers with disabled children who *do* spend all their time teaching and working with the child; they label such mothers "overinvolved" or "pushy."

A hardworking professional woman I know took her four-year-old cerebral palsied daughter for an educational assessment. The examiner administered a huge battery of intellectual and developmental tests and found that the child's scores ranged from above average to dramatically superior. Without asking for any background information, the examiner said accusingly: "You have certainly been pushing this child!" Until then, the mother had felt guilty for having a career, because she thought perhaps she ought to stay home all day, teaching her daughter. Now she was being criticized as though she *had* stayed home but overdone it. Always, it seems, mothers are told they are doing either too much or not enough, and it doesn't get easier as the children get older. Listen to Alexandra, the mother of a fourteen-year-old girl whose grades had dropped when she entered high school:

> My family doctor told me I wasn't pushing Sally enough. "You need to set up more structure for her, keep her to regular homework times, and so forth," he said. Because he felt I was intimidated by Sally, he sent me to a psychiatrist who was supposed to help me be a stricter parent. But the psychiatrist told me, "Sally picks up on your excessively high standards of achievement, and her lower grades are her way of protesting against them. Stay *completely* out of her schoolwork. Don't even ask her if she's finished her homework."

The ironies involved with the myth that mothers need the advice of experts in order to raise children are many. First of all, as we saw in Chapter 4, most of the honest experts freely acknowledge that human behavior is complex and that they usually cannot explain why a child from a problem-ridden home can turn out fine, but a child who seems to have everything can become a criminal.

Second, co-existing with and contradicting the myth that only the *experts* know the answers is the myth that mothers naturally know how to raise children (Chapter 4). The truth is that neither experts nor mothers know as much as each might wish; to a great extent, all of us fly by the seat of our pants and try to learn quickly from experience. But the proliferation of so-called experts on childrearing feeds a Bad Mother myth, because they make already insecure mothers (that is, most mothers) feel that only *the experts* know the right thing to do.

Ironically, many real mistakes that mothers make are based on bad advice they are given by "experts" or on their misguided attempts to follow that advice. Yet there's no shortage of experts willing to condemn anything a mother does, and mother herself often feels woefully inadequate. Plagued by impossibly high expectations for their behavior and/or trying to follow "expert" advice, mothers have developed intense anxiety and guilt. Children *are* harmed by parents' anxiety and guilt—that is one of the few principles on which mental health professionals *do* agree. Mother becomes unduly anxious around her children: instead of trusting her instincts and perceptions, she worries constantly about whether or not she is doing the right thing. But mothers cannot legitimately be held solely responsible for this harm, for *they* didn't set the unreachable standards. Ronni is a 31-year-old mother who told me this story:

> When my children were three and five years old, their father and I separated, and he was not very good about visiting or calling them regularly. My pediatrician said I should explain to the children that "Daddy really loves you a lot, even though he doesn't call," so that they wouldn't feel rejected by him. But my psychiatrist said, "Your ex-husband is very self-centered, and he really doesn't love anyone except himself very much. Don't tell the kids that Daddy loves them a lot, because that is teaching them that loving doesn't require any show of concern for the loved ones."
>
> I was so confused, because both of them made some sense to me. So I was nervous all the time. I just didn't know how to handle it, and the kids had a really bad time because of my anxiety. The five-year-old decided she had to take care of me, and she kept asking me what she could do to cheer me up. The three-year-old became a real behavior problem, because of having picked up my anxiety, I think.

The belief that only the experts really know the right way to raise a child damages mother-daughter relationships because it feeds a daughter's belief in her mother's inadequacy. (It does the same for sons; this myth applies to both mother-daughter and mother-son relationships.) Women's fear of not being naturally perfect mothers keeps them from sharing with their daughters their uncertainties and confusion, as we saw earlier. As a result, many daughters look at their mothers' imperfections and simply see a woman who couldn't manage to follow the experts' advice, rather than understanding her confusion, her struggle, and her good intentions. Some adult daughters, who achieved less in school than they now think they could have done, have told me they hold their mothers responsible for failing "to make me toe the mark." "She should have used tough love," said one. Others have said that their mothers should have followed the advice of experts to place responsibility for schoolwork squarely on the adolescent's shoulders. Many women learned to appreciate their mothers more once they themselves had children; through their own experience they learned not just how difficult, but how impossible it is to know what is right.

Mothers who feel that they aren't achieving Good Childrearing standards are not about to increase their pain by informing other people of their "failures." On account of this, rarely have mothers had a chance to learn that they are all in the same boat, all terrified of failing but pretty certain that that's just what they are doing.

Daughters shouldn't have to wait until they give birth before they begin to understand their mothers' frustration in the face of the myth that only the experts know what to do. Realizing how powerful the myth is, how confusing the experts' advice can be, and how hard most of our mothers tried to wade through that morass can take us a long way toward understanding and appreciating our mothers.

MYTH SEVEN: MOTHERS (AND DAUGHTERS) ARE BOTTOMLESS PITS OF NEEDINESS

"What does she *want* from me?"
— Countless men, about their wives, through the ages

Many stories and images promote the myth that women have unmeetable emotional needs and make ceaseless demands on other people. Mothers, the myth would have us believe, drain everyone around them of their love, autonomy, and self-respect. We know the tales of woman as witch, sorceress, Circe, Scylla and Charybdis, and Cleopatra; the fear of being faced with unmeetable demands is even entrenched in the Bible, such as in Ecclesiastes: "And I find more bitter than death the woman, whose heart ensnares and nets." Closer to our own day, Freud wrote that daughters feel intense hostility toward their mothers for not meeting (as no one could) their "insatiable" and "immoderate" needs.

Problems in relationships are routinely blamed on women's supposedly unmeetable needs for affection. In fact, women blame their own "neediness" for causing trouble. Rosalie had this to say about her relationship with her husband:

> Sam always wants me to be compassionate and supportive when *he's* upset, but when *I* need a little compassion and support, he throws up his hands and says, "What do you want from me?! Nothing is ever enough for you! *Nobody* could meet your needs!"

Since men are raised with the myth of women's neediness and most are also raised to be inexpressive, many of them worry that they won't be able to respond in kind to a woman's nurturance (or they may feel it's not masculine to do so). They worry, too, that if they can't respond adequately, she will reject or abandon them. Instead of acknowledging their fear of their own inadequacy, many men claim that women's needs are unmeetable, thus perpetuating the myth.

A husband who fears that he will lose his wife because of his emotional inadequacy will often deal with this fear by demanding endless demonstrations of loyalty, commitment, and reassurance from his wife. Yet the woman who responds by giving a man her all is vulnerable to criticism. She is labeled the smothering, engulfing woman/mother who overwhelms men and children with love and nurturance long after they have had enough, the "seductress" who uses her warmth and sexuality to control and manipulate men and children. And since girls and women absorb men's attitudes, in part as a way of pleasing them, they see themselves as men do. This reinforces their belief that their own needs (and those of other girls and women) are enormous.

Women's needs may seem enormous for other reasons. In general, women are brought up to be more expressive than men; we show what we want as well as what we have to give. Men's needs tend to be better masked—and are usually sensed and tended to by a woman (mother, wife, daughter, girlfriend) even before the man has to acknowledge having them. Marnie, a newly married woman, told me:

> The minute he walks in the door after work, my husband Bart expects me to know whether he needs to talk or to be left alone. But when I tell him I'm hurt because he doesn't take an interest in how *I'm* feeling after a day at the office, he says, "How am I supposed to know how you feel if you don't *tell* me?!" But when I do tell him I've had a rough day, he says I shouldn't burden him by "emoting all over the place."

Women have been encouraged to appear helpless, needy, and dependent, so that we would be attractive and unthreatening to men. For many men, this works—until the woman's neediness starts to infuriate them. As Suzette wrote in a letter to me:

> Allen loves to feel strong and protective when I burst into tears. But I feel like he allows me about thirty seconds of sympathy, and then he expects me to stop crying. If I don't, he rants and raves about my being such a "big baby."

Like the members of any undervalued or oppressed group, women sometimes do need extra support, because in addition to dealing with the ordinary problems of daily life, they have to cope with extra stresses and wounds. Our culture increases women's real needs for support and then uses those needs to "prove" that we are simply overemotional. This does not prove, however, that women *inevitably* have huge emotional needs.

A major reason for some women's intense needs for affection is that they, like some men, were inadequately nurtured when they were children. Therapists have reported that such children grow up feeling that they can never be loved enough. This makes it particularly hard for women, who are supposed to provide nurturance for others, despite feeling so needy themselves. In addition, unpleasant restrictions of various kinds have been placed on our mothers' lives, including—for most of them—the lack of real choice about whether or not to get married, have children, and stay at home to take care of them. Furthermore, the success of their marriage was considered to be mostly their responsibility rather than one shared equally with their husbands.

These factors in combination have left millions of women unhappy and unfulfilled. As Betty Friedan pointed out in *The Feminine Mystique*, each unhappy housewife in our mothers' generation thought her unhappiness proved that she was ungrateful, selfish, and unwomanly; each was isolated by that fear, because she wasn't about to let anyone else know about her "failings."

So many now-adult daughters were raised in this context. Small wonder, then, that mothers often turned to their daughters for attention, support, companionship, and, indirectly, confirmation that they were good, lovable mothers. Daughters more than sons were more likely to fulfill these roles because they, in turn, were being taught to raise their daughters to be nurturant and sensitive to other people's needs. According to Larissa, whose daughter is now a grown woman:

> My daughter was always my best friend. She was such a good, sympathetic listener—even when she was little. We'd have long talks while she helped me wax the floor or put up preserves. I don't know what I would have done without her.

The daughter in such a situation may begin to hide her own needs for nurturance as she tries to meet her mother's needs; then, since those needs are invisible, they go largely unmet, and she feels insufficiently nurtured. When the daughter grows up, she, too, may become a mother who turns to her daughter for solace.

Mothers and daughters often describe this development as "My mother is more like a friend to me than a mother." Such a relationship can provide a great deal of genuine closeness and sharing, but it becomes a problem if it involves a total reversal of roles so that the daughter always takes care of the mother, never vice versa. What is more dangerous than a moderate degree of role reversal is mental health professionals' claim that any daughter's nurturance of her mother is a sign of "fusion," of pathology, because this claim sullies the loving give and take that can characterize such mother-daughter relationships. (This point is the subject of Myth Eight.)

The mother-daughter role reversal occurs partly because the daughter takes care of her mother and partly because, in some ways, mothers tend to nurture their daughters less than their sons. Psychologist Elena Belotti says that mothers teach their daughters, in effect: "Everything is fine as long as I have to do as little as possible for you, so hurry up and learn how to fend for yourself." Although Renate is now in her late twenties, her recollection of this aspect of her mother's treatment of her is still painful:

> When I was seven years old and my brother was nine, he got more attention from Mama than I did—even when I was sick! When *he* was sick, she'd stop everything, make him chicken soup, and sit on his bed, playing board games and cards with him. But when *I* was sick, I just got the soup. She'd say, "Renate's so good at entertaining herself when she's sick." I really had no choice, because she never took the trouble to entertain me.
>
> I know that Mama loved me, and I knew it then. What hurt wasn't

thinking she didn't care about me but feeling like I needed from her some attention that she was proud of me for supposedly *not* needing—yet it was obviously a great pleasure for her to give that kind of attention to my brother.

   And then, whenever Mama was sick, my brother was nowhere to be found. I was expected to take care of Mama, but no one ever gave me credit for it. As she told Papa, "You don't need to take care of me. Renate's my daughter: she's *supposed* to be my right arm—and she sure is." She'd beam proudly when she said that, and I felt at once glad to be doing what she wanted, glad to be her "right arm," but wistful because I had to be so grown-up all the time. It never felt OK for *me* to need to be taken care of, and I was hurt because I thought she wasn't particularly interested in doing that for me.

Any time a daughter spends providing nurturance is time that she is not receiving it, and this can leave her feeling her own needs are unmeetable. Then she becomes a mother herself and is supposed to give her infant the nurturance that she feels she never had. It is like asking a starving woman to serve a feast. Daughter holds her mother responsible for failing her.

In addition, the presence of her infant daughter consciously or unconsciously brings back mother's memories of her feelings of being neglected, so that her loneliness re-emerges just when she is trying to take responsibility for her newborn. The combination of feelings can make it difficult to relax and love a baby. If that baby is not nurtured enough, the cycle is perpetuated. Woman after woman grows up feeling as though she will never be loved enough.

If mother and daughter understand why each other's needs *seem* unlimited, we won't be driven apart by this fear. But when mothers and daughters *believe* the myth of women's neediness, the myth creates a barrier between them; believing the myth, each is terrified of being sucked dry and used up by the other's allegedly limitless needs. Each feels daunted by the prospect of being expected to provide sufficient nurturing to the other; and each is likely to misread *some* need in the other as *boundless* need. Diane and Marie, a mother and daughter I interviewed, described the way this dynamic appeared in their relationship:

> *Diane:* When Marie was fifteen and her first real boyfriend broke up with her, I thought she'd never stop crying. At first, I held her and patted her back, but after an hour she was still sobbing. I felt so helpless. I just didn't know what to do. She seemed to need so much more than I

could give her. But, then, she'd always been like that, needing me so much, and I never felt up to the task. Sometimes I'd just run to my room and close the door. I couldn't stand to see her when she was so needy.

Marie: I felt the same way about her. One night when I was about seven, I saw Mom leaning on Dad and crying. She was saying, "I'm just a miserable, unhappy person." I don't know why she was upset, and she wasn't asking me for help. But she was always saying how great a help I was to her, how loving and sensitive I was, and I felt like I *should* have been able to make her happy.

Both Diane and Marie fell into a common trap of believing that we have to *do something* when someone close to us is upset. Often, however, the best thing to do is simply to be present and listen, or wait empathetically and lovingly. We feel helpless and useless if we believe we should be able to banish their pain. Marie had an added burden: no one, including her mother, had taught her that children are not supposed to be able to solve adults' problems.

Passing On The Emptiness

A case conference in which I participated involved four generations of women and shows how the emptiness is passed on and how it is blamed on mothers but not on fathers. The reason for the family's presence at the clinic was that the eight-year-old daughter was depressed, and the head therapist wanted to understand the family's history and dynamics before recommending treatment.

I'll call the grandmother Bree, the mother Resa, and the daughter Rosemary. According to the mother and grandmother, the great-grandfather (Bree's father) was jovial, and the great-grandmother was cold and hard. Bree married Cesar, a cordial but deeply depressed man. When they had children, Bree was determined that they not feel rejected by her, as her mother had made her feel; but she was unable to respond to their needs for warmth, since she took her father as a role model and acted jovial and chipper—but not warm. As her daughter Resa grew up, she planned never to have children, because she sensed that, like her mother, she had little love to offer.

Resa did have a daughter, however, and she clearly found the child primarily a bother, an obstacle to the satisfaction of her own needs. She went through the motions, doing a few of the "right things" like taking Rosemary for haircuts or buying her clothes; but the relationship between mother and daughter was basically empty, punctuated by frequent, angry outbursts on both sides.

In the conference, the chief psychiatrist laid all the blame for Rosemary's depression on the unmet emotional needs of the generations of women, each of whom focused more on her own needs than on those of her children. Neither the psychiatrist nor the women in the family asked, "Where was Bree's father's warmth? Did he ever even spend time with his family?" Is he remembered as simply jovial rather than jovial-but-remote because as a man he wasn't expected to be any more? And aren't Cesar's passivity and depression as likely contributors to Resa's brittleness as Bree's frenetic, chipper style? After all, depression seriously limits the emotional resources one can offer. Bree and Resa bear intense ill will toward their own mothers, because of their "unmeetable needs," and both idealize their fathers.

When Rosemary began spending more time with *her* father, who is an extremely loving parent, her depression began to lift. Her eyes started to sparkle, and she became more open and outgoing. What a therapist can learn from such cases is that either mother's *or* father's neediness can harm a child, *and* either mother's *or* father's capacity to love can help. This is an important lesson when we consider that therapists usually involve the mother of a troubled child in therapy but rarely try very hard to involve the father. This traditional approach both exaggerates the impact of mother's neediness and overlooks the potential for truly loving fathers to meet their children's needs.

MYTH EIGHT: MOTHER-DAUGHTER CLOSENESS IS UNHEALTHY

Women love connection. But in a society that is phobic about intimacy and extols the virtues of independence, we mistakenly regard connection and closeness as "dependency," "fusion" and "merging." So most mothers worry that they are keeping their children too dependent on them. When her child cries as she is left for the first day of nursery school or camp, mother fears that she has failed; she feels ashamed of her child's "dependence" on her and her "need to tie her child to her."

We live in a culture that values independence and rationality over closeness and emotionality. Furthermore, men are usually considered independent and rational, whereas women are considered dependent, eager for closeness, and emotional.

Given these assumptions, relationships between two women are often regarded as overly dependent, because both people are presumed to be unhealthily interested in closeness. In mother-daughter relationships, the danger of being branded "dependent" is intensified still more. An infant or young daughter is inevitably dependent on her mother. Even though mothers and daughters usually become more independent as the daughter grows up, they believe the myth and fear that they will be criticized or ridiculed for being "too close." The mother of a first-year college student explained:

> Laura and I have always been so close. Since she left for college last month, every time I walk by her room, I get all weepy. I know I shouldn't feel that way—I shouldn't be so upset. I guess we've been *too* close.

Unfortunately, no one assured this mother that her reaction was a normal, human response to separation from a loved one, not a sign of "too much" closeness.

In a similar way, for the mother whose child cries on the first day of school, memories of her own sadness the first day of school flood back, and she believes she is repeating the mistakes her mother made with her: "If only my mother had made *me* more independent," she thinks, "I'd know how to do that for *my* child." So she blames her mother and she blames herself.

But this thinking is destructive, because far more of mothers' and children's behavior is within the normal range than we have dared to believe. Sadness about separation the first day of school or camp is usually a sign of a mother-child relationship that is loving and worth holding onto, the security that comes from feeling you can turn to your mother, and a healthy fear of the unknown. How different would we feel if we lived in a society that encouraged us, on seeing a weeping child the first day of school, to think, "How sad for the child and the mother—but how lovely that they care enough about each other that it is hard to part!"

Do we really believe that sadness about mother-child separation is pathological, whereas sadness about the loss of a spouse is normal?

Despite the unreasonableness of "overly dependent," "fused" or "engulfing" as descriptions of most mother-daughter relationships, the belief that mothers and daughters cannot see themselves as separate from each other is pervasive. Many mothers and daughters have accepted this description of their relationship as accurate. We worry that any closeness between us proves that we are fused, but on the other hand, any distance between us or interruption of closeness is unfeminine, because women are supposed to be loving. In the recent novel *The Good Mother*, the main character wonders, "How could I love her without damaging her, I wondered. Not too much, not too little. Is there such a love?"

In our culture, growing boys are encouraged to become increasingly different from their mothers; growing up, for boys, means leaving the world represented by mother and the female culture. A man who remains close to his mother is likely to be regarded as less than a real man. A woman who remains close to her mother may be considered "too" dependent, but she at least is not accused of being unfeminine for that reason. So daughters get the message both that we are "too dependent" on our mothers and that we are supposed to stay close to them, but staying close is mislabeled "dependency." Mother and daughter cannot win. There is no room for our behavior to be considered healthy.

The myth becomes entrenched, then, that—unlike sons, who eventually separate from their mothers and enter the "real" world—daughters and mothers never achieve that separation. The experts assume such dependency to be unhealthy. They believe the daughter enjoys her dependency so much that she cannot grow up, and the mother wants to keep her daughter close by to meet *her* enormous needs. Women who are patients of therapists with such attitudes are directly affected by this approach, but few women escape the effects of the myth, learning the concept from friends who are in therapy or picking it up in the popular media.

Is it true that mothers and daughters cannot separate from each other? In general, no. On the extremely rare occasion, someone will be unable to recognize that another person is separate from oneself; that is indeed a serious problem and a severe psychological disturbance. It is *not* typical of most mother-daughter relationships.

When professionals—or we ourselves—talk about "the mother's inability to see her daughter as separate from herself," variously called "mother-daughter fusion," "merging," "enmeshment," "engulfment," or "symbiosis," we're usually referring to a mother's suppression of her own needs in order to tend to other people. But to be able to do that, a woman *has* to know she is a separate person; otherwise, she mistakenly assumes that the other person's needs are identical to hers. So, in fact, successful nurturing requires a substantial psychological separation of self from other. It's sometimes called "maturity." A mother's suppression of her own feelings can cause problems, but it does not necessarily decrease her sensitivity to her children's needs when they differ from her own.

A New Vision

A major force in encouraging more accurate and positive labeling of women's behavior comes from women like the Wellesley College Stone Center therapists' group (including Judith Jordan, Alexandra Kaplan, Jean Baker Miller, Irene Stiver, and Janet Surrey) and social worker Rachel Josefowitz Siegel. They have noted that the classic, influential theories about child development identify independence and separateness as the goals of emotional maturity. Although some independence is necessary (such as learning to feed and dress oneself, learning to protect one's body from harm), another important track of development has nearly been ignored. The growing ability to form and maintain relationships with other people is necessary both to survive (e.g., learning how to signal an adult when you are hungry so that you will be fed) and to enjoy life fully. Psychologist Janet Surrey calls this "relational ability." Despite the importance of relational ability, any deviation from independence is usually regarded in our culture as an alarming aberration rather than a valuable step toward deepening one's interpersonal relationships.

The Wellesley group has found that "women do not want to separate from their mothers. They want to keep that relationship authentic and add other strong and close relationships." Surrey calls this a "model of growth through addition and enlarging of relations."

Women who attend seminars given by Siegel, the Wellesley group, and others like them report feeling empowered, warmed, and optimistic about their relationships with their mothers and with other women. Many of us are told that problems with our mothers arise because we are *too* connected, and so we should move away emotionally; this contradicts the way we have been raised—to establish and maintain connections. We don't always recognize the contradiction; fed by the male superiority myth, our first reaction to being told we're too close to our mothers is likely to be embarrassed agreement. We may try then to win praise for dissociating ourselves from women and becoming more emotionally distant. Most mothers invest a great deal of effort in enriching connections with their daughters. When daughters mislabel those connections as problems, they tend to keep their distance from their mothers.

Ironically, many therapists and friends who have told us that we are "too close" to our mothers are the same ones who have encouraged our total devotion to the men in our lives. To make a man the center of one's life is not considered a pathological choice to be avoided at all costs (despite the Catch-22 that the average woman is supposed to be dependent on a man, and dependency is considered sick, so the average woman is sick), but to be close to one's mother is dangerous.

Homophobia Rears Its Head

Mother-daughter closeness can even be mislabeled as unhealthy because of homophobia, the fear of homosexuality. Mothers often have physical contact with their children, particularly when they are infants; most women find this contact pleasurable. For many North Americans, however, physical contact between any two people is riddled with conflict. Women who are already worried that our own needs are too great become preoccupied with such questions as, "When does touching cross the line between affection and sex? Is there such a line? If I feel warmth or pleasure when I touch my baby, is that naughty, selfish, or sinful? Should I not touch her?"

Some mothers fear that they themselves have lesbian tendencies, or that their daughters will become lesbians, if they provide any physical pleasure for each other. For this reason, many mothers limit their physical and emotional contact with their daughters severely. One woman reported:

> My mother announced to me, when I was just old enough to understand what she was saying, that she would no longer hold or kiss me, because it was time I learned not to expect warmth from the world.

This woman said that her mother did not treat her sons in that way but did the same with her other two daughters.

One of my students described a poignant, early memory:

> I was five years old, and my family was at a picnic. . . . We had just finished eating and had lain down to nap. I moved to curl up next to my mother and to place my head on her chest. She pushed me off curtly, telling me that I was too old for that sort of thing any more. I moved away, hurt and angry.

Her hurt and anger have only recently begun to subside. She realizes that her mother hadn't loved her any less but had been trying to do the right thing by physically distancing herself.

In some cases, someone other than the mother may set the limits. Some fathers may intrude because they are jealous of their wives' physical closeness to their daughters. Regardless of how much her mother then retreats, the daughter usually believes that her mother wants the distance. Not understanding society's prohibitions of homosexuality, daughter knows only that her mother has rejected her. Children typically respond to rejection by searching within themselves for the reason. They wonder, "What did I do to make her love me less?" Since we don't like to be around people who make us feel unloved (although we may keep trying to win their affection), we back away from our mothers.

In contrast, mothers and sons are encouraged to maintain some sensual/sexual tension between them, because our society is heterosexually oriented. Furthermore, because men tend to regard women as inferior, many women long for a close relationship with a male in which she can have some vicarious power. A mother's relationship with her son makes this possible. Out of her need to be needed by him she may intensify her nurturing, boasting that her son "never lifted a finger" to help in the house. According to the French writer Colette, her mother, Sido, said this about her daughter and son: "Yes, yes, of course you love me, but you're a girl, a female creature of my own species, my rival. But in his heart I never had any rival."

The myth that mother-daughter closeness is unhealthy is enormously destructive because it pathologizes what is probably women's greatest source of strength—the capacity to form loving, mutually supportive relationships.

MYTH NINE: WOMEN'S POWER IS DANGEROUS

Women's power is generally assumed to be dangerous, but men's is not. This is ironic. While most of women's power is used for other people's benefit—to nurture, protect, and teach them—a great deal of men's power is channeled for their own benefit into power lunches, corporate politics, war games, and violence against women. Because women have so much control over us when we are very young, and because mother-blaming is encouraged, many people think that women can control our lives in damaging, destructive ways. Furthermore, *any* expression of power by members of a low-status group tends to be regarded as "too much" power.

Mothers' power is limited almost entirely to the family, but even in that sphere, mothers are commonly misperceived as *more* powerful than fathers. Psychiatrist Dr. Teresa Bernardez has said:

> . . . the reality that marriage is protective of the mental health of men but not of women, that women and girls are increasingly victims of physical and sexual abuse and often found among the poorest of groups, is in stark contrast with the mythical power assigned to women in the family.

Mothers are among the most powerless people in our whole society; they know that most of their work is undervalued or unnoticed. Furthermore, once we understand how truly powerless our mothers feel, we see in a different light the ways in which they do have power over us.

On the rare occasion when mothers feel powerful they are usually terrified that their power is destructive. And daughters often think of mothers' power in negative terms: "She has the power to make me feel totally worthless, just by looking at me the wrong way." We don't think of the positive side of our mothers' power over us—their support, nurturance, and even empowerment of us—partly because mothers have so little power in the world outside the home and partly because motherwork gets so little respect.

Women in therapy frequently believe their mother's power is dangerous. Fifty-three-year-old Margo wrote to me in a letter:

> Every time I've made a major decision, I've dreaded telling Mother about it. It makes no sense, because she's *always* been supportive—and I haven't dreaded telling Dad, although he's sometimes been very skeptical about my judgement. I don't exactly know what has frightened me about Mother. It wasn't just the fear of disappointment if she didn't approve of me. It went beyond that. I really felt, somehow, that she had the power to destroy me.

We fear our mothers' power partly because we remember the great power she had over us when we were young. That fear may also be fed by our images of mothers as the bearers of life and our association of the power to give life with the power to take it away. When mother said we children had done something wrong, we were pretty powerless: we could not argue with her, we could not remind ourselves that mother was simply invoking a specific set of moral standards with which others might well disagree. Her words were law. When we were young, she had *so* much information that we didn't have but longed to know. After all, mother presented most of the world to most of us when we were very young. And most of what she told us was true ("That is a doggie"), important ("Don't cross the street when the light is red"), or interesting ("No two snowflakes are exactly alike"). To some extent, she still has the power of knowledge, because she's been through certain things that we haven't—empty nest, a forty-year marriage, aging, etc.

Adult daughters often react to their mothers as though they (the daughters) were still powerless: "She makes me feel like I'm an adolescent again when I visit her!" We must remind ourselves at crucial times that we are no longer as powerless as children— we can feed and clothe ourselves, we can look elsewhere for love, support, and approval if they aren't currently forthcoming from mother.

One way to achieve a realistic perspective on our mother's power is to understand that her anger and tension are not always caused by us. As long as we believe that we are the major source of her anger or tension, she retains the power to make us feel that *we* are deeply evil. Children characteristically assume they deserve whatever mistreatment they get. Some years ago, when I was waiting to hear whether or not I had gotten a particular job, I felt I was screaming at Jeremy and Emily all the time. I tried desperately to counteract the effects of my anger by saying, "Oh, kids, it's not you. I'm just so worried about this job." When our mother yells at us, we find it hard to believe the yelling is not really aimed at us in particular, not a sign of our failings; it's even harder when we are children.

When a mother seems to be wielding undue power over her daughter, the real reason is often hidden. It may be misdirected rage provoked by her husband; many women suppress such anger in order to appear feminine or to avoid male violence or because they're not sure their anger is justified ("Do I have the right to be angry that he *never* takes the kids to the doctor?"). Sometimes a mother takes out on her daughter the frustration she feels about the thousand limits on her own life because of being a woman, but few mothers are aware of this until it's suggested to them. In many of my workshops, I ask mothers how they feel about teaching their daughters "feminine" behavior; out pour the stories of ambivalence and pain. "Every time I tell her not to let men know how high her salary is, I feel so confused. I don't want her to scare men off, but it doesn't seem right for her to have to hide her accomplishments. I myself have never even had a job—my husband wouldn't let me—and *I* always felt ashamed that I didn't earn any money of my own." What may have seemed to this woman's daughter like her mother wielding undue power over her was really her mother trying desperately to transmit social expectations to her.

Strange though it may seem, mothers often fear their daughters' power, too. As the 41-year-old mother of a teenaged girl told me recently: "I know she notices everything about me, all my faults. No one knows better than Bonnie where my weak points are, and no one can be more ruthless than she about pointing them out." Our culture casts both women and girls in the role of enforcing social rules (as discussed in Chapter 4); this endows both mothers and daughters with the dangerous power to spot deviations and shame the deviator. Mothers and daughters fear each other's power because each generation has knowledge that the other one does not. A daughter can make her mother feel like a fool because of what she does not know—"You haven't heard the latest?!" In her turn, the mother possesses knowledge and wisdom not yet acquired by her daughter, intensifying the daughter's resentment of her mother's power. Knowledge does confer some power on each.

When my daughter Emily was nine years old and my son Jeremy was eleven, I had an experience that showed me how little I noticed my power to make them feel good (although I worried constantly about my power to upset them). I was taking Emily and Jeremy to weekly tennis lessons. Knowing nothing about tennis, I asked their teacher how they were doing; he replied that they were doing well but that Emily's progress was limited by her age and size. "Don't worry," he said, "as she grows she'll be able to do more, and it will be less frustrating for her."

On account of this information, my admiration for Emily grew. As I watched her try gamely to do what I now realized was extremely difficult for her, I felt very proud of what a good sport she was. When the class took a break, I said to her, "Emily, your teacher said that what you are doing is very hard for nine-year-olds. I really admire you, because you keep trying even though it is harder for you than it is for the other kids." I wasn't sure that she had listened to what I said. Many days later, Emily came up to me and asked, "Do you *really* admire me because I try hard at tennis?" and she looked delighted when I confirmed that I did.

That incident impressed upon me the power *to do good* that we have over our children. My remark had stayed with her for a long time. It had really mattered to her. We mothers are often surprised by our power to affect our children in positive ways, partly because our good mothering work is often ignored—until we *forget* to do it.

Like most mothers, I had believed that women's power is dangerous; even after the incident with Emily, I couldn't just relax and enjoy the beneficial effect I had had on her. Recognizing my power scared me to death, since like most mothers I felt that in most of my childrearing I was just scraping by, lucky to avoid messing Emily and Jeremy up completely. So it seemed to me very likely that my power would have some damaging consequences.

A woman is supposed to give nurturance (Myth Two), to live up to the role of giver and protector of life. But anyone who has a lot to give can inspire fear in those she nurtures; if she has the power to make them feel secure, then she can also pull the rug out from under them. If she withholds nurturance, their sense of security may collapse.

As we acknowledge that our mothers' power may be less dangerous *and* more growth-enhancing than we had believed, we can become better allies. Furthermore, changing our assessment of mother's power can improve our feelings about our own power. Twenty-five-year-old Lillian told me after a workshop on mothers and daughters,

> Now that I've had a chance to focus on some of the specific times that my mother ingeniously used her power to protect us from our abusive father, I seem to feel better about my own use of power. It doesn't scare me so much to think of myself as a powerful woman.

Fearing women's power over us more than men's is unwarranted, especially because the frequency of violent acts men commit against women, combined with men's greater political and economic power, certainly justify some fear of *their* power. We assume our mothers' power is evil, but we're less likely to assume that about our fathers' power—unless, perhaps, he is physically or sexually abusive (although, as noted earlier, even daughters of those fathers often manage to forgive their fathers and accuse their mothers instead).

The more self-confidence we have, and the more we feel loved and supported by other people, the less we fear anyone's power and the stronger we can be in urging them to use their power for good. Therefore, as we improve our relationships with our mothers, our fear of their power and of anyone else's is likely to diminish.

ASKING QUESTIONS ABOUT
THE BAD MOTHER MYTHS

As you think through what has happened in your mother-daughter relationship, and as you try to understand what is happening now, ask yourself these important questions:

- How *can* we lower the barriers between us as long as we believe that men are better than women, that only the experts really know how to raise children, that mothers and daughters are bottomless pits of emotional need, that mother-daughter closeness is unhealthy, and that mother's and daughter's power is dangerous?
- Can we stop automatically making negative assumptions about women? This form of prejudice is as bad as any other.

Thinking carefully about the myths enables us to reinterpret our mother's (or daughter's) behavior in a better and more realistic light than before. For instance, when we think our mothers can't let us go, are trying to merge with us or keep us dependent on them (Myth Eight), we are tempted to blame them. If we realize instead that what they have attempted was to *maintain a close relationship* with us, then we realize our potential to be allies, understanding that we have been shaped to label our interactions negatively and to demean both ourselves and each other. As allies rather than adversaries, we can better deal with aspects of the relationship that are frustrating or inhibiting, using the fine skills of communication and empathy which so many women have developed.

In some ways, the Bad Mother myths make it even harder than the Perfect Mother myths to see our mothers' humanity. But once we get some inkling of the pervasiveness and the power of the Bad Mother myths, we can begin to see how ludicrous they are. Turning back to the start of this chapter and reading these five myths aloud, all in a rush, is a good beginning; just doing that may show you clearly that very few human beings are so horrendous.

Then, think about one myth at a time, while assuming that most mothers are merely human. In regard to the male superiority myth, it can't really be true that most mothers are vastly inferior to fathers. In regard to the myth that only the experts know how to raise children, hasn't your mother done some good things, perhaps even *against* the advice of the experts? In regard to the myth that mothers and daughters are bottomless pits of emotional need, can't we recall times that we have unjustly equated our mothers' and our own normal, human needs with boundless neediness?

When we think about times we have felt close to our mothers, hasn't *some* of that enhanced our growth rather than tying us tighter to their apron strings? And aren't there occasions when the constructive, loving aspects of mother's (or daughter's) power were clearer to us than the destructive ones?

I am not suggesting that we replace a pessimistic but realistic approach to mother-daughter relationships with a blindly optimistic one. I am suggesting that we look at what *works* to break down mother-daughter barriers so that both mothers and daughters feel better about themselves. The woman-blaming, woman-hating messages are tantalizing. They tempt women with the promise that if we will dissociate ourselves from our mothers, we will be regarded as different from, and better than, they. By now we are depressingly familiar with this approach that divides women against each other. It is dangerous. It promotes both mother-blame and self-hate, in dramatic contrast to the empowering consequences of thinking about women in positive ways.

We cannot always distinguish fully between when mother or daughter really has done something bad or wrong and when the myth alone has made us think so. The key is always to *ask* ourselves whether one or more myths might be distorting our view, for that enterprise of asking will at least bring us closer to the truth. Because having poor opinions of each other is so destructive to the mother-daughter relationship and to both mother's and daughter's self-esteem, we should usually err on the side of giving each other the benefit of the doubt.

The Either-Or Tightrope

The co-existence of the myth that mothers are endlessly giving (Myth Two) *and* the myth that mothers are endlessly needy and demanding (Myth Seven) dramatically illustrates the narrow band of acceptable behavior for mothers; together, these myths make us misconstrue even modest needs in our mothers and daughters as unmeetable ones and misconstrue less than total support from them as emotional miserliness or even betrayal. Any giving that mothers fail to do becomes a sign that they are unnatural and unwomanly; conversely, even their normal desires become proof that their needs are unmeetable. Working in concert, the two myths pressure women to give unceasingly and to ask for nothing for themselves.

The narrowness of the band of acceptable behavior for mothers is part of the narrowness of that band for women in general. Females face a dilemma because of two sets of labels provided by society: the seductive-submissive-admiring-compliant kind (what I'll call the Type One labels) and the powerful-dominant-bitchy-cold-castrating kind (the Type Two labels). Who can imagine wanting to be classified either way? Mothers who try to live up to the Perfect Mother myths are likely to be given a Type One label; that is, if they try to be totally self-sacrificing and sweet, they will be considered overly emotional, over-involved, and smothering. Mothers who don't behave in that way will probably be considered Type Two, rejecting mothers. It is hard to find behavior in mothers that is simply appreciated.

Mothers are tempted to behave in accordance with the Type One labels for several reasons. First, this behavior is considered "feminine." Second, in its milder forms it *can be* associated with being warm and loving. Third, Type One behavior is more likely to please the people with whom one lives and works than is Type Two behavior.

The crucial issue is not whether mothers spend more time behaving in Type One or Type Two ways; it is that most women —especially mothers—continually monitor their behavior, afraid they are being either too warm or too cool, too intrusive or too laissez-faire toward their children. Every mother I have interviewed describes what I call the Either-Or tightrope that she walks, between feeling she shows her daughter too much love and feeling she doesn't show her enough. If she *is* loving, is she being "too close" (Myth Eight); if she is rather reserved, is she failing to be nurturant enough (Myth Two)? In spite of women's protests about these pressures, mothers' psychotherapists, families, and friends have not let up very much on the Either-Or pressure.

Never have I met a mother—no matter how much she was

admired by others—who has always felt confident that her mothering was just fine. And my own experience as a mother is the same. "Your child has asthma? I guess you know that asthma is caused by mothers' overprotectiveness," says a colleague who is a psychologist. "You let your twelve-year-old ride the subway *alone?!* Don't you *care* about her?" says a well-meaning friend.

Thirty-year-old Susannah came to me for psychotherapy, certain that she was a terrible mother because she alternated, she said, between "ignoring my kids and smothering them with affection." Like many of my women patients, her biggest problem turned out to be her harsh self-judgment: teaching her children to play on their own occasionally was not rejection, and missing them when they visited her ex-husband did not constitute overprotectiveness.

Daughters tend to grasp quickly how the Either-Or dilemma affects their interactions with their mothers: when anything a mother does can be classified in one of two negative ways, then any way she treats her daughter involves the same risk. Mothers walk a tightrope: if their daughters don't do the traditional, feminine, housekeeping tasks, they have failed to be demanding enough; but when their daughters want to help them with these chores, the mothers regard themselves as *too* demanding and selfish.

Many daughters moan:

> If I *don't* offer to wash the dishes after Thanksgiving dinner at Mom's house, she thinks I'm unfeminine and ungrateful. But when I *do* offer to help, she tells me not to bother, that she doesn't mind doing it, that it's really a one-woman job.

We have been shaped to think about mother-daughter relationships primarily in terms of the myths. Having journeyed through some of the major myths, you now have the beginnings of a new vocabulary, a repertoire of less mother-blaming interpretations of your mother's (or daughter's) behavior. You may not always choose to use your new vocabulary, but you now know that you have a choice.

6 ❦ Feeling Safe: Going Beyond The Myths

NOW THAT YOU have read and thought about the effects that mother-blaming and the myths have had on your relationship with your mother, you may already feel less angry or anguished about her. But you may not yet feel such relief, because intellectual understanding of the myths isn't enough to transform intense, negative feelings that have built up over the decades that you two have spent together. Overcoming the effects of years of conflict, alienation, fear, or guilt can be damned hard, so you may still feel that the best solution is to live three thousand miles away from your mother. Grasping ideas is one thing; putting them into practice is another.

As Karen, a young adult student, told me:

> I've learned so much about how I automatically blame Mom for things, and whenever I *think* about her I feel more compassion and less anger than I used to. But when I actually *see* her, she still gets to me. I still flare up instantaneously when she says certain things or looks at me in a certain way.

If, since starting to read this book, you've tried to behave differently with your mother or even to think about her differently, without success so far, do not despair. This chapter and the next two will help you begin to make your understanding of mother-blaming and the myths work for you.

First, we shall consider the stakes: how your life can be enriched by building bridges between yourself and your mother and what you stand to lose if you do not. Then, you'll learn ways to feel safe and secure in rethinking your mother-daughter relationship and possibly in attempting changes directly with your mother. Next, we'll consider some general steps that everyone can take toward overcoming mother-daughter barriers; these include ensuring that both daughter and mother feel supported and empowered as they start their work together, humanizing the daughter's image of her mother, and forging an alliance with her. And finally, we shall look at choosing and defining particular problems that need work, and deciding how to do that work.

As you read through the remaining chapters, remember that you can carry out most of the steps on your own, with a partner of some kind, within a group, or directly with your mother if she is living. You may need to modify some of the steps to fit your situation and to suit your style or needs. So I suggest that you read through this chapter and the next two, noting which steps strike you as most important or easiest to take, then deciding which order of steps seems best for you. Remember, too, that many techniques help you toward more than one goal—for instance, interviewing your mother may help support and empower either or both of you, it may humanize your image of her, and it may help you to forge a working alliance.

No one can say it will be easy; but if you conscientiously follow some of the steps I suggest, which other women have found helpful, the chances are good that you'll soon start to make some headway.

My son Jeremy created this proverb: "On a staircase there is only one real step. The rest are there only to help you along the way." The one big step you're wanting to take is to improve your relationship with your mother, but you can't expect yourself to take it in a single bound.

Similarly, if you talk directly to your mother about the problems between you, neither of you should expect always to know just how to respond immediately, on the spot. Remember the value of silence and time: allow both her and yourself periods of silence during which to consider what you have heard, how you feel, and what you want to do about it. Many unnecessary troubles come from feeling we have to rush to respond to criticism or a request from another person. Both daughters and mothers need to ask for time to be silent, time to wait, time to think and feel things through before responding. Asking for silence or time is a way to show respect for each other, a way of saying, "Making our relationship better matters enough to me that I want to accord it time and energy." Since we live in a culture that values quick comebacks and snappy patter, we don't often think to ask for time, but learning to do so can be invaluable in working out problems in relationships.

For some daughters, reading and thinking may feel like enough preparation for talking to their mothers directly. But many daughters need to talk first to other women, partly to rehearse what they want to ask or tell their mothers, partly to learn that their feelings are not unique or weird, and partly to brainstorm. The brainstorming can include hearing how other women feel about their mothers, how those feelings have changed and what changed them, and how other women feel about *being* mothers.

Fundamentally, most of us want to be less angry, want to feel closer and more relaxed in our relationships with our mothers. Life is easier when any relationship is like that. But we lose sight of that goal because we easily get caught up in laying blame or withdrawing altogether.

Most daughters will tell you, when they're frustrated: "You don't know MY mother. She's unbelievably manipulative, overbearing, dependent, cold, critical, etc." Most daughters will also tell you they've tried for decades to have Big Talks with her, to no avail. If you ask daughters to describe these Big Talks, usually they'll say they told Mother to "stop hanging on to me," "stop telling me how to run my life," "stop being so critical of me," and so on. Rarely does a daughter (or a mother) come right out and say, "I want to mend fences, to bridge the chasm between us. I want us to be closer. . . . under certain conditions, yes, but closer and more relaxed is my main wish." *Saying* that, acknowledging that, is absolutely crucial, because it puts you and your mother on the same team.

Why is knowing you're on the same side so important? Because we become defensive or paranoid if we believe that the other person wants to hurt us or to protect *herself* no matter what the cost to us. Once a daughter is committed to improving her relationship with her mother, her mother is likely to sense that commitment even before the daughter talks about it. If mother and daughter both want to improve their relationship, their shared vision of a better future can take them a long way. The way to a better relationship isn't always smooth and permanent. There will be struggles and intermittent backsliding. Hanging on to the knowledge of your commitment and your goal will help you through those rough times and will keep you from giving up and losing the progress you have made.

No matter how much insight you've gained, no matter how energized you feel for improving your mother-daughter relationship, some part of you probably still feels scared. And for some of you, fear, apprehension, and the wish to ignore the whole arena are still paramount.

CONSIDERING THE STAKES

If part of you wants to avoid thinking about or working on your relationship with your mother, consider these important points:

- You have a lot to lose if you give up.
- You have a lot to gain if you don't give up.

If you give up, you will lose whatever fragments—large or small—of better times that you and your mother might have had. You may also lose the opportunity to understand and accept whatever good parts of you that are like your mother. *Lie down in a quiet room, and imagine the consequences of giving up. Try to picture them as vividly as you can.* Imagine the next holiday or the next family gathering—notice the knot that forms in your stomach as you recall the anger, sadness, or alienation that you feel in her presence. Remember the exasperation you have felt when you thought you could do nothing to lessen these feelings. Ask yourself whether you want to feel so bad and so powerless again.

You may want to consider the ultimate question: how you will feel when your mother dies. At that time, most daughters who have given up feel terribly guilty, and many feel frustrated and angry that they have no further opportunity to make the relationship better. This lost chance is especially poignant, because after a person dies, our warmest, most positive memories of them are the ones that tend to flood back. A woman in her mid-sixties described this process:

My mother died after a three-year illness that gradually wore her down and changed her whole personality. She went from her warm, energetic self to being sharp, irritable, and passive. During those three years I was absorbed in adjusting to the changes in her. But after she died, wonderful memories of the mother I knew for more than 55 years came back to me.

The most important message I have heard from women whose mothers have died is that the *attempt* to resolve remaining problems is essential. As Kenna said:

When my mother told me she had only six months to live, we used the time well. Our relationship had always been stormy, and we never did see eye-to-eye on many moral and political issues. But during the last months of her life, our love and respect for each other remained clear and strong, even though we could not overcome all of the problems between us. After she died, what mattered most to me was knowing that we had done our best to resolve our problems. We had really tried.

In attempting to repair your relationship with your mother—or to revise your vision of it—you'll be better able to retain its warm, funny, or loving aspects, and you'll feel better about yourself.

Imminent death isn't always enough to enable mothers and daughters to break down all of the barriers between them. Some cold or rigid mothers become even more so as death approaches, but a daughter who has tried her best to break down the barriers is likely to be left with enriched memories of mother and in so doing to increase her understanding of herself.

On a less dramatic scale, about fifteen years ago my mother and I were uncharacteristically reticent with each other, leading to unnecessary emotional distance between us. When my first child was born, my parents, who lived a thousand miles away, came to visit a few weeks after the birth. Years later, I told my mother that I had been hurt because she hadn't offered to come immediately when Jeremy was born. She explained that she had feared that, if she offered to come right away, I would think she was intrusive and overprotective or that she lacked confidence in my mothering ability, so she had decided to wait until I asked her. I hadn't asked her to come right away, both because I was afraid of seeming too needy and because I thought that mothering came naturally, so I shouldn't need anyone at all.

If myths about women's neediness, women's power, and the

naturalness of mothering hadn't gotten in our way, and if we hadn't kept silent about that incident for so many years, we would have understood each other a lot better. Telling each other at the time about our concerns would have enabled us to base our decisions on *real* considerations rather than on fears about how our behavior might be misinterpreted or what it might "prove" about us.

If you don't give up on your mother-daughter relationship, you can gain the increased warmth and satisfaction that come from trying to improve relationships, and the enhanced self-esteem that comes from finding qualities in our mothers that we can respect and love. Since we so often think of ourselves as being like our mothers, finding more to respect in them increases our *self*-respect. And remember, too, that when we improve our relationships with our mothers, we feel like competent people who can have some effect on the world; if we can make real changes, no matter how tentative or small, in that relationship, then we feel better able to take on other challenges. We improve the way we get along with other women, including *our* daughters. If you're reluctant to work on your relationship with your mother, ask yourself what picture of mother-daughter relationships you are presenting to your daughter. And think about whether, if she were upset with you, you would want her to give up.

Lying down in a quiet room, imagine the positive results that might come from trying again. For example, call to mind in vivid detail the warmest, loveliest time you ever had with your mother —where you were, the sights, the sounds, the smells. If you were happy once, then perhaps you can be again. Molly, aged twenty, tried this exercise at a time when she and her mother had been "at each other's throats about my brother marrying outside our faith":

> Mother thought what my brother was doing was terrible; I didn't think it was so bad. For months, that issue overshadowed our whole relationship. Whenever Mother came to mind, all I felt was frustration and anger because, on account of her attitude, the family was being torn apart. When I lay down and pictured our nicest time together, I remembered our planning a family reunion when I was twelve years old. We shopped for decorations together, did the cooking, and made a collage of family photographs. Through it all, I felt so warm and happy and close to her. We shared so much. That memory reminded me that Mother was much more than "the-woman-who-is-causing-anguish-in-the-family."

Some daughters have fewer good memories to draw on. If you are one of them, recalling or finding out things about your mother other than her worst aspects can still be helpful. A student I'll call Nora described her difficult journey toward improved self-respect through understanding of her mother. She wrote in a paper, "I had been seeing my mother as 'crazy' and this was frightening to me. Would I be crazy, too?" Nora also blamed herself for the physical abuse she had suffered at her mother's hands, as well as the sexual abuse inflicted on her by a neighbor boy when she was four years old. Nora's efforts to learn more about her mother's life and about what had led her to mistreat Nora paid off.

By carefully exploring her own memories and listening to the stories of other abusive mothers, she learned that her mother was overwhelmed by having a large number of children, by the frustration of her own educational ambitions (she was forced to leave school after grade six), by her misery in an arranged marriage to a husband who beat her, and by her horror, confusion, and sense of powerlessness when she discovered that Nora had been sexually abused.

Nora's understanding didn't lead her to justify what her mother had done, but it did clarify her view of her mother as a woman who, under enormous pressures, coped in a way that inadvertently hurt Nora. More importantly, Nora realized that neither the sexual nor the physical abuse had been her own fault, nor had she deserved either one.

When someone who has endured the extremes that Nora suffered can feel better about herself by thoroughly exploring her mother's experience, there is certainly hope for those of us who have suffered less grievously at our mothers' hands.

Remembering good times with mother or learning more about her should help you to keep clearly in mind what you have to gain—or regain—as you prepare to work on your mother-daughter relationship. It's the reachable carrot at the end of the stick.

FEELING SAFE

Once you have considered what you have to gain from revising your view of your mother or from approaching her again, and what you have to lose by not trying, you have to figure out what will make your approach feel as safe as possible. After all, no matter how strong or optimistic we feel about the task ahead of us, we women too often try to ignore our apprehensiveness, especially about our mothers. The denial doesn't destroy our doubts and fears, however, and they are easier to overcome once we have faced them.

You can increase your feeling of safety in three good ways:

(1) *Humanize your image of your mother*. Reduce her from Perfect Angel or Wicked Witch, or both, to simply human. Dealing with a real person is always less scary than dealing with a larger-than-life character. Many techniques can help you humanize your mother: they may not all work for you; you will feel more comfortable doing some than others; and you may not need to do them all. Read through the section in Chapter 7 on "Humanizing Your Image of Mother," and choose what you think will be most comfortable and effective for you.

(2) *If you're balking at the prospect of trying again, try to figure out why that might be*. Are you so angry that you're afraid you'll lose control and do something completely horrible if you try to talk to your mother? If so, reread the section on anger in Chapter 2, and try to figure out what feeling underlies your anger. You will probably be more comfortable talking to her about that underlying feeling than about your anger—and you'll likely be more productive, too. You may need to express your anger first in a safe place with a nonjudgmental, non-mother-blaming person, so that your first attempt to reach your mother is not overshadowed by your overwhelming anger.

Perhaps you're blocked by the fear of further disappointment. You've approached her so many times, and nothing has worked. If so, reread several times the beginning of this chapter. Ask yourself whether you have honestly tried putting your mother and yourself on the same team before bringing up the problems that come between you. (This issue is treated in more detail in the next section of this chapter.)

You may feel too intimidated by your mother to approach her again. If so, try the technique used with great success by psychologist Dr. Albert Ellis. He suggests asking yourself, "What's the worst thing that could possibly happen?'' followed by the comment to yourself, "If that *does* happen, it might be painful, it might be humiliating, it might be depressing—*BUT*—IT'S NOT THE END OF THE WORLD!'' Our relationships with our mothers matter so much to us that we don't often stop to realize that, even if we approach them again and fail utterly, we probably shall survive.

Once you've identified your worst fears, you can take steps to minimize their bad effects. Are you afraid you'll be devastated if you make new efforts to get along with your mother and they don't succeed? Are you afraid she'll reject you or simply not love you any more than she seems to now? Do you fear that you'll burst into tears or explode with anger in front of her or that she'll make you feel guilty or ashamed of yourself? Most daughters have these common fears. What can you do?

You can try to work through them, to understand them fully; you may find that rereading Chapter 2 and reading Chapter 8 about specific feelings will assist you. Then you can face fully, ahead of time, how you will feel if nothing good happens when you talk to your mother or try to deal with her differently. This reduces the element of surprise that makes us feel so vulnerable. You can remind yourself that you're no longer a child, so you don't need her approval or her love as desperately as you used to. You may *want* them, but you don't *need* them as much. If she rejects you, now that you're an adult, you don't have to go to your room and sulk, feeling totally unloved; you can call a close friend, reread old love letters, go to a movie, do any of a million things that adults can do to remind ourselves of our basic lovableness and acceptability.

Is your greatest fear that you'll cry when you try to talk to your mother? If so, remind yourself—repeatedly, if necessary—that you may feel foolish or vulnerable, but: IT'S NOT THE END OF THE WORLD. Are you afraid she'll make you feel even more guilty and ashamed? Ask yourself if you *can* feel much guiltier than you already do. Are you afraid you'll have another fight with her? Ask yourself, "What's one more fight?'' At worst, it will be another fight, and at best, with your new approach, it might bring some improvement. Remember, you'll be going to her better prepared than before both to understand the sources of your own feelings and to understand and interpret what she does in less combative, degrading, or self-demeaning ways.

Maybe you're blocked because your mother has been so impossible to deal with for so long that you simply cannot imagine her ever changing. Dealing with her may seem impossible because she seems flawless, or horrid, or some of each; she seems superhumanly perfect or inhumanly evil. Your next step, then, should be to search for ways to see her as simply human, to find out in what ways mother is really a person. (See Chapter 7 section on "Humanizing Your Image of Your Mother.")

And if, after all your efforts, your relationship has not changed? At least you will not go through life tormenting yourself with the thought that you *might* have made a breakthrough if you had talked with her while applying your new thinking about mother-blaming and the myths.

(3) *Decide to take small steps.* Don't aim to eliminate totally the tension between you and your mother. *Visualize yourself taking one tiny, slow step at a time toward her.* Make a list of the tiniest possible steps you can think of—sending her a birthday card signed with your name but no added message; asking her a question about something in her life that has nothing to do with you or your relationship to her; smiling at her, once; stopping for just a second to think before you reject her next invitation to dinner (even if you go ahead and reject it). In choosing which small, first step to take, consider what would be easy for you but mean a lot to her. If birthdays are very important to her, try starting with a card on her birthday. If she seems terribly hesitant each time she greets you in person, try an immediate, unsolicited smile. And don't expect your small steps to have even small effects right away. Your mother may need time to understand that your changed behavior is just what it seems—a reaching out to her, not a cover-up or a meaningless gesture.

Small steps at this stage increase your own comfort about dealing differently with your mother. No law says you have to make major changes all at once, and the more hopeless you feel now about the chances for change, the more important it is for you to experience small successes. No one—certainly not we or our mothers—can make major changes all of a sudden, and if you feel you have to take a huge leap right away, you're almost certain to fall on your face. Neither you nor she will be prepared.

Each of these ways to feel safe takes time and careful effort on your part. Humanizing your image of your mother can begin suddenly and dramatically the moment you decide to *try* to see her as human rather than as perfect or impossibly bad, but the humanizing process is continuous. Ideally, it never ends, because we will always be pressured to apply the Perfect Mother myths and the Bad Mother myths to our mothers. The humanizing effort is a constantly needed antidote.

In a similar way, confronting and trying to resolve interpersonal problems is rarely easy, and, in virtually everyone, doing so produces fear and apprehension. Trying to resolve a problem *before* we have identified what makes it hard for us to try is like attempting the high jump wearing work boots. As we deal with each mother-daughter problem, then, we shall need to stop and identify what is blocking us. This pause is not a luxury; it is an absolute necessity.

Understanding mother-blaming and the myths certainly gives us a framework that makes it easier to spot the real causes of mother-daughter problems. *Because* they are *interpersonal* problems and are often decades old, however, many of them will require a great deal of dismantling work. For that reason, we must realize that the steps we take will often necessarily be small. But even when they are tiny, at least they are forward, not backward. As in football, every step toward one's own goal is far more heartening than a rush in the wrong direction.

A RELATIONSHIP BUILT FOR TWO

Obvious though it may seem, we often forget that relationships involve two people. Sometimes we spend so much time focusing on ourselves—our shortcomings, problems, and needs—that we overlook the ways our lives are affected and enhanced by others. Developing ideas, resolving problems, and enjoying life can be done, to some extent, on our own. But such efforts are very limiting when they take place completely *in the absence* of specific work to improve our connections to important people in our lives.

Often the message we hear from a therapist or anyone else is,

"If your mother won't respect your need for privacy, you'll have to stay away from her!" rather than "I know your mother is driving you crazy; here are some suggestions for guarding your privacy without abruptly and totally shutting her out." Then we become self-righteous and impulsive, rushing about demanding that others meet our needs. Many people in therapy hear reasonable suggestions to "Identify what you really want in order to feel good" and misinterpret them as "I have the right to demand what I want, and I should always get it!"

Trying to resolve issues with your mother is pointless if you think about only your own needs or anger. If you fit that picture, try some of the humanizing and alliance-building exercises that are outlined in Chapter 7. After all, if *you* describe your relationship with your mother as explosive or distant, she probably feels the same way and is no more eager than you for another explosion or another empty encounter. And why *should* she make an effort to have a serious talk with you, if she thinks she has nothing to gain from it?

For example, you may note *to yourself* that your mother's overachieving style has undermined your self-confidence. But you can't realistically expect your relationship with her to improve if you begin with that kind of one-sided announcement. Why? Because most people don't respond well to anger, criticism, or accusations, especially in close relationships. Making your life or your relationship with her better is not all up to *her*, nor is it solely up to you to figure out the problems in your relationship. However, if your fundamental longing is not just for freedom from problems but rather for a better *relationship* with her, you simply have to offer her more than the information that she's driven you mad.

Remember, chances are she's spent years worrying about whether or not she was a good mother, whether she truly harmed you, whether you *think* she did terrible things to you, whether you —more keenly than anyone else—saw her failings as a mother. If you now add your accusations to her self-doubts and self-recriminations, you know what she'll do. You didn't need to read a book to find that out. Like any sane human being, she'll respond with some combination of anger, denial, self-blame, guilt, and depression. Those feelings do not increase her ability or inclination to work on thorny relationships.

Even if part of you feels that she deserves to suffer, remember that you *want* to make progress in your relationship with her, and accusing or criticizing her gives her nothing to work on, nothing to do but feel horrible, powerless—and powerlessness paralyzes. She'll feel paralyzed by the apparent impossibility of making up for the damage she's done to you. The worst crime you can accuse most mothers of is that they made their children unhappy. To most mothers' way of thinking, nothing they can do could atone for that.

Just as *you* have begun to take *small* steps toward change, *she* too needs to feel she can take small steps that might make a difference. She needs to feel supported and empowered in order to face your shared barriers. We all need to feel supported and empowered in order to do that kind of work. Two of the most important sources of empowerment will be: (1) her belief that the two of you can truly form an alliance about at least some issues and (2) her hope for a better relationship with you in the future.

SUPPORT AND EMPOWERMENT

What are some steps we can take to feel supported and empowered enough to approach our mothers about specific problems? A combination of *further education and rehearsal* can be extremely helpful.

Further Self-education

Before you talk to your mother, you may want to *explore your feelings and expectations carefully by talking with a partner, a friend, a sister, other relatives, a group of women, or a good feminist counselor.* You will learn more about yourself, both by hearing *their* perspectives on your specific unresolved issues and by hearing the kinds of concerns they have about *their* mothers or daughters. You may join an ongoing group or consider forming one yourself. You may form one by word of mouth among friends or co-workers or by advertising in church, synagogue, or community group newsletters or in women's newspapers and magazines.

Whether you work with one other person or with a group, very informal, unstructured discussion opportunities can be productive. However, you may want more structure, more sense of direction. If that's the case, you might each read this book or other books and articles about mothers and daughters (see the Bibliography at the end of this book for some suggestions) and use the chapter topics and the steps in this chapter and the following ones as starting points for discussion.

For example, using Chapters 4 and 5, *discuss ways that the mother-myths affect your own lives, the way you think about your mother and, if applicable, about yourself as a mother.* Hannah realized that the time her father had bought her a figurine of an angel when she was seven years old and sick in bed had stayed with her as a vivid memory of his warmth toward her; she had difficulty thinking of any single illustration of her mother's warmth that seemed as dramatic to her. She commented, "I guess that the difference is partly because my mother was *usually* warm and loving, and Dad was more reserved. But I think I also expected her always to be nurturing and loving, and I didn't expect so much from him." Thinking about her perceptions of her parents in relation to the endless nurturance myth changed Hannah's view of her mother by drawing her attention to the warmth her mother had shown her but that Hannah had hardly noticed.

As a next step in self-education, try to *describe your mother.* Focus on the problems that plague your mother-daughter relationship the most. You may wish to use the technique I used in my course: write down the first three words or phrases that come to mind when you hear the word "mother." Then, write a lengthier description of your mother. And finally, complete the sentence, "In regard to my mother, I wish. . . ." If you are working on this with another person or in a group, each of you can do these things, and then you can circulate the descriptions (you can do this anonymously in a group if you wish), so that you can see commonalities and differences in your relationships with your mothers. After each of you has read the descriptions, you can discuss the material as a way to help see mothers as human beings.

Chapter 7 has an entire section on "Humanizing Your Image of Your Mother," much of which involves self-education or work directly with your mother. Two such helpful exercises are mentioned here, because they are particularly useful when you are working with someone other than your mother, whether with one person or a whole group. First, each of you should *reinterpret the negative descriptions of mothers as strengths or, at the very least, as faults that are not aimed at hurting the daughter.* Second, *watch for instances in which the daughter's descriptions of her mother's positive features might have grown out of the daughter's feeling that she has to be her mother's protector or press agent for her Perfect Mother.* Of course, all mothers have some faults, not just good features that have been mistakenly labeled, and what a daughter describes as her mother's good points may be truly good. But these exercises help us see mothers in some reasonable perspective, without the preconceptions imposed by our culture.

The group can establish some ground rules for itself. One rule should be to *prohibit mother-blaming and use of the myths to "explain" why they are upset with their mothers.* We are then forced to search for new ways to think about our mothers' behavior and motives and about the ways we interact with them. For example, if a woman says that her mother upset her because she is so demanding, the group members mustn't let the daughter get away with that. "Danger! Bottomless Pit myth!" they should warn. Then the daughter has to identify a specific, concrete instance of her mother's behavior. Group members or the partner should join with the daughter to consider whether that instance is proof of the mother's unmeetable, unreasonable needs or whether it can be understood some other way. In some instances, the partner or group may agree that a mother is wrong to refuse to see a therapist or talk to her friends about your father's extramarital affair, for example, and to insist on talking *only* to her daughter. Few daughters would want such total responsibility for meeting their mother's needs. The partner or group in this case can help the daughter go beyond simple mother-blame. Instead of saying, "Yes, your mother really is impossible!" they can encourage observations such as, "Perhaps your mother believes that a good woman never says bad things about her husband outside the immediate family, no matter what he does to her. So maybe you can let her know that it's perfectly fine to tell others, that at least *you* won't think she's wrong if she does that."

Sharing Perspectives and Solutions

A second useful rule for self-education sessions is to take some time near the end of each meeting to *discuss specific steps that each of you has found productive in dealing with her mother.* How did Mary tell her mother that she wanted to talk about her mother's criticism of Mary's lover? Exactly what words did Jane use to ask her mother if she *really* loved Jane's sister best? Encourage the group members to brainstorm, each woman suggesting words she might use. When we can't imagine how we could actually raise a sensitive subject, this kind of exercise unblocks our creative juices.

We are each other's best sources of ideas for techniques and for highly specific "how-to" ideas. In my courses and workshops, women who describe to the group what they consider an intractable problem find that other women can suggest ideas they hadn't thought of. Overwhelmed and frightened by the desire to scream, "Why can't you let me run my own life?" at mother, we can't imagine how else we could get the message across—and so we say nothing at all. But many's the time I've watched one woman listen to another's description of the way she handled a problem and exclaim, "That's it! That's how I could say it. I really never thought of putting it that way."

We must remind each other not to be too grandiose: We're not looking for grand success stories about sudden resolutions of problems that have existed since childhood. We can educate— and, therefore, support and empower—each other best with statements like:

> I realized that my mother doesn't have all twelve of us for Thanksgiving dinner because she loves to suffer and have back pains from all the work. I now see that she's afraid she'll be criticized as a bad mother if she *doesn't* invite us, *and* she does love to have us all with her, because she enjoys her family. Once I understood that, I caught myself last Thanksgiving having a knee-jerk, guilt-and-rage reaction when I saw her tired expression. I couldn't bring myself to be very supportive or warm toward her, but I did feel I understood the real Mom a little better, and I felt good about that.

Rehearsal and Role-play

Work in a group or with a partner is also ideal for *rehearsal and role-play*. Have each woman in the group choose someone to play the role of her mother and describe what she regards as her mother's worst characteristics to the "mother." Then, let them rehearse the daughter's approach to her mother. The other members should take careful notes so that they can give the daughter feedback about both the constructive and the risky or destructive things she does.

A method of rehearsal which maximizes your chances of doing *constructive* work and which minimizes *destructive* interactions is an approach called "expressive training." The principles and step-by-step directions for expressive training are outlined in Appendix A. I hope you will read them carefully before you try them out, but I shall illustrate them here. As I pointed out in the section on "A Relationship Built for Two," if we approach our mothers— or anyone else—with threats, demands, or criticisms, we are probably doomed to failure. When we are hurt or angry, though, we are inclined to do just that. So we need to find a way to say how we feel that enables mother to listen to us *and* shows her what she can do to make things better between us.

According to expressive training principles, if I say, "Mom, you're always interfering in my life," that's a criticism and she will probably either tune out or counterattack, "That's because you have such lousy judgment! Look at that creep you married!" But if I keep my remarks to a simple statement of *how I feel*, rather than *what she does*, I make a good start: "Mom, I feel hurt when you tell me that I have to get rid of my husband. I feel hurt because I'm having a rough time with him and would appreciate your support, and when you give me such strong advice, I feel like you don't think I have very good judgment." In those sentences, you have not only described your feeling but also told her what specific step she took that led to your feeling; you have done it without attacking her, just by saying she gave you strong advice. If she's halfway open to hearing you, you may be pleasantly surprised by how well she responds when she doesn't have to defend herself against criticism or attacks. When you attack her, she has difficulty paying attention to your needs since she has to protect herself from you. In the absence of an attack, she may say, "Well, let me know when you *do* want some advice," or she may pick up on your comment that what you really would appreciate is a little support.

If you state your feeling and its cause clearly, but your mother doesn't respond well and instead goes off on an angry tangent, hauling out old grievances or intellectualizing like crazy, come back to your simple statement of feeling and cause. Repeat it once, and then say, "I just wanted you to know how I feel and why. I don't expect you to react right now to what I have said. But I would appreciate it if you could think about it a little, and maybe we can talk about it later on." This technique is so simple, but in our talk-mad society it's rarely used. Your mother may be relieved to hear you make a short statement *without* expecting an immediate reply or instantaneous action. One way we can show genuine respect for each other is to ask for and offer each other time to digest each other's heartfelt words.

Some mothers won't respond very well, even when you choose your words carefully. They may reply, "I treat you like you don't have good judgment, because you *don't!*" I won't pretend that all mothers act like a dream when you find the magic words. But at the very least, when you have to interact with your mother you'll like yourself *better* if you state your feeling and the cause of your feeling simply, with dignity, and without making threats, demands, or criticisms. That is a valuable lesson. It keeps us from confusing our own shortcomings with hers. It allows us to separate *our* tendency to act provocatively or hurtfully from *hers*. When *we* act in positive ways, we see that our mother-daughter relationship may not be a mess because both mother and daughter are seriously flawed. But keep in mind that seeing her flaws by now need not lead us back into mother-blaming; ideally, it will lead us to further exploration of what made her the way she is, mythical baggage and all. But even when we can't reach that ideal, freeing ourselves from the ritual of attack and counterattack, in which we easily can become involved, is useful and empowering.

The techniques of expressive training are useful in rehearsal with someone *other than* your mother, but they are also invaluable for the times when you talk directly to her. (And, no doubt, you'll find them useful in your other relationships as well.)

Consider letting your mother know that you want to be able to talk to her about the barriers between you, and suggest that she might want to form a mothers' group and do similar kinds of work to what your daughters' group is doing. You might have the two groups meet together after they have met separately for several months. Use your creativity to arrange interesting exercises for the combined group. For instance, give the members of each mother-daughter pair the chance to learn about each other's views of their problems. Make sure that each member of a mother-daughter pair in the separate groups has role-played her version of one of their problems. Then, in the combined group, have the women who pretended to be the mother and daughter role-play the scene together as the actual mother and daughter observe. And finally, encourage the real mother and daughter to play the scene and get feedback from the rest of the group.

Now you have a framework for thinking about many of the specific problems between you and your mother; you now understand mother-blaming and the myths. By considering what is at stake, how to feel safe, and how both you and your mother can feel supported and empowered, you have prepared yourself to put that framework to use.

7 ❧ Mending the Relationship

YOU MAY BE planning to talk directly with your mother about the barriers between you and may already know how you plan to approach her. Or you don't yet—and may never—want to have such discussions with her; perhaps you wish you could, but *she* has refused to do so or is no longer living. You may fall somewhere between these two extremes. However you are feeling right now, in preparing to work on particular mother-daughter problems, you should read carefully through this chapter and make sure to take the three essential steps that will be described here. You must:

1. *Humanize your image of your mother,* because whether you discuss your problems with her or whether you just try to think in new ways about them, you need to see the real woman behind the mother-myths;
2. *Forge an alliance with your mother,* either in fact or in your own mind; and
3. *Choose and define a problem* on which to begin.

HUMANIZING YOUR IMAGE OF YOUR MOTHER

. . . the more you love your children, the more shocked they are to discover that you possess a single strand of ambivalent—or negative—feeling. Insatiable for this love we expect to be absolute, we cannot forgive its mere humanness.

—Marilyn French, *Her Mother's Daughter*

Could a greater miracle take place than for us to look through each
other's eyes for an instant?

—Henry David Thoreau, *Walden*

Humanizing your image of your mother includes becoming
aware of the full spectrum of her characteristics and behavior.
Some daughters think of their mothers mainly in idealized terms,
others mainly in blaming or demeaning ones, and still others in
some of each. We tend to be less frightened of, and less angry at,
ordinary people than we are toward those we regard as larger-
than-life—whether in good ways or bad ways.

This section includes a variety of techniques for modifying
your image of your mother in order to eliminate her mythical
proportions. After you've read through them, try the ones that feel
most comfortable for you. You may also think of others. Most
daughters begin with the general techniques for "Demythologiz-
ing Mother." If you think of your mother primarily in idealized
images, you will probably want to focus on the techniques for
"Considering Your Mother's Struggles" (the real-life problems
that have confronted her). If you think about your mother primarily in blaming or demeaning ways, the most important techniques
for you will probably be those for "Considering Your Mother's
Worst Aspects"; as you attempt to understand their nature, you
may find them less uniformly and thoroughly horrible than you
thought. To end the humanizing work on an optimistic, growing
note, all daughters should work on "Finding Qualities to Respect
in Mother."

Demythologizing Mother

In scaling mother down, or up, to human proportions, we have
to tear away the mythical material that cloaks what she is really
like. You might begin by looking directly at the way you (probably unintentionally) use the myths to categorize and label her
behavior; in doing this, you may want to use the helpful psychological technique of exaggeration for the purpose of clarification.
*Make a list of as many things your mother does as possible, and then
classify each bit of her behavior as either Angelic or Witchlike*—
referring back to Chapters 4 and 5 as needed. You'll probably find
that some of her behavior doesn't really belong in either category;

trying to *force* everything she does into one category or the other will help you to see many of her simply human aspects.

One woman complained at the start of a mother-daughter workshop that she couldn't stand to visit her mother's apartment, "because she always insists that I eat a huge meal." I pointed out that she had omitted that complaint on her "Angel or Witch" list. She replied, "I started to write it down, but then I thought that, really, it's neither Angel- nor Witchlike behavior, really, is it?" I told her that, had I only heard her tone of voice and seen the look of complete exasperation on her face when she described her mother's pleas for her to eat, I would have been sure that her mother had tormented her about food. For that reason, I pressed her to include the conflict over food in the "Witch" column of her list. During the period for discussion of their lists, the other women in her small group heard her say:

> I realized, as a result of having to put *all* aspects of my mother's behavior on that list, that some of what she does really isn't terrible enough to justify my reaction. So if she wants so badly to feed me, and I can't simply say, "No, thank you," instead of deeply resenting *her* for pushing the food at me, I guess I also need to look at why I feel so guilty and angry about the whole issue.

As long as mother is assumed to be more *or* less than human, we can't expect ourselves to be only human or assume we *can* be just that. If mother *could* be perfect, or we really believe she *ought* to be, then we'll ask nothing less of ourselves. And if we think her destructiveness is of superhuman proportions, our deepest fear is that so is ours. The Angel-Witch polarities keep us from asking our mothers all kinds of questions we would easily ask of anyone at a party.

You probably already know more about your mother than you think you do, and you can use this knowledge in humanizing your image of her. Based on what you know, *make a systematic search for common ground*. Ask yourself which of the following you share with her: values, fears, political attitudes, types of friends, religious beliefs, favorite foods, sources of joy and of frustration, mannerisms, gestures, physical features, sense of style, etc. You may want to make a list of the ways the two of you are alike. You probably have some unreasonably high expectations and unreasonably low opinions of yourself, but at a gut level you know that in important ways you are "just a person," so finding commonalities between your mother and yourself should help you to humanize your image of her.

Seeing mother as just a person is often lovely and moving. Fearing less intensely that she'll find us inadequate or infuriating, we can enjoy learning about her with interest, as we would about anyone else. *Try to recall what you know about your mother's childhood,* since children seem very human to most of us, and we are less likely either to worship or condemn them than adults. I remember my mother telling me just a few years ago that as a little girl, she had longed to have a puppy because she wanted to cuddle it. I had always known my mother hated cats, and I'd assumed that extended to all animals. When she told me of her childhood wish, all in a rush I had a glimpse of her as a cuddly, wistful little girl—neither a perfect, idealized mother nor one with the power to create all the world's evils.

She told me another story about her childhood, one that showed a quite different side of her. In first grade she shared a locker with a little girl who always got to school before she did. The other girl regularly left her lunch, containing a large dill pickle, in their locker, and when my mother opened the locker, the heavenly smell wafted out. Every morning for months, my mother ate that little girl's dill pickle. For a child who was otherwise very well-behaved, this was an unusually mischievous thing to do! I now had another vivid image of my mother's humanness, involving neither idealization nor blame.

WRITING YOUR MOTHER'S BIOGRAPHY

By far the most valuable humanizing work you can do is to *write or tape your mother's biography.* Thinking about mother as a person begins with understanding that she did not magically appear in her full-blown, adult state, unrelated to her own childhood, the family who raised her, the wider environment in which she grew up, and the history of both her family and her culture. If your mother is living and willing to talk to you, I strongly urge you to interview her in person. Often your very *request* to hear her life story actually humanizes *her*—not just your image of her. This demonstration of their daughters' interest has made many mothers act less angry and distant. They feel less need to protect themselves from what they consider their daughter's superior attitude or disinterest in them; and they are relieved of the need to seem perfect in order to get their daughters' respect.

If, for any reason, you don't interview your mother directly, get her life story from people who have known her well. Or you could interview someone else's mother while having her interview yours, then trade notes. The changed perspective that can result from this exercise may astonish you. As essayist Anna Quindlen recently observed,

> My friends speak about their mothers, about their manipulations and criticisms and pointed remarks, and when I meet these same women I can recognize very little of them in the child's description. They usually seem intelligent, thoughtful, kind. But I am not in a position to judge. To me they are simply people, not some lifelong foil, a yardstick by which to measure myself, to publicly find Mother wanting, to privately find the fault within.

Ask your mother (or the people you are interviewing about her) to tell you everything about her life that she can remember, beginning with the circumstances of her own birth. (If she'd rather start by talking about *her* parents, begin there. Sharing with her an interest in your common ancestors is a good way to begin to find common ground with her; she may then relax when she talks about her own life.)

Before you begin, carefully study Appendix B; it includes the issues psychologist Karen Glasser Howe suggests that her college students cover in writing their mothers' biographies, as well as additional questions I have designed, some of which are focused on the mother-myths. Of course, feel free to modify them as you choose. Howe says that writing their mothers' biographies helps her students understand more about their mothers and feel more compassionate and closer to them.

Ask your mother about her experience with you from the very beginning. Spend substantial time on the period before you were born, because you're not likely to know much about that part of her life. How did she feel the day she got married? How did she feel about changing her last name? What were her expectations of marriage? How was her first year of marriage? What surprised her, disappointed her, thrilled her? Did she feel self-confident about being a wife, a cook, a housekeeper? Did she plan to get pregnant? How did she feel when she found out she was pregnant —what were the reasons she was happy, *and* what did she fear?

What kind of pregnancy did she have? What were you like *in utero*—did you kick or were you quiet? What was your birth like? How did she feel the first time she saw you? (Let her know that if she felt nothing, that just puts her in the company of a lot of other mothers, and it doesn't prove she's unnatural.) What were those days in the hospital like before she took you home? Does she remember the first time she was left alone with you, at home? How scared was she? What did she enjoy about you as a baby, and what drove her crazy about taking care of you? How did she feel about the restrictions that go with being a mother? Did she ever tell anyone how scared she felt, and if so, how did they react? Did she think she was a bad mother or an inadequate one?

When your mother reaches the point at which she became a mother, let her know that you realize that no woman ever found mothering a breeze, and you want to hear what it was like for her. You aren't looking for Truth here but rather for her memories, her point of view.

Ask her where she got advice on mothering. Who gave it to her, and what did they say? How did it work for her? (Or look on your mother's bookshelves for the childrearing advice books that she used when you were little. Read them yourself. You will get an idea of the "shoulds" she tried to put into practice.)

During the interview, pay close attention to her reactions. When she gets a twinkle in her eye, you'll *want* to ask more. But don't be chased away when she gets tense or looks sad or angry. She may be tense or sad because in the past no one wanted to hear about a particular experience, or no one has cared enough to listen. Tension, anger, and sadness are signals that something is waiting to emerge, perhaps to be healed. Sometimes you must make a mental note of what was going on when the negative feeling appeared, wait a little while, and return to it later.

I had read some excellent books about the difficulty of being a mother, and my own mother had always been open to talking about her experiences. But only after I systematically questioned her about her struggles did I glimpse whole, unsuspected vistas of her life—and, therefore, of both her humanness and our relationship.

On the positive side, I was surprised to learn how happy she was when I was a baby. Because I had adored my babies but felt overwhelmed by responsibility and physical exhaustion, I had assumed she had felt the same way. But she explained that during the era in which I was born, doctors instructed new mothers not to climb steps and to get plenty of rest. Today, women are pressured to be superwomen—to give birth, climb off the delivery table, and go cook supper while nursing their newborn. In contrast, my mother says that her need to rest was legitimized by her doctor, so she didn't feel guilty about having her mother and another woman help her out; this freed her to enjoy her baby.

On the negative side, I had never known that my mother had trouble breastfeeding me. When she told the pediatrician that I had colic, he told her that she was at fault, that she was making me nervous. That authoritative explanation made *her* nervous, and her milk dried up, apparently fulfilling the doctor's assessment of her inadequacy. For my mother, this trouble was created by a lethal combination: her individual, personal insecurity, the myth that mothering should come naturally, and the myth that only the experts know best about babies.

Considering Your Mother's Struggles

When we see people from a distance, we seldom see their blemishes. An important way to overcome idealization of your mother is to consider closely her struggles, the real-life trials she has faced. For as long as I can remember, my father has had a sign in his office that reads: "Be kind, because everyone you meet is fighting a hard battle." Yet we are often blind to our mothers' brand of battles. A mother has enormous responsibilities—the duty to evaluate our progress, the duty to point out where we need to change or improve, the socially sanctioned right to penalize us when she thinks we have gone too far astray, and the duty to know when to stop doing these things. So perhaps we shouldn't be surprised that, in focusing on what we expect her to do for us, we often overlook her struggles—or even the fact that she *does* struggle.

Furthermore, many mothers feel pressed to live up to the idealized images of motherhood, so they hide their difficulties from us. Many have also been told that children shouldn't be "burdened" by information about their parents' imperfections or uncertainties. The result is that most of us don't hear much about the realities of our mothers' lives, and that information gap keeps us farther apart. The more we know about another person, the closer we usually feel to them—because we're more likely to discover what we share with them.

An experience I had a few years ago uncovered the battle of a woman who occupied a very powerful position. This story is the most dramatic illustration I have experienced directly of the humanity behind what seemed to be an invulnerable woman. She was my boss, not my mother, but like a mother, she seemed larger-than-life. This woman had been promoted to a job that no woman had held before; she supervised a large number of employees, each doing sensitive, complex, and important work. One day, I heard that she was scheduled to have eye surgery. I wanted to get her a little gift. Since the only thing I knew about her personal life was that she loved music, I got her a musical key chain. That then seemed insufficient, so I hit on the idea of getting a small gift to appeal to each of her senses (except vision) so that she could enjoy them during her recovery. I bought a small cake of lime-scented soap, a velvet doo-dad to feel, and some jellybeans for taste.

I heard secondhand that she was very touched by my gifts, because she thought I knew she was frightened of losing her eyesight and was trying to give her the message, "Even if you do lose your vision, you still have all your other senses to enjoy." I wished I had thought of that, but I hadn't known her well enough to be aware of her fear. I don't believe she had told anyone at work that she was afraid. Since we thought of her as powerful, we never suspected that she, too, had fears.

Since mothers often try to conceal their troubles and faults from their daughters, and since they have the power to make their daughters feel both wonderful and terrible, many daughters mistakenly assume that their mothers are invulnerable and all-powerful. As you begin to explore your mother's struggles, keep in mind that some of the difficulties mothers most frequently describe are uncertainty about how to care for children, isolation, physical exhaustion, sense of inadequacy, overwhelming sense of responsibility, and fear of failure. Other struggles with which many mothers have to cope include difficulties because of racial discrimination, poverty, disability or illness, unaccepted sexual preference, having many children, a child's disability or illness or death, being a victim of abuse in childhood or currently, being underpaid or overworked or undervalued or sexually harassed on the job, divorce, abandonment, poor relationships with other family members, responsibility for other family members, and frustrated ambitions and dreams. Any mother has been plagued by at least some of these burdens.

So, *think about how the adversity your mother faced might have affected her treatment of you.* Do you remember times she seemed too tired to play with you or exceedingly irritable or very emotionally needy? Could those have been the times her burdens were heaviest? If you're not sure, ask her, or ask people who knew her then. For example, remember that, according to current estimates, at least one-third and probably closer to one-half of all mothers were the victims of some sort of abuse—sexual abuse as a child, sexual assault as an adult, or battering by a mate. Since the effects of abuse include poor self-esteem, insecurity, and fearfulness, a huge proportion of what daughters have regarded as their mothers' faults are likely to have resulted partly from their having been victims of violence—but the daughters never knew.

As we learn about our mother's struggles, the bad things she's done to us usually seem less destructive, less malicious, and even less serious because we understand their sources (her worry about an impending divorce, her concern about where our next meal was coming from, etc.). We can better appreciate the good things she's done when we know that she did them in spite of adversity, that she didn't sail serenely through motherhood, that childrearing took effort and tears and strength and ingenuity. If we can find these buried qualities in her, we can discover them in ourselves as well.

These humanizing techniques will apply to very specific problems between you, some of which will be discussed in Chapter 8. For example, learning about her struggles or her viewpoint may shed important light on your belief that your mother wasn't as nurturant and supportive of you as she should have been. A close friend told me that she recently realized that, compared to her peers' descriptions of their relationships with their mothers, hers was pretty distant. "Oh, I know," her mother said.

> That's because your pediatrician told me that it was important for me to teach you to be independent, and I tried very hard to do that. Just lately, I've realized that, in trying to make you independent, I shut you out emotionally. I guess there are ways to be independent but still loving

and connected, but I have only begun to learn for myself what those ways are. And in my family, with ten of us kids, both of my parents were too busy to be very close to us emotionally. They just didn't have the time.

Considering Your Mother's Worst Aspects

Considering your mother's worst aspects, if properly done, can actually reduce your tendency to blame her or put her down. As we saw in Chapters 2 and 3, blaming and demeaning someone are quick-and-dirty, but ultimately unproductive, ways to deal with someone's unappealing or hurtful behavior toward us. Understanding and even personal growth can come from our attempts to stop taking the easy way out and really try, as the native American motto goes, to walk in the other person's moccasins.

You can do this in various ways, all of which involve trying to project yourself into your mother's situation. If you are very angry at or alienated from her, you may not be eager to try these exercises, but the results are worth making the imaginative leap. At the very least, they acquaint you with another part of life, another space on the wheel of human experience. At best, they also bring genuine understanding of your mother's life. Simone is a writer of 72, who tried walking in her mother's moccasins by writing a short story about their relationship:

> She had always been very hard on me, making me take responsibility for the worst and hardest chores on our farm. I grew up feeling like Cinderella in her pre-fairy-godmother period. I wrote a true-to-life story about my relationship with Mother, but the magazine that had commissioned the story said it was too downbeat and the mother was too one-dimensional and rotten.
>
> My first reaction was, "But that is what she was really like!" In order to get my payment for the story, I added some new material about the mother supposedly being frustrated and lonely doing hard farmwork. I thought that the added bits were complete fiction. But years later, I talked to a woman who had known my mother when she married my father; the woman told me that Mother had desperately wanted to be a concert pianist, but Dad forbade it. She was already an accomplished musician when they met, but he wanted her to help with his farmwork. All she had ever told me was that she played the piano for fun.

As stories like this illustrate, we often know more about our mothers than we think, once we correctly interpret years' worth of signs, hints, and innuendoes.

You can choose from among a number of specific techniques for exploring your mother's worst aspects. You might *ask her outright why she treated you as she did during a particularly painful incident*, how she felt and what she thought at the time. This may be too daunting a task at this stage, but sometimes illuminating information hasn't been revealed simply because no one has asked about it. Or, like Simone, *write (or imagine) a story about your mother's life*. Include everything you can think of about her, but especially *try to make her a sympathetic character;* this may be hard if you don't feel great about her right now, but you'll find the effort worthwhile. A woman named Phoebe said after a workshop on mothers and daughters:

> When I started writing about my mother, all I could think of were the things she does that irritate me. But since the assignment was to try to make her a sympathetic character, I really dug into my memories—and the first thing I remembered that was good was the smell of her chicken soup. That brought back a whole flood of good feelings, including how soft her cheek felt when I was four years old and had a fever.

If just trying to make her a sympathetic character doesn't work for you, try this: think of the worst thing your mother has ever done to you. (You may wish to refer to the notes you made at the start of the book.) Then, imagine that you were the one who did it. *Now, write a short story in which you explain why the character behaved as she did.* Or, if you prefer, just jot down a two-line explanation of the character's motives. *Or, find other women who have done similar things to their daughters, and interview them to find out what led to their behavior.* My student Nora began to understand what had led her mother to beat her only after she talked to other abusive mothers.

Finding Qualities to Respect in Mother

So far, the humanizing exercises have involved either learning more about your mother's life and struggles or trying to understand what led to her upsetting behavior. Now you can focus more specifically on her good points—not what seem to be her superhuman qualities but just her human good points, such as her sense of humor or her talent for word games.

First, see if you can think of reasons she deserves your respect; some of the material you learned in finding out about her struggles may be helpful here. An early-middle-aged woman I'll call Stacey learned at age seven that her mother had a severe emotional disturbance that sometimes made it impossible for the family to have company in their home. In the 1950s, when "mental illness" carried a far greater social stigma than it does now, her mother took her aside for a serious talk and said:

> Honey, I want you to know that the reason I sometimes do strange things is that I have what is called a "mental illness." I have tried very hard to fight this thing, but I really can't help it. I know that when I'm acting strangely, you can't have your friends over to the house, and I don't want them to think it's just because you don't like them. So I want you to feel free to tell the friends you really care about that my mental illness is the reason you don't bring them home with you to play.

As most children would do, Stacey took her mother's words as a matter of course. Not until she turned forty, spurred by the discovery by psychiatrists that her mother indeed had a disorder that was beyond her control, did Stacey appreciate the sacrifice her mother had made for her. Stacey grew up in a very small town where her mother still lives, facing daily the consequences of Stacey's having told her friends about her mother's problems. The townspeople still think that mental illness equals insanity, and Stacey's mother has suffered a great deal because of the ignorant misconceptions about her that have spread through the town. Stacey told me:

> Not only do I wish that people would stop gossiping so viciously about my mother, but I really wish that they would stop and think about what she did. She knew damned well that, when she gave me permission to tell, word would get around pretty fast, and people would distort the truth. And that's what they've done in some unbelievably grotesque ways.
>
> Instead of people gossiping about Mother behind her back, by all rights they should give her a medal for heroism.

If reasons to respect her don't immediately come to mind, try other methods. Ask other people what *they* respect about your mother, or think about features you admire in other women, then consider whether they might apply to your mother. Or use your imagination—pretend you have to write her response to a "Help Wanted" ad explaining why she deserves to get the job, or write a presentation speech for an award to be given to her. The job or award can be of any kind; you might begin with something that seems trivial, like her fondness for hummingbirds. Go on from there to think about what that tells you about her—that she has tender feelings for small creatures or a reverence for nature, for instance.

At least some of the humanizing techniques work for most daughters, but unfortunately, some mothers are at the really dreadful end of the spectrum. What can their daughters do?

Impossibly Difficult Mothers

> An eighty-year-old woman was told, "You can't be eighty years old!" and replied, "What do you mean? I have a 53-year-old son!" She said this while sitting on the couch next to her 54-year-old daughter.
> —story told to me by a friend

Your mother, like the one quoted above, may have done such hurtful things to you that her image can't be humanized very much. On the spectrum of mothers, these are the ones we're most tempted to go on blaming. But even if you are unfortunate enough to have a mother like this, your image-humanizing efforts are still important. Why? Because, as I wrote in Chapter 2, blaming her takes some immediate heat off of you—"She's the problem, not I!"—but as long as you regard her primarily as your Mother, and your Evil Mother, you are still poisonously bound to her. You'll go right on feeling terrified of being like her, or believing that you are. As long as your view of her is mostly as "My mother, the mother," your identity is tightly bound up with hers. Although humanizing your image of her may not make her any more lovable or palatable, try to understand how she got the way she is. Then you'll see the ways in which the forces that shaped you, including your own special, individual characteristics, are different from the forces that shaped her. You may discover that she was powerfully shaped, for example, by the male superiority myth; then, even if that same myth affected you a great deal, you can remind yourself that she never has gotten out from under its influence, whereas at age 25, or 45, or 65, *you already know that the myth is false.*

In trying to understand whether mother is truly impossible to work with, we have to try first to see her not as someone who suddenly existed as a full-fledged, monolithic mother the minute we were born but as someone controlled by her culture. Ironically, many women who forgive Sigmund Freud for the awful things he said about women, because he was a product of his time and culture, cannot do the same for their mothers.

Some of you may have a mother whom you consider, after careful thought, to be thoroughly unforgivable; there are, of course, some quite vicious mothers and some psychotic mothers. If nothing we have discussed seems to help, then so be it. But before giving up, let us consider an example of how we can think about a really destructive mother. As you read the story, put yourself in the young daughter's position, because if your mother was truly terrible, you probably doubted your own worth, as this child did. This is a continuation of the story of Resa and her daughter, Rosemary, who were described in Chapter 5. Rosemary had been brought to a clinic for treatment of her depression.

> When Rosemary was eight years old, her divorced mother's relationship with a man called Mike was in trouble. Resa involved Rosemary in this, urging her to beg Mike to stay with them.
>
> During one argument between Resa and Mike, Rosemary crouched in the corner in the other room, hungry, shivering from the cold and from fear, trying to block out their screaming. She remembers her mother coming into the room after some time and saying "*I* can't do anything with him. *You* try!"

What do we make of Resa? If we think back to the description of her parents and grandparents from Chapter 5, we recall that Resa's mother and grandmother were rather frenetic, cold people— chipper, at best. Her father and grandfather were more pleasant and gentle but minimally involved in the family. Because of the male superiority and endless nurturance myths, Resa's mother and grandmother look responsible for her difficulties, even though her father and grandfather probably contributed to her ungiving, self-centered character too. And thanks to the male superiority myth, Resa believes that she has to have a man—hence, she told her husband to leave so that she could be "independent" only after she had latched desperately onto Mike.

You may want to blame Resa for what she is doing to Rosemary. Or, you may want to absolve her of blame on the grounds that *her* parents and grandparents are at fault. Which view you take will depend in part on what you think about free will. Some of you will say that Resa is a blameless victim of circumstance, unavoidably shaped by her past, powerless to change. Some of you will say that, as an adult who chose to have a child, no matter what has been done to her, she has to take responsibility for not harming her child.

Whichever view you take, however, Resa's treatment of Rosemary clearly grows out of her own needs, not out of her daughter's inadequacy: it's not her daughter's fault. If your mother seems irretrievably horrible, try to think of yourself as Rosemary, and realize that you may have hated or blamed your mother in an effort to prove that you did not deserve what she did to you. If you can understand this, then even if you don't end up loving or forgiving your mother, you will probably feel a lot better about yourself, and you won't base your improved self-esteem on the shaky foundation of tearing someone else down. If only your self-esteem changes, that's a lot.

Humanizing your image of your mother may begin with changes primarily in your thoughts—such as catching yourself using the mythical images and reminding yourself that your mother is neither Angel nor Witch—although changes in your feelings may well follow. Forging an alliance with your mother, whether directly with her or within yourself, in the form of changed attitudes toward her, is likely to be a more emotional process. The humanizing process changes the power balance between you: she comes to seem more nearly equal to you in power, being neither far more admirable nor far more despicable than you. Forging an alliance implies a somewhat equalized balance of power but has more to do with emotions, with a shared feeling of closeness or commonality between you.

FORGING AN ALLIANCE

Improving a mother-daughter relationship requires the efforts of both mother and daughter. Forging an alliance between the two of you is, therefore, extremely important. Many of the techniques discussed so far will help create this alliance, will help you to realize that you are on the same team.

It's impossible to exaggerate the importance of this step; as therapist Nikki Gerrard has written, it does both people more good if we think of ourselves as building an alliance than if we think of one of us as "helping the other out" or singlehandedly diagnosing and solving the problems we share.

The initial steps you can take to forge an alliance with your mother involve "Getting Started; Looking at Obstacles," "Confronting Your Mother's Power," and "Clarifying Your Respective Responsibilities."

Getting Started; Looking at Obstacles

If you wrote or taped your mother's biography, you have already begun creating an alliance with her. If you haven't yet done the biography, consider doing so now. A lot may change as she sees that you take her seriously enough to ask about her life, to listen to her answers, and to consider her an important source of information, a partner in your effort to make sense of your life and of the relationship that you two share. Many women who have loved reading novels and documentary histories about women have never asked to hear their own mothers' stories. For alliance-building, *that* you ask matters more that *what* you ask.

If your mother doesn't bring up the subject herself, *ask her specifically about her view of the relationship between the two of you,* in the same way as you interviewed her about her life generally. Ask her to name a couple of things you have done that have brought her joy and a couple that have caused her grief. Remember that this is an interview, not yet a time to trade viewpoints or debate issues. The more you know about her view of the problem, the better you'll be able to assess the work you'll need to do together.

You may want to pretend that you are not her daughter if you don't like something she says about you—because the relevance of the interview for forging an alliance is that you have the chance to *listen intently and build up a picture of how you and your relationship with her look from her point of view.* Your mission is to gather information. Convince yourself that you are a stranger who's just met her at a cocktail party and is listening to her describe her daughter and herself. This kind of listening should give you a good idea of the aspects of your relationship that concern her the most, and she'll speak more freely if you can listen in a nonjudgmental and undefensive way. This is *not* the time to interrupt with, "But Ma, I *don't* do that!" or "You *always* liked my sister better!"

If you plan to have some conversations with your mother about the barriers between you, I suggest that you review the section on "A Relationship Built for Two" in Chapter 6. That will help orient you as you decide how to broach the subject with her. A good way to start is by telling her that you want your relationship to be closer or more relaxed, and that you would like her to set aside some time for the two of you to talk about how to make that happen. Suggest to your mother that the two of you think of your relationship as a kind of kinetic sculpture that will always be changing because of things beyond your control—like aging, societal expectations, etc.—but that can to some degree be shaped by the two of you.

Give her time, if she needs it. Tell her you'll call her in a few days to find out what she has decided. If she says she's not interested, you can urge her to tell you why she's reluctant, because once the reason is named, you may be able to deal with it fairly quickly. If she tells you that she is afraid that you'll tell her all the things she has done wrong as a mother, you can assure her that is exactly what you do *not* plan to do. Or, you might give her this book. Say that you have read it, and suggest that you talk after she has had a chance to read it, too. Even if she needs more time or if you never do overcome her resistance, you will feel better for having asked her why she's reluctant to talk. You may understand, for example, that what she feels is fear rather than disinterest in you or such intense anger at you that she can't imagine talking to you about the relationship.

If your mother is adamant about not discussing the relationship with you, she may need more time, and *she* may raise the issue with you if she can choose a time when she feels ready. But even if she doesn't, you will find in this section some more indirect ways to forge an alliance with her. One of them is the following:

Whether or not you do her biography and whether or not she agrees to talk to you about your relationship, you can tell her about some of the material from Chapters 3, 4, and 5 in this book.

You might start with a small step, such as describing the polarized images of mothers, the ways that mother-blaming results from both the Perfect Mother myths and the Bad Mother myths. She is likely to understand quickly, since she will have experienced them herself, and then you will have a shared framework. *Reassure her explicitly that you don't want either to idealize or demean her.* It may be the first time since she became a mother that anyone has named the stereotypes, called them bad, and said or implied, "Let's go beyond them."

You may want to describe some of the myths to her, perhaps focusing especially on the ones that you think have affected her the most. By having this kind of discussion, you make it clear from the outset that your purpose in talking to her is to begin a journey of exploration *with* her; therefore, she'll feel less need to try to maintain herself on the mother-on-pedestal position or will be less afraid of being in the put-down, cast-aside one. You can have this conversation with your mother even if she doesn't want to discuss your relationship directly.

Consider spending some time talking to her about her current emotional state. Because mothers are supposed to take care of other people's needs, we rarely think to ask them what *they* need; because they are supposed to help us deal with our fears and work toward our goals, we don't usually ask them about their fears and aims. For that reason, when we *do* ask them such questions, we show our mothers in a very moving way that we want to be allied with them. Freda Paltiel, who is Health and Welfare Canada's Senior Advisor on the Status of Women, suggests that you *ask your mother to describe her real self in terms of her "needs, risks, and tasks":* What are her needs, both in her relationship with you and otherwise? What risks does she feel she is taking, both in working on her relationship with you and at this point in her life generally? Are there risks she *wants* to take? What tasks does she want to accomplish, both in her relationship with you and in general at this point in her life?

Confronting Your Mother's Power

Now you must confront head-on the issue of your mother's power. Although the humanizing exercises may have equalized the balance of power between you *in your mind*, your mother needs a chance to work on that issue by herself and possibly in conversation with you.

As we saw in Chapter 5, mothers do have certain kinds of power over their children, and in our culture everyone is urged to regard that power as dangerous. Precisely *because* it is regarded as dangerous, many daughters and sons are overly sensitive about it, mistakenly labeling mother's displays of interest and concern or offers of advice and nurturance as her misuse of power. You must bring this issue out in the open. Talk explicitly about the unfairness of mother's power being so quickly damned as destructive. Also, tell your mother what kinds of power she does have over you—the power to inspire you or to make you feel loved, as well as the power to make you feel inadequate or ashamed, and so on. Daughters are often surprised to find that their mothers don't realize how much power they still have over their adult offspring. In fact, as described in Chapter 5, mothers usually feel quite powerless.

Until we realize that mother is not omnipotent and certainly does not feel she is, that her power is not as dangerous as we think, and that we are not powerless in relation to her, we cannot forge a true alliance. One way we deal with mother's power is to try to reduce her impact on us through mocking her, as Portnoy did. Novelist Rebecca Goldstein wrote: "I've transformed [my mother] into a parody . . . in the attempt to dilute some of her awesome strength."

I recently recognized that I was exaggerating, in my own mind, my mother's power and her destructive use of it. I had been feeling distant from her and wanted to call and say how much I loved her. It startled me to notice how hesitant I was to make that call. When I thought about why, I realized that I was very much afraid that she would make light of my expression of love, *even though* there was no reason to expect this. In fact, she has usually been very warm and expressive toward me. But what if she should be busy or preoccupied when I called? The prospect of being rejected by our mothers can be shattering—no matter how remote it seems or how old we are.

Be sure, too, to give your mother a chance to describe the power *you* have over her. A typical mother told me, "With one look or comment, my daughter can make me feel like an old fool *or* like I'm really OK." In responding to pressure to regard our mothers' power as dangerous, we daughters often fail to consider the influence that we have over them. But in order to build a true alliance with them, we have to know how we affect them as well as telling them how they affect us.

You and your mother need to base your alliance partly on your understanding of the limits of each other's power. Since both mothers and daughters are women in a misogynist culture, we don't have much power to improve each other's lives. We don't like to acknowledge this, because we usually wish we *could* help each other a great deal more. Often we are reluctant to tell each other about our needs, because we don't want to reveal each other's powerlessness. So discuss with your mother what you *wish* you had the power to do for each other, and acknowledge the frustration and powerlessness you both feel because, for instance, *you* can't make the rest of the family show more respect for her mothering work, and *she* can't arrange for you to receive equal pay, protect you from sexual harassment, or force your husband to treat you with respect. All of this is very painful to consider, but the best emotional context in which to do so is the assumption that mothers and daughters *want* to be closer to each other, want to overcome the barriers between them, and that *these are worthy, healthy aims.*

Clarify Your Respective Responsibilities

Now you and your mother should discuss what *are* and what *are not* your responsibilities. For instance, suggest that both of you *do* have the responsibility to:

- respect each other's strengths
- respect each other's right to be imperfect without being considered a failure or betrayer
- understand that much of what you have done to enrage or hurt each other came not from ill will but from cultural attitudes reflected in mother-blaming and the myths

Also establish that both of you recognize that, for example,

- a mother is *not* responsible for meeting all of a daughter's needs (Myth Two)

- a daughter is *not* responsible for establishing and maintaining a mother's good reputation through her impeccable behavior (Myth One)

Then look through Chapters 4 and 5, and see whether either of you has been holding yourself or the other person inappropriately responsible for the consequences of any of the other myths.

Since your goal is to be closer to or more relaxed with your mother, you will have to screen out mother-blaming messages. Even though *you* may now be careful about attributing all your problems to your mother, other people won't take such care. You'll need sensitive antennae to twitch a warning when the destructive messages come your way.

For example, as I prepared to write this chapter, a famous author appeared on television to publicize her latest book, in which she claims that successful Superwomen are insecure because of *their mothers'* needs for overachievement and the daughters' "enmeshment, their inability to separate from their mothers." Such statements are often made with such authority that it is hard to see the mother-blaming errors in them. Once you understand that you must screen out such messages, you'll be halfway to establishing and maintaining a true alliance with your mother. With that alliance as a foundation, you are now ready to go beyond thinking about the myths in general and to work on the mother-daughter problems that specifically plague *your* relationship.

CHOOSING AND DEFINING A PROBLEM

Once you have humanized your image of your mother and forged an alliance with her—either directly or in your own heart —you may find that some of your problems will diminish. But some are likely to need more patient, prolonged work. You can do a great deal of the work described in this section on your own, by talking with someone other than your mother (a friend, a therapist) or by talking with her directly. In any case, the basic steps to follow are:

1. Identify one problem at a time
2. Identify the feelings you have about the problem

3. Identify the sources of the problem and of the feelings about it

Remember that you are beginning a process of teaching yourself and your mother about each other. Either one of you can identify a problem, but be sure to consider both your and her feelings about it and both your and her perceptions of its causes. You may find it easier to begin by identifying a troublesome feeling that you have about your mother, trying to describe its causes, and then attempting to find out what your mother's feelings and beliefs about its causes are. (You will probably want to turn back to Chapter 6 and review the principles and techniques of expressive training, which will be very helpful.)

Remember that the problem you choose need not be your most serious problem; you may feel more comfortable beginning with a somewhat minor issue that you (both) can handle. You may wish to begin with something that came up as you worked on your mother's biography.

One mother-daughter pair discovered during the biography exercise that they had very different ideas about the meaning of "independence." The daughter defined it as "no more than a couple of visits a month," while the mother thought her daughter could remain independent and still see her every week. Both mother and daughter felt great relief when they both identified as the *cause* of the problem their specific concern about the frequency of contact. They discussed their different views of how frequent visits should be; this was more constructive than accusations about the daughter not caring or the mother being too demanding. In a series of discussions, the daughter described her amorphous fears that her mother wanted constant involvement with her and that "nothing would ever be enough"; the mother described her fear that her daughter really wanted nothing to do with her. Primarily, both felt fear—for the daughter, fear of engulfment, and for the mother, fear of rejection. What turned out to be the specific *cause* of their problem was that they hadn't bothered to tell each other their real wishes and fears. Each was making mistaken assumptions about what the other wanted.

A widowed, 78-year-old mother and her daughter had an almost opposite experience. The mother fell and broke her hip, and she went to stay with her daughter when she was released from the hospital. On their way home from the hospital, they got into a terrible quarrel, over an apparently trivial matter. When a visiting nurse came to check on the mother several days later, the mother burst into tears and began to describe her wish to live on her own, which she thought would hurt her daughter's feelings. The nurse called in the daughter and helped them to talk about how they each really felt.

They began politely, each saying truthfully that she loved the other, didn't want to upset her, and felt terrible about the quarrel they had had. At that point, the nurse urged them to acknowledge any other feelings they had. The daughter said, "I'm so confused, because I wanted Mother to feel at home here, but she seems so tense, and I don't know what to do." The mother replied, "I do feel tense here, but that's because I'm used to being on my own. When my insomnia is bothering me, I hate having to worry that my bustling around with my walker in here will disturb or worry the other people in the house." So each woman was guessing about how she was affecting the other, and neither had said before what her worst concern was. The nurse told them they had made a good beginning, and she arranged for a social worker to come to the house the next week.

The social worker made a series of visits, during which she told the women that their concerns about each other's feelings were admirable, but their denial of their own feelings was causing the tension between them. Over a period of weeks, the mother was finally able to express her longing to live on her own again and to admit that her reluctance to say so was caused by her wish to avoid seeming ungrateful for her daughter's care. The daughter was able to say that she had thought a good daughter should be able to make her mother completely comfortable in her home, and she felt miserable because she couldn't seem to manage that. Once she knew what her mother really wanted, she stopped feeling her mother was "impossible," and the tension between them subsided a great deal.

When you and your mother choose a problem together, remember that there is a big difference between agreeing on *a problem* and agreeing on the *source of the problem*. For example, try to avoid saying, "The problem is that you can't let go of me." That is an accusation and a criticism (see Chapter 6 section on Expressive Training), so she's unlikely to agree with you and will probably become defensive. Instead, define the problem according to expressive training principles. For instance, one daughter said, "I'd like us to talk about the fact that I *feel* guilty—and then angry about having to feel guilty—because you chide me if I go one day without phoning you."

In choosing problems to work on, you may want to review your list of the worst things your mother has ever done to you, and see which ones plague you the most, or consult any notes you made while reading this book. If possible, ask your mother to make a list of the worst things you have ever done to her. You might also want to review the list of myths in Chapters 4 and 5, considering which ones might be creating or exacerbating the problems between you. Then recast what happened, minus the myth(s). For instance, if she always told you the people you dated weren't good enough for you, ask yourself whether she *might* have been trying to be the all-knowing, completely protective mother (Myths Three and Two). Put yourselves in each other's shoes: if you had been the mother, what would you have done in this situation? Was there any way she could have done just the right thing? And what does she wish *you* had done when the problem first arose?

These kinds of analyses or conversations can be difficult, because women often find it harder to see beyond the myths in their own mothers' lives than in anyone else's. As I have mentioned, hundreds of women have each told me that *her* mother is the only masochist in the world. Through their awareness of the myths and mother-blaming, many such daughters have been able to understand their mothers' "Look what I sacrificed for you," *not* as proof that they revel in misery and martyrdom but as a perhaps justified, if misguided, plea for recognition and appreciation.

Another way to start work with your mother is to spend a little time with her and note when problems arise and how you feel. This is especially helpful if, when you *think* of your relationship with her, you feel so upset, numb, or alienated that you can't focus on specific problems.

Suppose, for example, you notice that both of you become tense when you discuss how often you talk to each other on the phone. As you see it, she can't let go of you and makes you feel guilty for not calling her enough. Try assuming instead that she wants to stay connected with you. Ask yourself what myths might have transformed that wish for connection into what seems to you like her inability to let go and her wish to make you feel guilty. That is the task that Gina, a woman in her mid-thirties, set for herself:

> I had a long talk about this with my best friend, and we realized that the myth that mother-daughter closeness is bad was making me suspect my mother of wanting "too much" closeness, and the myth that women's power is dangerous made me accuse her of *trying* to make me feel guilty.

Gina never even found it necessary to talk this through with her mother. The insights she got through talking to her friend about the myths made all the difference. The next time she had a busy week at work and didn't phone her mother, Gina got out of her old rut. When her mother called her, instead of saying her usual, "Oh, ma, why do you have such a fit when I go *one* week without calling you?" she tried, "Hi, ma! You've been on my mind all week, but they've been driving me crazy at work, and I just didn't feel fit for human conversation."

Nothing Gina said to her mother was untrue. She didn't pretend to be thrilled by her mother's call, nor did she carry on a lengthy conversation with her. What she did do was to avoid complaining or accusing her mother, and that had two important results:

1. *Something* happened between them besides complaints, accusations, and demands—when you create that space, connection and warmth sometimes seep in; and
2. Gina adopted a new attitude toward her mother, one that left open the possibility that her mother's motives might be better than Gina had assumed.

In exploring or even in trying to identify your feelings, try to remember or reconstruct the first time you felt this way about your mother. For instance, if you are phobic about telling her anything about your lovelife, think back to the first time you felt uncomfortable doing that. What had you said, and how did she respond? You may find that your upsetting feeling is now outdated if, for instance, you told her a boy had kissed you on the first date, and she expressed shock and dismay. Now that you are 45 years old, she may be less shocked, and even if she isn't, you may be less devastated by her reaction. But even if your feeling is not outdated, recalling its origins can help you to understand it better.

If you haven't done so before, ask your mother how she would describe the *development* of the problems between you. Did you always clash, or did you get along well until a certain point? When was there a change for the worse? Does she recall what caused the change? And, importantly, did mother-blaming and the myths play a role in the change? Her answers may help the two of you to identify the sources of the barriers between you; at least they will give you a starting point for your work. Let's look at some examples.

One daughter whose mother refused to talk to her about their relationship asked her mother's sister when the mother-daughter problems had begun. The aunt replied:

> When you were eleven years old, your teacher told your parents that he was concerned about you, because you weren't yet interested in boys. Your mother had been a very popular girl in high school, and when this teacher said authoritatively that your lack of interest in having boyfriends was a problem, she was very worried about you. She didn't want you to miss out on the fun she had had, and she was afraid that her delight in your academic success had retarded your social development. That was when she started pushing you to go to boy-girl parties, against your wishes.

From her aunt's account, this daughter understood that her mother had been trying to be a good mother. That knowledge was helpful to her, although her attempts to talk to her mother about the problem never did succeed.

If your mother feels that your relationship took a dramatic turn for the worse when you hit adolescence, you will need to explore together what it was about your reaching *adolescence* that provoked conflict. Were you expressing normal adolescent, hormonally based increases in aggressiveness that you hadn't learned how to handle? Was she frightened by the prospect of you as a sexual being—did she feel unable to teach you how to protect yourself from the vulnerability that accompanies sexuality? Did she fear that you would be sexually aggressive and that her friends would hear about it and think she was a terrible mother? Once you ask such questions you can easily see how your problems might have been aggravated by such myths as "The Measure of a Good Mother is a 'Perfect' Daughter."

You may identify your marriage as a point at which your mother-daughter relationship suddenly took a downturn. Both Roberta and her mother, Marsha, agreed that Roberta's marriage to Stephen had been the beginning of a painful series of conflicts between them. Marsha said:

> Roberta's marriage made me a mother-in-law. And when Stephen put me down, Roberta sometimes joined right in. When I told her privately that that hurt my feelings, Roberta said that I had taught her that a woman must always take her husband's side. And she was right: I *had* taught her that. Why should she side with me? Who ever got any respect by siding with a mother?

Marsha had seen that her daughter acquired status by siding with a man instead of with her mother, but she hadn't yet realized that that was a result of both her and her daughter's belief in the myth that men are superior. Marsha saw that later, as she and her daughter discussed how the myths had affected them, and much of her pain was relieved. Until then, she had known only that her daughter often mocked her and that she herself had somehow helped make that happen—but she thought that her own stupidity and her daughter's dislike of her were the roots of the problem.

For her part, Roberta felt frustrated and angry: "I have to be loyal to my husband, but I have an obligation to my mother—and I *care* about both of them." Looking at the list of myths, Roberta and Marsha immediately recognized that the myth of male superiority had played a major role in the development of the tension between them.

A daughter's divorce is often a turning point for mothers and daughters. It can turn the relationship in either direction. It turns for the worse when a daughter, feeling vulnerable and believing in the endless nurturance myth, falls into the trap of expecting her mother to stand by her one hundred percent and feels betrayed by anything less. Or the negative turn can come from the mother's side. Many an unhappily married mother is threatened by a daughter's divorce, because it shows her that she, too, has a choice: she doesn't *have* to put up with unhappiness. Having that choice both attracts and frightens her, and this confusion makes her angry. She may resent her daughter for provoking her ("unfeminine") anger and making her think about the frightening prospect of living unsupported by a man.

When daughter divorces, mother may pull away. Sherry was 27 when she and her husband decided to go their separate ways. Her mother reacted by stopping her weekly telephone calls:

> I'd known for a long time that the relationship between my parents was emotionally very distant, but not until I told my mother about my divorce did I realize how bad things were between them. She got very shrill and started lecturing me about how a woman's place is with her husband, no matter what. I knew she was trying to convince herself, and I was sad that she couldn't see that. The only way she could run from her wish to leave Dad was to stay away from me.

Some daughters have found that just waiting is helpful, until mother realizes that daughter isn't pushing *her* to leave her marriage. Other daughters have told their mothers explicitly, "I left Fred, because leaving was right for me. But that doesn't mean that I think you should leave Dad. Only you can make that decision."

Most mothers will hesitate to encourage their daughter to leave a miserable marriage. But when the divorce is a *fait accompli* a mother may feel freer to admit to herself and her daughter that marriage is not perfect; she no longer needs to try to persuade her daughter to stay in the conventional married role. One of my students describes her experience:

> . . . after six years of marriage, I called my mother one day and told her that I was leaving my husband. I told her that I was fed up with nurturing a man who was not capable of returning the nurturing. She understood what I was saying. . . . The separation and divorce left me feeling vulnerable, but free [to stop pretending marriage is perfect], as it did my mother. Our relationship began to feel truly loving and I felt her acceptance of me. I began to develop more self-esteem and greater satisfaction in my job.

As you work on particular problems, from time to time you will have to take measures to keep up your motivation. Remind yourself what you're working toward by recalling a time when you and your mother had a good relationship. Also remind yourself that you don't have to choose between telling your mother how you are feeling and trying to increase the closeness or reduce the tension between you. The two are not mutually exclusive. For example, you can tell her you don't like her criticism of you *because* it gets in the way of your enjoyment of your time together.

After choosing a problem to work on, trying to identify your and your mother's feelings about it, and discussing what you each regard as the sources of the problem, it will probably help to read how other mothers and daughters have worked on issues together. Once again, even if you are not working directly with your mother, you can benefit from learning about the kinds of thinking and insights that other women have found useful. The following chapter consists of stories about mothers and daughters and how their work has gone.

8 ❧ What Mothers and Daughters Have Done

A RELIABLE SIGNAL that our mother-daughter relationship needs mending is our emotional distress—or our mother's. We began this book with a look at the upsetting emotions that daughters feel, then we examined the mother-blaming myths that cause or aggravate them; now we have come full circle—back to the emotions themselves. But now, with the help of the language of the myths, we can take a fresh, active look at what to do about those painful feelings.

Sometimes alleviating the anguish can be accomplished quickly through insight and sharing, but sometimes it requires sustained, long-term efforts. Reading these stories of mothers and daughters should give you some idea of how you want to proceed; I hope you will feel how real are the possibilities for change. Not all of the stories are about problems that are easily solved, because mother-daughter problems can be so complex and delicate; but all of the examples do show you how a mother, a daughter, or both have worked on some difficulty between them and have been able to achieve some improvement even when they have not eliminated the difficulty altogether.

I can't discuss all of the key feelings and issues that can plague any stage of the mother-daughter relationship, from the daughter's birth through the mother's and the daughter's aging; however, I have chosen a variety of examples from different stages. Some of these stories will hit closer to home for you than others, but I encourage you to read them all, because other women's ways of thinking or speaking or acting may be useful to you, even if their concerns differ from yours.

A PRINCIPLE FOR ALL FEELINGS

Anguish in our mother-daughter relationships usually results from a rift between us, so we need to focus on ways of repairing the rift rather than on laying blame. A daughter may react to some disturbance or interruption in her connection to her mother by feeling ambivalence, betrayal, despair, anger, guilt, sadness, or numbness and alienation. Too often, we aren't even aware that our unmet need for connection is the problem. To illustrate this, feminist therapist Nikki Gerrard described what happened one Sunday in her house:

> My six-year-old daughter was whining about being bored, and I got irritated and angry. I wanted to scream at her, spank her, and maybe send her to her room. I thought that her bad behavior was a sign that she couldn't play on her own, and I was feeling that I was a bad mother for not having taught her how to do that.
>
> Suddenly, something clicked. I realized that I was assuming that her independence—or lack of it—was the issue here, and I was so focussed on that that I hadn't wondered what else might be going on. I thought about what makes *me* cranky and irritable, and I realized that often it's because I'm uncomfortable about a break or a distancing in a close relationship. So I took my daughter in my arms and said, "I love you." I told her that she was precious to me, and I stroked her hair. She sucked her thumb and lay there like a contented cat. After awhile, she got up, went outdoors, and played. A rift in our relationship had been repaired, and now she felt fine.

This is a good and useful model for all of us. I have tried it many times myself, including with my daughter and with my mother. Recently, my daughter was upset about the trouble she was having with a school project. I called from the kitchen into the family room, "Emily, why don't you look it up in the encyclopedia?" Silence. "Honey, do you understand what the assignment is? You could call one of the other kids in the class and ask them." Irritated outburst from Emily. Then I remembered Nikki's experience with her daughter. "Emily," I said, "I'm sorry you feel so frustrated, and I wish that I could help." She was relieved: her school assignment had upset her, she had taken out her irritation on me and then felt bad about that. When I stopped trying to find exactly what to do for her (Myth Three) and instead just tried to be warm and supportive, she was reassured because her irritation hadn't damaged our connection for more than a few minutes.

The relief that comes from repairing damaged mother-daughter connections was experienced by Janice and her mother, Marjorie, whose relationship was plagued by the myth that the measure of a good mother is a perfect daughter. Janice thought that her mother was trying to force her to follow social rules for selfish reasons; her mother's angry behavior had seemed to her to be her mother's heartless attempt to make her fit an acceptable mold.

When Janice's lover, Aaron, moved in with her and her two pre-teen children, Marjorie was terribly upset. She thought that Janice and Aaron were selfish for not waiting long enough to make sure that their relationship would last, and that the children would be hurt if Aaron later moved out. Also, having been extremely sympathetic through Janice's previous relationships with men, Marjorie said that, frankly, she did not want to get her hopes up this time. She had been agonized when Janice's previous relationships dissolved, and she was upset at the prospect of listening once again to Janice's anguish about a broken relationship. Says Janice:

> My first reaction was hurt. I felt rejected, then angry. I wondered—and asked Mom angrily—why she couldn't be happy that I was so happy. Why couldn't she see that Aaron was wonderful to the kids and that they adored him?

Janice wanted Marjorie to feel as she felt. She longed for her mother's support and approval and felt betrayed when they did not come. But in her wish for Marjorie's support, Janice was being insensitive to her mother's feelings. Marjorie's feelings were understandable and were not aimed to hurt Janice, as Janice finally realized:

> When I calmed down and put myself in my mother's position, I figured that I would probably have felt the same way. I get fed up with friends who repeatedly go through a period of elation at the beginnings of relationships, followed by longer times when they need my support as the relationship turns sour.

So the first step that made a difference was trying to see the situation from Marjorie's point of view. Janice then put that understanding into action: she called Marjorie and said, "Mom, I wish you could rejoice with me, but I understand why you can't, and I respect your feelings."

For awhile, Janice thought that the problem was solved. She felt very mature about acknowledging the different feelings that she and her mother had. But then she realized that she also felt estranged from her. After spending some long nights fearing that her next step might fail miserably, Janice picked up the phone and called her mother again:

> I *told* her that I was feeling distant from her and didn't like that, especially since we've usually been so close. I said that I was still happy with Aaron, and so were the children, but that I felt uncomfortable because she and Aaron, two very important people in my life, felt totally unconnected to each other. I told her that I didn't expect her to jump on the next plane and move in with us for six months so that she could get to know and love Aaron. I didn't ask Mom to change her feelings. I just said that our estrangement pained me, and I wanted to be close to her again.

Four months later Marjorie spent a weekend with Janice and Aaron. Although nothing is perfect, and she does not yet adore Aaron—and may never do so—she does know that Janice wants to stay close to her. Finding a way to avoid simply blaming Marjorie for their estrangement, and finding a way to live with her own decisions even though they were *not* what her mother wanted freed Janice from the resentment she had previously felt toward her mother. A great deal of energy was released from self-doubt (for not pleasing her mother) and from mother-blaming, freeing Janice to use that energy to maintain and strengthen the bond with her mother.

For Marjorie's part, she now felt less pressed to approve and participate wholeheartedly in everything Janice did, but she also learned that her daughter's involvement with a new man did not mean that Janice had stopped caring about her relationship with her mother or respecting her mother's opinions.

These stories illustrate the need for us to keep in mind that much of the distress in our relationships with our mothers comes from our longing for more connection with them.

AMBIVALENCE

We have looked in detail at the power of the polarized mother-images to make us deeply ambivalent about our mothers. When strong ambivalence is a characteristic of your mother-daughter relationship, you'll probably find it useful to consider how the two sets of myths can feed that feeling. For example, the Perfect Mother myth of mother's endless nurturing attracts us to our mothers, even as the Bad Mother myth of female inferiority may make us want to dissociate ourselves from them.

A daughter's ambivalence about her mother often appears or becomes particularly pronounced in adolescence, when her wish to have nothing to do with her mother is intensified by her need to feel grown-up. My editor Janet Goldstein recalls her mother saying to her, when she was a teenager, "I can't even stand in line with you at the movies right. I either stand too close to you or not close enough!" When daughter wants her mother near, they are both plagued by the worry that closeness is unhealthy, and when they *are* close, each fears being overwhelmed by the other's "enormous" needs.

Teenaged girls usually want to stay distant from mother in order to hide their increased sexual and aggressive feelings; but the confusion those feelings arouse makes them long more than ever to feel protected and supported. A mother who knows what her daughter feels is a potential source of comfort. But if the daughter's fear of her mother's disapproval is too great, her mother's knowledge about her feelings can also be a source of fear and shame, with which she copes by trying to shut her mother out. The daughter may experience her mother as a human mirror who will not retreat respectfully into shadow.

As adults we often moan, "When I'm with my mother, I feel like I'm fourteen years old again." We believe that our mothers see through us, see what we want most to keep hidden. We may feel that our maturity and independence have never been recognized by them. Ideally, mothers and daughters can find ways to be close, loving adults who interact as equals. Gina's story in Chapter 7 about her phone calls from her mother is an example of this kind of successful resolution.

Ambivalence can unexpectedly rear its head with surprising

intensity, often after a period of equilibrium and general close-ness. As your mother ages, you probably begin looking after her in certain ways, helping her out, checking on how she's feeling. Although in fact you may just be continuing your mutually caring relationship, you may worry that you have participated in a "role reversal," that you now "mother" your mother. You and your mother may want to stay close but you worry that such mother-daughter closeness is unhealthy. Rosa, a mother-daughter work-shop participant, put it this way:

> After my mother's arthritis got so bad, I started doing some of her house-work—especially the things she had to kneel down to do. I wanted to help her, but I worried that she'd feel uncomfortable having *me* take care of *her* instead of the opposite; and I felt strange, too. Sometimes the strangeness really got to me, and I'd take it out on her, getting really irritable.

The strangeness, for Rosa, was not caused only by the change in her role, for strangeness in itself needn't be upsetting; her nega-tive feelings also came from her belief that a grown daughter and her mother should be independent of each other. As Rosa ex-plored her feelings and recognized her ambivalence (evidenced by her mixed reactions of caring and anger), she gradually under-stood the effects of the myth that mother-daughter closeness is unhealthy. Furthermore, she saw that her feeling that she ought to be endlessly nurturant, combined with her fear of giving too much, threatened to paralyze her emotionally.

Rosa also saw that two myths had allowed her to take care of her father *without* feeling ambivalent. Because of the male supe-riority myth, she felt privileged to help him, and because of the endless nurturance myth, she felt very womanly for doing so. Rosa said:

> I realized that I've never felt irritated about taking care of my father since his heart attack. I'm afraid the difference is that I expect so much of her, but not of him.

Weeks after the workshop, Rosa called to tell me that she had talked to her mother both about how strange her caretaking role felt and how much she appreciated all the caretaking her mother had done for her over the years. Her recognition of the power of the myths had resolved much of her ambivalence, and her energy was freed so that she could show her mother some appreciation and respect.

By acknowledging her discomfort to her mother, rather than taking it out in anger at her, Rosa established a new phase in their relationship. Although the changes involved some reversal of power and responsibility between them, they came closer to being psychological equals. They did this by straightforwardly acknowledging their human reactions—Rosa's discomfort and resentment, and her mother's discomfort and sorrow about her loss of physical ability. Rosa's mother had felt less deserving of her daughter's respect than when she was better able to take care of herself, but Rosa reduced the pain and isolation they both felt when she managed to acknowledge her own feelings in a respectful, dignified way.

Women whose mothers are too ill or disturbed to have the kind of conversation Rosa had with her mother have told me that just understanding the way the myths affected their feelings has helped to relieve some of their upsetting feelings. For instance, would you feel the same if such an incident were happening instead between you and your father, or between a father and a son? One woman vividly described the double standard for older people in this way:

> I see the same pattern in all my friends' families, as their parents get old. The father—even if he's been a bloody tyrant all his life—is respected as he ages. His maddening habits (both the lifelong ones and the new ones he acquires as he ages) are considered his idiosyncrasies. But the mother—no matter how much she slaved to keep the family together and to take care of everybody—is called a bitch and "an impossible person to deal with" when *she* is difficult.

You'll feel less ambivalent about taking care of your mother if you try to redress the balance, to fight against a complete power switch—or at least focus on respect for her. You can sometimes achieve this by asking her to do what she *can* do—tell you stories from her past, or tell you what you were like when you were little or what she wanted to be when she grew up or what she's done in her life that makes her proud. This is a good way to combat the pressure from our youth-mad culture for us simply to withdraw from older people, to stop caring.

You can also acknowledge her status as a resource person

because of her age. Mothers can help demystify the process of aging for us. A few years ago my mother told me that, because of her hearing loss, she feels isolated when unable to hear a conversation that is going on right in front of her. I hadn't realized how much of the world we can miss because of changes that go with aging. Any discomfort or irritation I might have felt when her hearing problems caused me inconvenience was partly mitigated by my greater understanding of her experience and by my respect for her honesty in talking about it.

BETRAYAL

Daughters commonly feel betrayed by their mothers because the myth of male superiority leads mothers to undervalue or even demean both their daughters and themselves. In her early twenties, Genna came to such a realization in the aftermath of a shopping expedition with her mother:

> For so many years, I'd loved the times that Mom and I went to the beauty shop or clothes shopping. Then, one day, I felt horribly let down because she made a cutting comment about a beautiful suit that I bought. She said, "You'll certainly make me look dowdy when you show up in that flashy suit." I couldn't believe it—my mother was jealous of me.

Genna felt disappointed and betrayed—and those feelings about her mother were too painful to ignore. She knew that in order to feel comfortable seeing her mother again, she would have to find some way to come to terms with what had happened. She knew that if she simply told her mother how hurt she was, her mother would say she was ridiculous to respond that way to a compliment. Genna discussed the matter with an old friend, and together they identified Genna's feelings:

> My immediate reaction had been to feel guilty for outdoing her. Then, I felt angry at her for making me feel guilty. And then I got mad at myself, because part of me was glad to outdo her. Finally, I saw how much pressure she had put on both of us to get men's approval and how that drove us apart. That's when I realized that, in addition to the warmth and the sharing in those expeditions, there was a frenetic quality, because the whole point was to make ourselves attractive to men!
> My mother's concern with men's approval was something *she* had picked up from *her* mother. I knew, because I had often heard my grand-

mother talk about "looking nice for the menfolk." Memories started to come back to me—all those years I felt so proud of being thinner than she was but at the same time felt I could never be as strong and competent as she. And I recalled many times that she had shown her jealousy of me for being young and thin. I felt really cheated: why had we spent so much energy competing with each other for my Dad's and my brother's approval, and each of us feeling like we had lost?

At first, I blamed her: *she* had trained me to do this! But I had noticed in my friends' families how the mothers thought they were *supposed* to teach their daughters to play up to men, and I finally saw that my mother wasn't so different in that respect. I also saw that it was no more her *fault* than the fault of my friends' mothers that they were that way. I felt more like we'd been duped together. And my resentment of her slowly began to fade. It didn't disappear entirely, because I still wished she had been strong enough to keep from being duped, but it did get somewhat better.

In a variation on the male superiority theme, because mothers think they should raise conventional daughters and sons, their daughters often feel betrayed. As 29-year-old Becky recalled:

> I never felt like *my* anger was legitimate, like it could lead to anything good. My brother's anger could, though: if I yelled and screamed, I got put down for it, but if he yelled and screamed, my parents buckled under and gave him whatever he wanted. And as for sex, the message I got from my parents was simply "Don't!" but my brother was given condoms and proud, knowing looks by our dad. I knew my parents were worried about me getting pregnant, but that worry seemed to get in the way of their making me feel anything good about my sexuality. It became only a burden to me.

Many women discover that their mothers thought they should teach their daughters to look up to men more than women even though they disliked some aspects of the female role and did not really want to compete with their daughters for men's favor. Mothers have sometimes found ways to opt out of the competition and get out of the female tasks that they hated the most.

When I was growing up, I heard my mother say repeatedly (and, to my surprise, shamelessly), "I couldn't sew on a button!" So I became the home "tailor," sewing on buttons and hemming skirts and slacks for the family. I believed that my father thought I was better than my mother in this way. I felt embarrassed for her and at once proud and guilty for having outdone her. Not until the year I turned forty did I understand what had really happened. I asked Mother, "You know how you used to say you couldn't sew on a button? I just realized—*anyone* can sew on a button—including you, right?''

"Sure," she said, with a grin, "but I wasn't gonna get stuck doing all that!" She had had no interest in competing with me for the title of Sewing Queen, but I had been sufficiently caught up in the race for men's approval that I felt smug about beating Mother at a game she wasn't even playing.

Some traditional therapists believe that intense mother-daughter competition for males' attention is inevitable and healthy, and that the competition is crucial in helping the daughter escape her "enmeshment" with her mother and enter the "real, public world" represented by her father. This belief is not true, however. It is childish to believe that loving father more must mean loving mother less; that belief is fed by the myth that men are superior—so why would anyone *want* to stay close to mother?

Because women are devalued, both teenaged boys and girls are driven to prove they're different and separate from their mothers; a daughter wants to show how different she is from her mother, but she also resents her mother (perhaps unconsciously) for bearing the message that both of them are less worthy than men.

You may want to think back over key moments in your childhood when you were disobedient and rebellious against your mother. Ask yourself whether you might have been resisting some of the traditionally feminine things that your mother felt she should teach you. Lori, who now has two children, bristled every time her mother gave her recipes or cooking advice:

> I felt like she was telling me that, without her help, I'd be a lousy cook. One day, a woman at work was talking about how much she hates to cook, and it hit me: *I* hate to cook, too! All those times when I was a kid, my mother would call me into the kitchen, with a big grin on her face, and say, "Let's bake some cookies together!" I think she thought that's what mothers were supposed to do. I never wanted to bake, but I didn't want to hurt her feelings. Now I know that I always hated working in the kitchen, and I resented her for acting like it was so much fun.

Like many daughters, Lori felt betrayed by her mother's participation in the myth of men's superiority; she thought her mother's cooking was a sign of submission to men's expectations for women to do the cooking. The recognition of that myth as a source of the trouble is the first step toward overcoming our feeling that mother has betrayed us.

DESPAIR

In Chapter 2, I told the story of Ellen, who despaired of pleasing her mother, Sue, in regard to Ellen's trip with her boyfriend. If despair is the major troublesome feeling you have about your mother, you may want to review the story of what Ellen and Sue did to overcome that despair.

In addition to being concerned about not pleasing mother, daughters despair, often unconsciously, because they see their mothers as victims and feel powerless to help them. In approximately one-third of North American families, the father physically abuses the mother; in a larger number of families, he humiliates her. Here, the daughter's dilemma is even more painful. At age thirty, Alison looked back on her adolescence with a father who frequently insulted her mother:

> It tore me apart. I hated him for insulting her, and that made me want to side with her. But I fled from the humiliation-by-association. When Dad intimidated Mom, I hated her for not standing up for herself. To me, her weakness meant that all of us women had to suffer our shame in silence.

For many daughters, decades pass before they realize how the myths of male superiority and the dynamics of male domination may have operated in their family and why their mothers deferred to their fathers in important ways. You can start to understand by asking your mother what she thought would have happened if she had refused to be so deferent. A woman who asked her mother that question reported: "Mother said that she knew she had more sense about managing money than Dad, but she let him make the financial decisions because she didn't want to make him feel like he wasn't the man of the house."

Because children usually feel powerless to help their mothers, they are likely to respond to their mothers' victimization by developing behavior problems or becoming detached. Many children, however, hold on to the feeling that they ought to be able to protect and save their mothers. Daughters are particularly likely to feel that way, because of their nurturant self-image. For these children, feelings of powerlessness can lead to despair, and these feelings can be carried through a lifetime. Often adult daughters do not realize that they are no longer powerless.

Marianne, a Black civil rights activist, realized how deeply distressed she was because of her inability when she was a child to stop her mother's suffering at the hands of a racist employer:

> Mama and I had always talked about some of the awful things that white people did to our people, and Mama's teaching was what made me become so active in the civil rights movement. But sometimes I hated being around her when she'd come home from work worn out from fighting off the sexual advances of her foreman. I couldn't stand to think of her suffering and not be able to help, so I'd just shut my feelings off.

At age 36, Marianne reached a crisis in her life. The more people she had helped through her civil rights work, the more she despaired about her past failure to help her mother. When she assisted an older Black woman in winning a sexual harassment suit before a local Human Rights Commission, Marianne realized that sexual harassment was one of the problems her mother had had to deal with; she could no longer avoid seeing how, for years, she had distanced herself from her mother's pain because she was powerless to help. Now, at last, she had the power and therefore felt no need to pull away from her mother's suffering.

Marianne called her mother and asked to come for a visit, during which she explained her insight. "Mama wasn't surprised," she said. "She'd known all along why I backed off. But *I* felt better for knowing what had come between us, and after that I didn't have to keep my distance so much."

At difficult times in our own lives, we may despair when we find mother doesn't give us what we want and we don't know why. Because mothers so often hide their troubles, we can't figure out why mother is emotionally distant, try though we might. Those are usually the most important times to ask mother directly what is going on in *her* life. One of my students realized, soon after having a baby, that her mother wasn't meeting *her* needs because she had other problems on her mind. The student had been longing for her mother's approval of the way she took care of the baby, and she had been disappointed when her mother said nothing about it. She saw the reason when her mother and grandmother came together for a visit:

Part of this visit is to make sure that Grandma has a chance to see her great-granddaughter. All along I have been hoping that my mom would say, "You are doing a fine job with Alexandra," while she herself has been searching for reassurance from me that she is being patient and nurturant with her mother.

This kind of understanding teaches us that mother "neglects" us not because we're bad, not because she disapproves or doesn't care, but because she is a human being who is trying hard to cope within the narrow boundaries of the supernurturant female role. Despairing daughters must realize that those narrow boundaries and women's lack of power in the wider society limit both mothers' ability to meet their daughters' needs and daughters' ability to protect their mothers.

ANGER

Anger is a big part of so many mother-daughter relationships partly because mother-blaming encourages it and partly because anger is a common reaction to any unpleasant feeling. When we feel ambivalence, betrayal, despair, guilt, or sadness toward our mothers, we are likely to get angry at them for "making" us feel those ways. As we learned in Chapter 2, an important step in understanding and overcoming our anger is to identify the underlying feelings that may be fueling the fire. What follows are some of the most common anger-provoking situations that daughters encounter with their mothers.

"I Can Never Please Her"

We've already looked at some examples of the daughter's need to please her mother, in order to show that mother has raised a good daughter (Myth One).

A painful situation is that of the overweight daughter, who gets caught in the conflict between her mother's need to have a "presentable" daughter and her own struggles to become independent and develop a sense of identity. The mother of an overweight daughter feels inept because her daughter doesn't fit the current feminine ideal, so she thinks she ought to do something; she may also worry that being overweight harms her daughter's health. But her offers of advice only highlight the daughter's "failure" of self-control, increase her self-loathing, and establish mother as a handy target for all of this frustration. Twenty-year-old Amanda was one of my clients and told the following story:

> Mother wanted me to lose weight for my own sake, sure—but also for *her*, and I couldn't stand being her route to her club ladies' praise: "How nice! Amanda has finally lost some weight!" I felt like a piece of meat.

Using some of the techniques in this book, Amanda finally sat down for a heart-to-heart talk with her mother:

> I knew that basically Mother cared about me a lot, and telling her to get off my back hadn't worked, so I took a different tack: I tried to find out about *her* point of view. I asked her to stop talking about what being overweight might do to *me*, and asked her what my extra poundage meant to *her*. At first, she thought it had nothing to do with her own feelings. But when I asked directly if she felt like a failure for not being able to produce a slim daughter, she burst into tears and said, "I don't know what I've done to drive you to eat so much. Do you eat because you're unhappy, or is it just that I never taught you enough self-control? And also, if you're too fat, you'll never get a husband, and I'll never have any grandchildren."

Once her mother's worries were out in the open, the two women could talk about how unfair it was for both of them to be judged —or to judge themselves—by the shape of Amanda's body. They became partners. Amanda reported:

> Mother sometimes still says she wishes I would lose weight; but she doesn't hate me for being "proof" of her failure as a mother, and I don't feel like she's trying to control my eating habits simply for *her* selfish reasons.

I have heard similar stories of daughters who believe their mothers "hate" them for marrying out of their faith, for choosing not to have a child, or for choosing women as lovers. Daughters in such situations often deal with their mother's disapproval or discomfort by intellectualizing or attacking her: "She's being irrational!" "She's homophobic!" "She cares more about what her super-religious brother thinks than about how I feel!"

A daughter's choice of partner or decision not to have children can threaten her mother, but eliminating mother's and daughter's *misinterpretations* of each other's feelings can reduce some of their pain.

A daughter who had been married for five years to a man of a different religion told me that her mother hated both her and her husband. I had talked to her mother and knew that she did not hate her daughter but considered herself a failure for not having raised a daughter who would marry within their faith; her mother said openly that this was a question of feelings—of failure, of fear that she would somehow be punished, and so on. Her daughter raged about her mother's hypocrisy and irrationality.

"Your mother never claims that her reaction is logical," I told the daughter, "but what's most important is that you both love each other and want to reduce the tension between you. The one thing you never do is to let each other know you care. Each of you clings to a five-year-old grudge, and although it's been an excruciating time for you both, perhaps you can now create a calmer kind of connection. Why don't you begin by assuming that she doesn't hate you or want you to feel guilty but does want to get along better with you. You know, *she* believes that *you* hate her. I never saw such a family for avoiding showing that they care."

The other daughter in the family had said something similar to her mother, and the next time mother and daughter talked on the telephone, the tension was reduced. Each woman felt less rejected, and each was willing to believe that the other wanted to reestablish a connection. They have not simply lived happily ever after, but their recognition of each other's desire for acceptance and for reconciliation has helped repair some of the hurt from the past.

A mother's negative reaction when her daughter makes a nontraditional life choice can so upset the daughter that she doesn't give her mother credit for having good intentions. Most mothers want their daughters to be happy, and mothers who cling to traditional beliefs believe that the quickest route to happiness is the most traditional one. Fortunately, daughters are finding ways to show their mothers that the traditional route does not necessarily bring happiness and that nontraditional ones sometimes do. Help began to come with Betty Friedan's *The Feminine Mystique*, in which traditional women described their dissatisfaction with their lives, and help continues to come both from individual women's stories and from systematic research revealing, for instance, that marriage, childrearing, and other traditional choices are not good for everyone.

"She Knows Things I Don't Want To Hear"

Part of a mother's role is to warn her daughter when there is danger ahead. Unfortunately, that makes mother the bearer of the bad news, news the daughter may not want to hear. When I was a very young woman, my mother told me that a man I was involved with had hugged her "too closely." I pooh-poohed her concern: "Oh, Mom, you don't understand. He's just a warm person —and he's European. That's how they act." He turned out to be a womanizer of the most deceitful sort—but I hadn't wanted to hear her warning because it punctured my little happiness balloon.

I had been angry, wrongly believing that my mother was abusing her power over me; what she said would have helped me if I had been able to listen rather than blame her for interfering. Daughters who are doing their very best to *start* an intimate relationship want to believe they'll live happily ever after. We don't want to hear from mothers who can foresee the misery ahead of us if we have a partner who is a batterer or an alcohol or drug abuser or a compulsive gambler or womanizer. When we do hear from them, we are pushed to acknowledge that the realm of relationships is not as safe as we want it to be. We mourn this loss of our innocence, and anger about loss—even inevitable ones—is a normal part of any mourning process. So we turn on our mothers in anger when their counsel leads to that loss.

"She's Too Bad" and "She's Too Good"

Like most daughters, you have probably sometimes resented your mother for being a poor role model and sometimes resented her for being too good a model, setting a standard you could never meet. Adult daughters resent mothers who were poor role models for tasks like childrearing. The exasperated young mother screams at her children, recognizing her mother's words and inflections, and blames her mother for failing to teach her better ways to cope.

Women's isolation from each other has made us exceedingly dependent on what we learned at mother's knee. When a daughter who is trying to create a good relationship or raise a family finds herself repeating her mother's mistakes, she may nourish a festering resentment of her mother. As a young woman told me, "When my brother and I used to fight, Mother would become hysterical and shriek that we were going to kill each other. I refuse to act that way when my kids fight, but I don't know what *to* do. I sure didn't get any clues from her."

Who, in most cases, led the daughter to believe that marriage and motherhood would be the answer to all her needs, would mean living happily ever after? In most cases, mother did some of that teaching.

Many daughters who aspire to have it all resent their mothers, who were full-time homemakers, for failing to teach them how to combine a professional career with a fulfilling family life. A mother-daughter workshop participant said:

> My mother was a Supermom, right down to baking cookies every Thursday. The way she did it, mothering was a full-time job. But now that I'm a mother *and* have a paid, full-time job, I can't for the life of me figure out how to be as good a mother as she.

When the mother has kept her own aspirations within the narrow traditional limits for women, she mirrors the poverty of possibility in her daughter's future and may draw her daughter's rage for that. Said one daughter:

> Mom did everything for Dad and for us kids, but she never did anything for herself. I adored her, and that narrowed my vision of what I could be, because I was so intent on watching her as a great mother that I didn't learn much about the richness and variety of life choices from her.

Daughters may find it maddening that their mothers seem to handle so easily the tasks that the daughters find difficult. Rarely does a woman find marriage or childraising easy. If your mother tried to conceal from you her difficulties, dilemmas, or problems, she may even have become afraid to acknowledge them to herself. You may feel that she sailed through all her problems; you may have thought something was wrong with you when you could not sail smoothly through your thorny problems.

When you "fail" in this way, you may resent your mother for having protected you from reality, for leaving you unprepared to be a wife and mother, for not showing you how to cope. You may feel even more isolated from your supposedly perfect mother than from other women, at a time when you most need to turn to her for advice, information, and compassion. Rebecca felt this way about her mother and finally told her so:

> Mom was shocked to learn how afraid I was to tell her about my insecurity about motherhood because I saw her as such an example of perfection. She'd tried so hard not to "burden" me by telling the truth about some of the difficulties of being a mother. But once she really understood that her perfect image was making me upset, out came story after story of her own struggles. She was relieved to tell me, and very gradually I began to stop hating her for being perfect.

If your mother gets tense when you tell her you are frustrated as a wife or mother, don't assume that her tension reflects her disapproval of you. She may be feeling ashamed for not being able to teach you how to flourish in those roles or for not having helped you avoid the traps and limitations she knows all too intimately.

"She's So Critical Of Me Sometimes"

We want always to be able to lean on our mothers. The endless nurturance myth is so powerful that we feel enraged when we don't get what we want from them. Less commonly acknowledged than the *mother* who can't let go of her *daughter* is the fury of the adult daughter who expects endless nurturance from her mother when the mother is looking for some rest from the long decades of maternal responsibility.

In a brilliant paper called "We Are Not Your Mothers," social worker Rachel Josefowitz Siegel writes that people expect all older women to be motherly, so we even turn to older women who are *not* our mothers, expecting understanding and advice—and getting angry if it's not forthcoming; when our own mother fails us, we can't imagine that she might want a break from advising and supporting.

After I read Siegel's paper, I caught myself turning to my mother and other older women for support, without letting them know that I'd gladly return the favor. Once I realized this and started asking, "And now, how are *you*?" I heard about both sorrows and joys I hadn't suspected they felt. Asking our mothers that question, and truly wanting to hear their answer, decreases their resentment of us; we now are offering something back to them.

Certain times in our lives place us at special risk for feeling undernurtured. When a mother offers advice about baby care, her daughter assumes that her mother thinks she's incompetent. Only if her mother can describe some of the uncertainties she herself felt at such a time is her daughter likely to understand that her mother's offer of advice is not a sign that her mother thinks she's doing badly. When Erica's mother did not volunteer that information, Erica took matters into her own hands:

> I couldn't stand it any more. She kept showing me how to change Tammy's diapers, how to burp her, how to hold her. Until Mom came to visit, I thought I was doing okay.

When Erica finally got up the nerve to tell her mother how she was feeling, she learned that her mother had felt just as insecure with her first child.

We are especially vulnerable to feeling undernurtured when an intimate relationship ends. A mother who seems cold or withholding at such a time may have a host of reasons other than that she doesn't care. If she thought you and your partner were poorly matched, she may be biting her tongue to keep from saying, "I always thought you were wrong for each other." Or she may be afraid of seeming intrusive, or she may simply not know what to say or do—a typical feeling for anyone trying to respond to someone else's loss. If the relationship that ended was anything other than a traditional, heterosexual, legal marriage, she may feel out of her element and be particularly unsure about the right thing to say. Knowing these possible explanations won't stop you from longing for her support, but they will give you some ideas to consider in understanding her behavior.

Anger is such a powerful emotion that we're hard-pressed to settle down and figure out what lies beneath it. And we're at a greater loss if the object of our anger can't explain *her* behavior. Consider the following story of how a daughter-in-law's anger at her mother-in-law's hostility toward her was based on mistaken explanations:

> My mother-in-law never seemed to think that anything I did was good enough for her son, Harold. She raved about the presents that "Harold" gave her, although she knew that I had shopped for them. "I'm so unfortunate," she'd moan, "because daughters-in-law just never treat you

well." This hurt, because I went out of my way to be warm and attentive to her. After 25 years, I simply gave up.

Then, one Christmas Eve, the family asked her to talk about her early childhood. Ruth's father was a rich, charming, but good-for-nothing man. Ruth's parents left her and their older son in Ireland when they came to the United States to build a new life. Ruth spent most of the first five years of her life with her grandmother. "Did your parents write to you from America?" I asked Ruth. "No," she said, "because I couldn't read. And I forgot what my father looked like."

According to Ruth, "When I was nearly five years old, my brother and I were put, unaccompanied, on a ship coming to America. When we landed at Ellis Island, I recognized my mother but not my father. As they rushed toward me, I asked my mother, 'Where is my father?' My father was rarely home and was very distant from us emotionally.

"My mother had a suitor who adored her, but she would not leave my father, because she was afraid that her suitor might abuse me; that was what *her* stepfather had done to her."

Trapped in a loveless marriage in a foreign country, burdened with financial worries and a husband who was not a good provider, Ruth's mother had little energy and love to give Ruth. And her father gave Ruth nothing at all.

Hearing the tale did not make Suzanne, the daughter-in-law, feel more accepted by her mother-in-law, but it did make clear to her a very important point: Ruth's treatment of her was largely a manifestation of her miserable early life, since her childhood experiences had left her feeling empty, hurt, and cheated. That did not make Suzanne more anxious to spend time with Ruth, but it helped take the sting out of Ruth's rejection of her.

GUILT

Daughters describe feeling guilty about not making up to their mothers the isolation, the devaluation, and the humiliation they have endured because of being women and of being mothers. Our impotence in this regard damages our sense of power to affect the world. Still worse, we feel guilty when we realize that we, too, have often joined in demeaning mother.

A daughter often knows that her mother is unhappy but feels she cannot help, as in the example of Marianne, the civil rights worker, in the section on "Despair."

That other people or institutions have caused our mother's

unhappiness doesn't keep us from feeling bad about our limited ability to help, especially if mother seems to have sacrificed *her* life and happiness to do all she could for us. Jody, who is now 41 years old, writes:

> About five years ago, something I'd barely noticed suddenly jumped right out at me. My otherwise lovely father had a habit of putting my mother down. I can't tell you how many times I'd heard him relate the story of my mother's mispronunciation—forty years ago!—of a novelist's name. As Mom and Dad got older, while she quietly but carefully lowered the amount of fat in his diet, he started telling "jokes" about how ugly old women are. It had taken me years to see the sexism in my own family and to think about how much it had hurt my mother when I joined in the laughter at her. I felt so guilty when I realized it.

Jody had a series of long talks with her father, and once he realized how his putdowns affected his wife, he toned them down quite a bit.

It helped Jody to recognize that she had not initiated the mockery of her mother; both she and her father had been influenced by the myth of women's inferiority. Understanding that process did not mean overlooking or minimizing the ways that she and her father had participated in demeaning her mother, but it released some of the energy that had been tied up in Jody's guilt so that she could use it productively to change both her and her father's treatment of her mother. We are better able to help our mothers when we understand the causes of their problems and therefore can see what needs to be done.

The daughter who worries about her mother's happiness feels especially guilty about separating from her. As Ladonna, a college student, explained,

> I had been my mother's protector for so long that when the time came for me to go to college, I was afraid she wouldn't be able to get along without me. She isn't very happy with my father, but she thinks she shouldn't talk about that to anyone outside the family. I'm afraid she will be alone, and I feel guilty about that.

We may be able to encourage our mothers to find other confidantes, or they may do that themselves. In any case, as both Jody and Ladonna found, feeling guilty helps no one.

Another source of the guilt that daughters feel toward our mothers has arisen primarily in recent years. When we have a successful career and they do not, we feel discomfort. When Janet turned thirty and was promoted to manager at the large bank where she worked, she wrote to me:

> I feel so guilty. My mother works as a secretary just down the street. She stayed home and took care of my five brothers and sisters and me until a couple of years ago. She would have loved to have a better-paying job with more responsibility, but she never had the chances I had.

I suggested to Janet that she and her mother have a talk about what prevented her mother from getting a job earlier. Later, Janet wrote that from that talk she learned that her mother had wanted to work earlier:

> But my father said everyone would think he wasn't a good provider if he let her get a job. So, to keep him happy, she stayed at home. And here I'd been thinking that just the responsibility for taking care of us—our very existence—was to blame for my mother's lack of a chance to do what she wanted.

The phrase "I feel guilty" causes problems. Guilt has a stagnating effect; all we can do is stew in it. Guilt immobilizes us, and confessions of guilty feelings can be counterproductive, because saying "I feel guilty" makes us feel that we *have* done something to make amends. As long as we describe ourselves as terrible daughters and claim to feel guilty about it, we think we have shown what good people we are. The danger is in believing that acknowledging guilty feelings relieves us of the responsibility to right our wrongs or to figure out why we feel "guilty" when we haven't really done anything wrong. (For instance, we may feel guilty for being unable to protect mother from demeaning treatment, as discussed earlier. If that is the cause of our "guilt," we need to be aware of it so that we can direct our anger against the true impediments to mother's happiness, rather than feeling that we ourselves are the cause.)

Nikki Gerrard suggests that the word *guilt* is often used when another word is more appropriate. Next time you start to say you feel guilty, ask yourself whether another word seems better. Often, the better word is either *ashamed* or *sad*. *Shame* implies that you have failed to meet a standard, so once you know that you feel ashamed, you can take some action. You can ask, "Whose standard is this that I feel I've failed to meet? And is it a reasonable standard?" So instead of saying, "It's Sunday, and I forgot to call my mother. I feel so guilty," you can see whether "calling Mother every Sunday" is your own standard, hers, or someone else's.

Wanda asked her mother how she felt about her regular Sunday calls. To her surprise, she learned that her mother felt limited because she had to stay at home and wait for Wanda's call. Mother and daughter were able to get away from a rigid schedule that neither of them liked, while acknowledging that they both valued frequent contact. If, unlike Wanda's mother, your mother values the predictability of your Sunday calls, you can take other action. For instance, you may be able to explain to her that you sometimes don't call because you are exhausted from work or need some time alone, not because you're avoiding talking to her.

If *sad* seems a better word than *guilty* for what you feel about your mother, you probably feel somewhat estranged from her— in that case, too, you can take some action, this time in the form of strengthening the connection between you (see "A Principle For All Feelings" earlier in this chapter).

At a 1988 conference on motherhood at Goddard College, a woman named Carol told the following story the morning after she heard a presentation on mother-blaming. Carol was raised by her mother, who ran her own business during the Depression. Carol had always resented her mother for giving her gifts in the form of cash instead of her personal time. After the mother-blaming panel, Carol had telephoned her now 84-year-old mother, who lived fifteen hundred miles away, and said:

> You know I've been angry at you for fifty years because you always gave me money or presents instead of your time. Well, I just realized that, because of your experience during the Depression, from your perspective you must have thought that cash was the most valuable thing you could have given me.

According to Carol, her mother listened, was silent for a moment, and then asked in a small voice, "Does that mean you are not mad at me any more?" Carol assured her that she was not, that the purpose of the phone call was to tell her that she was *not* angry but was sad that her anger had come between them for so long. A barrier between them had been surmounted, and both mother and daughter felt better.

FEAR

Two of the primary fears of adult daughters in relation to their mothers are the fear of displeasing her (or even losing her love) and the fear of becoming like her.

Our fear of displeasing mother is intensified by the myth that women's power is dangerous: if we displease her, we feel, some horrible fate will befall us. For some daughters this fear is partly based in reality, because they have very critical, demanding mothers. But all daughters ultimately fear losing their mothers' love. The daughter in feminist writer Robin Morgan's novel, *Dry Your Smile*, says as her mother lies on her deathbed: "She does have power. She has the power not to love me." More than anyone else, mother is *supposed* to love us—and love us no matter what —so we are terrified to think that maybe she doesn't. If she won't love us now, then who will after she dies?

Surprisingly often, a daughter benefits by telling her mother how frightened she is of failing to meet her standards or of disappointing her in some way. Dina, age 33, explains why:

> My Mom was amazed that I worried so much about her opinion of me. One by one, I listed all the things about me that I thought she disapproved of, and as I did that, she recognized that her standards really are very high. But it got her thinking, just to hear how long the list was. She told me that she guessed she'd been pretty rough on me, but that hadn't been her intention. As we talked, I learned that she set such high standards because she was trying to be a good mother by making me measure up to what girls are supposed to be. She had bought into the idea that she would have failed if I weren't very sweet, patient, giving, skinny, and high-achieving though modest and unaggressive.

The fear of becoming one's mother, or becoming like one's mother, has been called *matrophobia* by poet Adrienne Rich. We fear repeating mother's mistakes. Because nobody knows better than we how abject and ashamed her disapproval makes us feel, we fear our own power to make others feel that way. Working through the mother myths on her own the year she turned forty, Arlene saw that her fear of becoming like her mother was

> a convenient focus for my fear of ending up living a very limited life and not being valued very much, like so many women of my mother's gen-

eration. That insight has made it a lot easier for me, because I realized that I wasn't afraid of *my mother;* I was afraid of being treated the way she was. I also feel less fatalistic now—where I used to know I was destined to end up like Mother, I now know I can shape my life differently. I don't have to accept the traditional "feminine" limits or put up with disrespect. I no longer have to fear that whatever happened to her will inevitably happen to me.

Particularly pronounced in North America's youth-mad culture is daughters' fear of aging, as our mothers age before our eyes.

In a similar way, Aviva, who is now in her early thirties, has been frightened by signs of age in her mother. Aviva is noticing the effects of gravity and time on her own body:

> I can't spring out of bed as fast as I used to, and I sometimes forget familiar facts. When I look at my mother, my love for her is mixed with fear, because in her face, body, and functioning I see my own future and my own mortality. And we all know that in America, old women are the least respected people.

Aviva eventually realized that her fear was exaggerated by the male superiority myth; she counteracted this myth by a conscious decision to think in terms of valuing her mother more than ever because of her experience and wisdom. This reduced her fear of her mother, because if her aging mother could have *her* respect, she feels,

> by the time I get old, maybe old women will get more respect. I'm taking one small step for me, hoping it will be one giant step for womankind.

SADNESS

Two of the most poignant causes of our sadness about our relationships with our mothers are our knowledge of what has been missing in their lives and our sense of the distance between them and us.

In her study of women whose mothers had died, doctor of theology Martha Robbins reported that one of her most striking discoveries was that the women mourned more over their mothers' lives than over their deaths. As one of my friends, now in her mid-thirties, said:

> I cannot tell you what pain I feel when I see how much my mother is under my father's thumb. She waits at home every day for the moment when he walks in the door after work. All her energy is focused on his dinner. What should she make? Will he like it? Will he even notice it? I could get angry and say she's neurotic or cowardly or stupid—and I do all those things sometimes; but mostly I just feel so darned sad for her.

For such sadness, we must try to come to terms with our own limitations. Yes, we can urge Mom to get a job, to do volunteer work, to think of herself as a worthy person for reasons other than her great pot roast. But since she was raised in an era quite different from ours, possibly nothing we can do will change the way she lives.

What we *can* do, though, is to try to change how she *feels*. My friend acknowledged, to herself, how boring her mother's life seemed to her, but then tried to see her mother's point of view. Raised in a society in which a good woman sits and waits for her man to come home for dinner, her mother's self-worth revolves very much around her pot roast. So, my friend began to ask her mother about pot roast recipes. She reports:

> I used to feel bored by conversations like that, because I—like most people—was caught up in thinking that cooking and housekeeping were unimportant, easy tasks. But now, every time she starts to talk about her recipes or her needlepoint, I remind myself that what she's really doing is trying to convince herself, and me, that she does something worthwhile. And that makes it less boring and very moving, so now my increased appreciation for what she does comes through, and I can tell that she feels that.

My friend now doesn't feel so much the need to mourn her mother's life.

My friend has also found a way to repair the mother-daughter rift caused by her accepting the myth of women's inferiority. If her mother went daily to an office, my friend wouldn't have to be so concerned about the limitations of her mother's life. In the section called "A Principle For All Feelings" earlier in this chapter, I emphasized the importance of repairing broken connections between mothers and daughters. Listen now to the story of Maria, who was saddened by what she misperceived as her mother's withdrawal of love from her:

> I told my mother in anger 18 years ago, when I was 14, that I was having a sexual relationship with another girl. Until recently, I believed that it

had taken my mother seven years to stop disapproving of me because of this. I just thought she was homophobic and condemned me for loving another girl.

But recently, I thought back to the comments my mother made years ago—"I'm concerned about your committing yourself to something that could limit your potential later in life, for which people will reject you" and "I think you'll regret not having children" (since having children was a rare option for lesbians at that time). I had blocked out what she really said back then, and all I could think of was that she hadn't simply said, "That's just terrific!" I began to wonder whether in fact she may *not* so much have disapproved as been genuinely worried about my happiness. After all, it has taken me seven years to find a partner who makes me happy, and my mother has relaxed now that she sees me in a good relationship.

Maria told her mother about her changed understanding of what had happened between them, and her mother confirmed that she had been primarily worried about Maria's happiness. She was able, too, to say that she had had to deal with some surprise and some guilt—she had worried, "Have I messed up my daughter?" —but her major concern had been for Maria's happiness.

NUMBNESS AND ALIENATION

As I described in Chapter 2, when upsetting feelings—especially but not only hopelessness—overwhelm us, we often simply go numb or feel alienated from our mothers. The story of my friend in the previous section (the woman who now appreciates her mother's pot roasts) demonstrates how our sense of hopelessness about our mothers' lives can distance us from them; so, too, can our feeling that trying yet again for greater closeness is pointless. When we don't know what else to try, and the pain of broken connections is too great, what can we do *but* go numb? I hope that some of the steps and techniques in Chapters 6 and 7 and this chapter have suggested ways that you can open new doors.

Let's look at an example of a daughter who went numb not so much from pain as from a surfeit of anger. Jocelyn and her mother, Beth, had had terrible arguments from the time Jocelyn began to approach puberty; at that time, although a psychiatrist had told them that they were competing for the attention of

Jocelyn's father, he had not told them how to work out ways to enjoy their mother-daughter relationship *aside from* the focus on the father. When I saw the mother and daughter years later at a lecture I gave on mothers and daughters, they described the father to me as a very cold man. With so little warmth and attention from him to go around, mother and daughter had competed with each other for scarce resources. But now that the daughter was an adult and could get warmth and attention outside her immediate family, the fierce mother-daughter competition wasn't so necessary.

Once Jocelyn left home, Jocelyn and Beth had masked their continuing rage at each other under what they thought was a lack of love for each other. Once Jocelyn moved away, the visits between mother and daughter were so rare that they both were afraid of spoiling them with outbursts of anger. So they held it all in, never really getting at the roots of their mutual anger, and letting the efforts to hold it in create a wall between them. Sparked by the lecture, Jocelyn and Beth worked on their relationship, and Beth wrote me a letter in which she said:

> I had always thought Jocelyn was an impossible person, and she thought the same about me. Once we realized that we had had to compete for the minimal approval of the high-status person in the family—my husband—we saw that the evil was not all within us. We had both been afraid he would reject us, which would have made us feel worthless. Recognition of those shared concerns has now created a bond between us. These days, when we are together, we don't hold anything back. When we need to argue, we argue. But the difference is that now we know there's a lot of love between us. And it's great not to have to feel numb any more in the presence of my daughter.
>
> At the ends of our visits, when the time comes for us to part, we can now say to each other that parting is always hard, that we usually feel there is much left undone and unsaid, but that we love each other.

In similar ways, as described in the section on anger, identifying the feelings that underlie numbness and alienation—and the myths that fed those feelings—enables mothers and daughters to build bridges between them.

All of the stories in this chapter are about different ways that mothers and daughters have tried to mend their relationships, with varying degrees of success. Naturally, mothers and daughters will differ in the techniques they use and the pacing of the repair work, but most mother-daughter relationships—like richly woven tapestries—are worth mending.

9 ❦ *It Is Only A Door*

> Emotionally healthy women who have the best
> connections with their mothers also have the best
> connections with other women.
>
> —Dr. Janet Surrey

> [I]f we step outside socially imposed injunctions, then
> . . . daughters and their mothers wield powers for one
> another's help as well as harm. They may even make of
> one another revolutionaries.
>
> —Nancy Mairs

AS WOMEN, OUR vision of ourselves, our feelings about ourselves, our pride in ourselves are inevitably affected by our vision of, and feelings about, other women. We are all the more profoundly affected by women close to us, women with shared experiences or similar features or gestures—most especially our mothers. Some days I notice that the way I move my hands or the inflection in my voice is my mother's. And because I love and respect her, the gesture and inflection somehow seem right and fitting; they have a place, they belong in the world. Without feeling a need to be like her in all ways, I can enjoy aesthetically and emotionally the symmetry, the resonance that comes from this. In part, it's a way of connecting, of weaving a strong and richly textured cloth that stretches between us and through time. The weaving began before us and will continue after us.

Sharing strengthens us. Like it or not, we *are* involved with the woman who raised us, whether we want to be like her or want to avoid being like her at all costs. But even for avoiders, all daughters can gain from discovering what features, what gestures, what styles, what values we *can* love or respect—rather than hate and reject—in our mothers. And as Pulitzer Prize-winning author Alice Walker has written, "We are together, my child and I. Mother and child, yes, but *sisters* really, against whatever denies us all that we are." Sharing is easier once we see our shared humanity and our shared dilemmas beyond the myths.

BEYOND THE MYTHS

In a sense, much of this is about forgiveness—of our mother and ourselves—because we have been misguided by the myths of mother-blame. This is about accepting the only-human nature of both mothers and daughters in a world that simultaneously raises us to heights of an unattainable ideal and consigns us to some-times appalling depths of devaluation, demoralization, and pow-erlessness.

As I have said, going beyond the myths allows us to think of our mother as someone other than "My mother, the mother—the woman who is only my mother and of no significance apart from that." When you can think beyond her as a mother, you'll find that all kinds of questions come to your mind. Feminist author Judith Arcana heard her mother's answer to an unusual question and was astonished by what she learned:

> One day, when I visited her as she lay in bed looking particularly frail, smaller and lighter than she ought . . . she told me about a friend of hers who'd taken a psychology class . . . [and] found the class silly . . . . The instructor had asked each person in the class to name an animal they'd like to be, if they could choose. . . . I said, "Come on, Ma, think about it —what animal *would* you be, if you could?" She thought for a time and said, "I'd like to be that big yellow spotted cat, you know, the one that runs faster than all the others."
>
> I was so unprepared for this revelation that I could only cry, cry for the contrast between the bedridden woman and the golden yellow cat. My mother the martyr, a woman who put her husband and children before her from the day of her marriage, would be a cheetah, racing over the African savannah.

Think over your relationship with your mother since you became an adult. Imagine how different that story might have been if:

- you hadn't suspected that every indication of closeness be-tween you was really evidence that

1. your needs and hers were too great (Myth Six);
2. your mother was trying to control you (Myth Eight); and
3. wanting the closeness itself was wrong (Myth Seven);

- you hadn't had to worry that, even as a grownup, any false move might humiliate your mother (Myth One) and might invalidate, in her mind, the kind of life she has led (Myth Five);
- society hadn't made it hard for you to acknowledge your "unfeminine" sexual and aggressive feelings (Myth Three) so that you needed to *blame* your mother for either appearing to handle her feelings so easily and skillfully that you could never match her *or* for handling her own feelings so poorly that she taught you nothing helpful for handling your own;
- society didn't judge you so much on the basis of your wife-and-mother roles (Myths One and Two), making you either blame your mother for setting impossibly high standards by her own Supermom example or blame her for being a lousy role model;
- you hadn't expected her to know automatically what your needs were, and to meet them (Myths Two and Four);
- you hadn't assumed that she could have been—and could still be—a good mother if she'd only listened to the experts instead of to her own instincts or doing what *her* mother did (Myth Six);
- you didn't feel torn *between* allegiance to your mother and allegiance to your father; between allegiance to your mother and allegiance to your husband; and our culture didn't push us so hard always to choose the man (Myth Five);
- your mother hadn't been so limited in her options (Myth Five) that *you* feel guilty about your own success;
- you weren't afraid that any show of strength or assertiveness by your mother was a sign of her destructive power (Myth Nine).

THERE'S VALUE IN EVERY STEP

As you begin to work on your mother-daughter relationship and choose the techniques and timing that feel right for you, remember to regard each step you take as valuable in and of itself. Don't aim to settle everything in One Big Talk. Go slowly, and don't try to do too much at once; if you do, you'll be working under too much pressure, and your efforts will be counterproductive. And *don't* think ahead to how many steps remain to be taken. I used to wake up in the morning, look at the huge list of tasks I had to accomplish during the coming day, and feel exhausted before I got out of bed. Then I had what seemed at the time to be an amazing insight: I didn't have to perform *all* of those tasks simultaneously every minute of the day. When I pictured the day as a long line rather than as a single point, I realized that I only had to do one thing at each point, and no human being should be expected to do more than that. I also saw that, even if I didn't finish on that day everything from my list, I would still have done some things, and there was value in that.

Be sure you don't make the mistake of assuming that this is a recipe book of easy steps that work magic—and that something must be wrong with you if you don't immediately succeed. This book is intended to suggest a way to begin to make changes in your mother-daughter relationship. As you begin to think differently about your mother and are less burdened by mother-blaming myths, your attitude toward her will change for the better. Chances are she will sense that and will respond.

So realize that each step will help you along toward your final goal, but each step will also bring its own benefits that will probably stay with you. For instance, humanizing your image of your mother will be a relief, even if you never approach her directly about the problems between you. A mother who lived in a series of foster homes as a child and raised four children alone might be so bitter or overwhelmed that her daughters cannot discuss directly with her the problems that come between them; but at least her daughters can understand more about how unrealistic they were to blame themselves for their mother's rages or depressions.

Remember, too, that even defining your "ultimate goal" for a relationship is tricky; in any relationship, both people are always changing, so that a step may not end where you thought it would. Homespun philosopher David Friendly has said that working on a relationship is like being on a turntable: you set out walking, and by the time you finish a step, the ground beneath you is pointing in a different direction.

Keep in mind the limitations of the approach I have described. In a single book it is not possible to describe every type of mother-daughter problem or anticipate every result if you do try these techniques. Furthermore, the degree and speed of your success in using these techniques will *not* depend just on you; they will depend partly on the history of your relationship with your mother, what your father or your mother's other partner is or was like, whether or not you have siblings—and if so, what they are like—how much support you can get from other people while working on these issues, the fragility or strength of your self-esteem, and the degree of stability in the rest of your life and your mother's life. Your race, religion, and social class, your ethnic roots, your sexual orientation, your age, and your state of health will probably have important effects, too (although thorough research on *how* those important sources of variation work remains to be done). For instance, in a 1988 symposium on biracial children, Barbara and Robin Miller pointed out that Blacks more than whites in North America regard wisdom as coming from the older generation, and so Black daughters may be more inclined than white ones to feel genuinely respectful toward their mothers.

Remember, too, that if your mother has died or for some other reason you can't talk to her, you can modify most of the techniques I have suggested.

We often hear that people never really change; but that should not lead to dire predictions about changing your mother-daughter relationship. Although people's basic characters do tend to stay the same, some people do make significant changes under the right circumstances. Lifelong alcoholics stop drinking altogether; some people make major career changes; some become more mellow and some more assertive over time. Psychologist Karen Howe reports that nearly every student who wrote her mother's biography said, "I feel like I have met my mother for the first time"; that is a major change that can give rise to even more significant ones.

Furthermore, we don't usually need major character changes in mother-daughter relationships, because the characters are not the major sources of trouble. Instead, we must understand the need to go beyond the myths and learn a different set of questions and procedures for understanding our relationships.

THE FEAR AND THE EXHILIRATION OF OPENING DOORS

Beware, because getting to know your mother or seeing her in a new way will change you—at the very least, you'll learn more about yourself. No one can predict how much or in what ways you will change; the changes may be sudden or gradual, immediate or delayed.

A student in my course on "Mothers" experienced a sudden, dramatic change after reading the first book I had assigned—Adrienne Rich's *Of Woman Born*. The student wrote:

> Since adolescence, matrophobia—the fear of becoming one's mother—has been a significant force impelling me toward change and growth. My mother's barrage of criticisms, her reserved self-expression, and her tears provoked by most confrontations were interpreted by me with ease: "God forbid I should be as mistrustful as my mother. Or as fragile and weak."
> . . . I did not attribute my mother's depression and plaguing self-doubts to the daily war she waged. Instead, I judged her acts as compromises and struggled with a nagging fear of powerlessness in the face of ardent wishes and goals for my future. I was not thinking to acknowledge her role as victim but freely identifying her victimization of others.

For another woman, whom I had interviewed, the change was delayed. She telephoned me weeks later to say:

> Last night I began asking myself why I only focus on the ways my mother has upset me. Then I remembered what you had said about how easy it is to blame our mothers, and I was flooded with memories about good, funny, or touching things my mother had done for me. Then I had a moment of precious insight. I remembered that they used to call *my mother's* mother the Iron Woman. My mother's mother was so cold to *her* that I guess it's a miracle that *my* mother was ever able to show me any warmth at all.

Yet as Adrienne Rich says in her poem "Prospective Immigrants Please Note," there are no guarantees about where change will lead, for "The door itself/makes no promises./It is only a door." But it is likely that when you walk through the door that leads away from mother-blame, you will experience a surge of energy, as what was bound up in your own mother-blame is set free. If you feel better about your mother, and if your relationship with her improves, consider taking one more step, putting some of that increased energy to use in wiping out the myths. Some of you will talk to one or two other mothers or daughters at a time, telling them what you have learned and suggesting what they might do in their own relationships. Others of you will refuse to listen to jokes that demean mothers and women in general, will challenge the opinions of scientists and other "experts," or constantly question casual comments based on assumptions about women's limitless ability to nurture, their limitless neediness, or their destructive use of power.

I hope that some of you will directly challenge and oppose the institutions that perpetuate the myths. The position of mothers and all women will be enhanced by every step you take toward ensuring equal pay and reproductive freedom for women, every improvement in daycare facilities and facilities for ill or older people, every blow you strike against sexual harassment or against the devaluation of old women and poor women, every struggle you join to protect the rights of disabled women, women of color, immigrant women, lesbian and bisexual women, or women patients in the mental health system.

A BEGINNING

Let me end by telling you about one of the small steps I took years ago toward my mother. One day my son, Jeremy, then seven years old, had had a difficult day at school. That evening, my mother telephoned long distance from her home and talked to Jeremy for awhile. A few minutes later, Mother called back because she was not sure whether I knew about the upsetting incident that Jeremy had described to her. She wanted me to be alert to any particular needs he might have that night. She then asked to speak with Jeremy again, just so that they could have a pleasant chat and she could remind him that she cared about him during this stressful time.

Now people may roll their eyes and talk about overprotective, interfering grandmothers, or, at best, fleetingly register the fact that Grandma had done a nice thing for her grandson. I put myself in Jeremy's place and imagined how I would feel if my grandmother took the trouble to call me back just to talk, at a time when I felt I had had a rotten day.

I *could* say that my mother did a nice thing. Or I could say that my mother did something out of deep compassion and genuine caring about other people. To call what she did "naturally feminine and nurturant," just part of a mother's job, would not do her justice. Few people do such compassionate, considerate things anyway, and no one is better served if, when mothers do them, we hardly take notice because it is what we believe they are supposed to do.

That evening I found myself filled with pride and warmth for my mother. I appreciated how much we women have to work with, even if our nurturance and compassion have sometimes been taken advantage of and used against us. Taking care not to let ourselves be abused or ignored because of how we are, we can feel proud of our warmth and strength, and proud of each other's. I told my mother how I felt, and she seemed surprised but warmed by my appreciation and respect for her.

When we respect our mothers more, we gain more self-respect, and when we see the injustices they have suffered, we increase our own humanity. Because we see the pain—or the potential for pain—in which we share, we also glimpse the ways we can use our common humanity and strength to empower each other. Poet Susan Griffin recalls: "I remember my fury at the constrictions placed upon me as a child. I remember the look of innocence on my daughter's face. . . . And that when I realized I'd given birth to a girl my heart opened to myself and all the suffering of women seemed unreasonable to me."

In the past, the pain of that opening and viewing has led many women to retreat to the traditional rules for raising and restricting daughters; that retreat was encouraged by a society that refused to acknowledge its unfair treatment of women. But mothers' and daughters' support of each other, women's support of other women, and women's and men's growing acknowledgment of this unfairness give support to all of us. With such support, we can face the longings in our own and our mothers' pasts and shape something better for our mothers, ourselves, other women, and the coming generations. As you begin, I wish you well.

Appendix A:
Expressive Training

The most important principle of expressive training is that someone who wants to improve her relationship with you can do it better under the following conditions:

- She is not bombarded by threats, demands, or criticisms;
- She is not overwhelmed by long, intellectual discussions or explanations of problems between you;
- She knows what concrete steps she can take.

The techniques for expressive training are straightforward and specific. Don't expect yourself to be able to implement them perfectly right away, however, for some of them are deceptively simple and require a great deal of practice and thought. The techniques are:

(1) Choose mother or daughter to be the "actor" for a scene.

(2) Have the actor write at the top of a sheet of paper a very brief description of a typical problem—for example, "Mom gives my twins milk, even though I have told her that they are allergic to it."

(3) Have the actor identify and write down one, two, or three *feelings* she has about that problem—for example, "anger" and "worry."

(4) Have the actor write down a *concrete cause* for each feeling. Concrete causes exclude threats, demands, criticisms, and

intellectualization. They *must* be events that everyone would agree have taken place. For instance, the actor cannot write, "because my mother doesn't care about my kids' health" or "because Mom thinks I'm an incompetent mother"; those are criticisms and leave too much room for interpretation. A concrete cause would be "because she gave them milk after I had shown her the doctor's report, which confirmed that they are allergic to milk."

> *Special Note About Anger:* Since anger is a secondary emotion, a concrete cause of anger would be "When she gives them milk, I worry that they will get another ear infection, and because she's already given them the milk by the time I find out about it, I feel helpless, and *feeling helpless makes me angry.*"

(5) Have someone play the "receiver." If the actor is the daughter, the receiver will play her mother, and vice versa. Instruct the receiver to try to prevent the actor from focusing on and describing her feelings and their causes. The receiver can criticize, change the subject, weep, intellectualize, or do anything to try to divert the actor from simply stating her feelings and their causes.

(6) Before the role-play begins, instruct the actor to name her feelings and explain their causes. She should write them down. When the role-play begins, she is to try to avoid doing *anything* other than state what she has written on her chart. This gives her practice in avoiding threats, demands, or criticisms or getting involved in intellectualization or changes of topic. Advise the actor that an excellent way for her to end a scene is to say, in the face of the receiver's onslaught, "I just wanted you to know that that is how I feel and that is why I feel that way. You don't need to respond right now." This approach is useful not only in role-play but also in real life, of course. Your real-life "receiver" will probably need time to think about what you have said, and out of respect for her—as well as in the hope of making real change—you need to grant her that time to absorb what you have said.

(7) Before beginning the scene, the actor may wish to tell the receiver what kinds of responses she usually gets from her mother or daughter.

(8) Ask the other group members to be "directors." Each director makes notes about what actually happens during the role-play and gives the actor feedback of the following kinds, once the scene has been played out:

Feelings—"You said before the role-play that you had two feelings. During the scene, you stated the first one very clearly, but you didn't mention the second."

Causes—"You explained clearly and concretely the cause of your first feeling, but you didn't describe the cause of your second one," or "You described the cause of your second feeling, but you didn't say what feeling it produced in you."

Off-track Behavior—"Near the end of the scene, you made a threat when you told your mother you'd never bring the kids to see her again," or "You didn't stick to your feelings and their causes. You let her involve you in an intellectual discussion about the merits of different kinds of allergy tests."

Appendix B:
Guidelines for
Mother–Daughter Interviews

THE INTERVIEW QUESTIONS*

1. When and where were you born?
2. What were your parents like? (such as ethnic, religious, economic background)
3. What were the important influences on you as a child?
4. What was your relationship like with your mother? your father?
5. What is/was your relationship like with my father?
6. Did you work outside the home?
7. What are your main interests?
8. Are there some things that you have always wanted to do but never had the opportunity?
9. Student: Add two questions here of your own.

QUESTIONS ANSWERED BY STUDENTS*

1. What are your earliest memories of your mother?
2. What is your relationship like with her—in the past and now?
3. What messages or advice did she give you about being a woman?

Questions designed by Karen G. Howe, expanded from material in Sue Cox (Ed.), *Female Psychology: The Emerging Self*, 2nd ed. New York: St. Martin's Press, 1981.

4. In what ways are you like or unlike your mother?
5. What have you learned from doing this biography assignment? Are there areas of your mother's life experience that you have learned about for the first time? Do you have any new understandings about your mother now?
6. How do you feel about your mother now?
7. What was your mother's reaction to being interviewed?
8. Other comments.

ADDITIONAL QUESTIONS FOR MOTHER'S BIOGRAPHY†

1. While you were raising your children, what did *you* think that being a good mother meant? What did you think a good mother should do?
2. What was hardest for you about being a mother? What was your worst fear?
3. Did the experts ever give you information that went against what you thought or felt was right? Did you ever get different information from different experts?
4. Did you think that mothering should come naturally to you? If so, how did that belief affect you?
5. As a new mother, how did you feel (both positive and negative factors)? (If she doesn't raise these issues, inquire about whether she had feelings of isolation, fatigue, loss of freedom, fear, need for help of various kinds, concerns about changes in her marriage, concerns about her identity or about the interruption of her ability to carry out her dreams or ambitions. Ask also about whether she felt love, closeness, delight, or fascination with her children.)
6. Did you want your daughter (me) to be like you? Why or why not? If yes, in what ways? If not, in what ways did you most want her to be different from you?
7. How do you feel now when you look at your daughter and notice that in some way she *is* like you?
8. How do you feel now when you look at your daughter and notice that she is different from you in some way?

†Suggested by Paula J. Caplan.

9. Is it hard for you to support your daughter when she needs support that you never got or when she has opportunities that you never had? How does that feel?

10. How do you feel when your daughter does something untraditional or unusual?

11. Did you ever feel that your daughter betrayed you or let you down?

12. When have you most felt estranged from your daughter (or even felt that you had lost her)? Did that change? If so, how and why?

13. What are the pros and cons of having your daughter ask you for your advice or want your approval?

14. (If she is or was married) Have your husband and daughter ever seemed to take sides against you? Have they ever made you feel left out or inadequate or inferior?

15. What values or lessons do you hope you have imparted to your daughter?

❧ Notes

The numbers preceding notes refer to page numbers on which the quotes appear.

xi: Since I failed . . . Pat Conroy, *The Prince of Tides* (Boston: Houghton Mifflin, 1986), 94.

Chapter 1
1: How are we . . . Letty Cottin Pogrebin quoted in article by Ingeborg Day, "Daughters and Mothers," *Ms*, June 1975, 79.
1: the plot is not . . . Marcia Westkott, "Mothers and Daughters in the World of the Father," *Frontiers* 3 (1978), 16.
2: Angel in the House . . . Gerda Lerner, *The Female Experience: An American Documentary* (Indianapolis: The Bobbs-Merrill Company, 1977); Karen Payne, ed., *Between Ourselves: Letters between Mothers and Daughters, 1750–1982* (Boston: Houghton Mifflin, 1983).
4: my earlier writing . . . Caplan, *Between Women;* Caplan and Hall-McCorquodale, "Mother-Blaming" and "The Scapegoating of Mothers."
5: "She's a masochist . . ." Paula J. Caplan, *The Myth of Women's Masochism* (New York: E. P. Dutton, 1985 and New York: Signet, 1987 [paperback edition with additional chapter, "Afterword: A Warning"]).
6: Only a few books . . . Adrienne Rich, *Of Woman Born;* Judith Arcana, *Our Mothers' Daughters* (Berkeley: Shameless Hussy Press, 1979); Phyllis Chesler, *Women and Madness* (New York: Avon Books, 1973); Phyllis Chesler, *With Child: A Diary of Motherhood* (New York: Berkeley Books, 1981).
6: Some writers . . . Nancy Chodorow, *The Reproduction of Mothering: Psychoanalysis and the Sociology of Gender* (Berkeley: University of Cali-

fornia Press, 1978); Luise Eichenbaum and Susie Orbach, *Understanding Women: A Feminist Psychoanalytic Approach* (New York: Basic Books, 1983).

6: A daughter hides... Eichenbaum and Orbach, *Understanding Women*, 51.

7: *My Mother/My Self* ... Nancy Friday, *My Mother/My Self* (New York: Delacorte, 1977). For thoughtful evaluation of some of the mother-blaming literature, see Pauline Bart, "Review of Chodorow's *The Reproduction of Mothering*," in *Mothering: Essays in Feminist Theory*, ed. Joyce Trebilcot (Totowa, N.J.: Rowman and Allanheld, 1983), 147–152; and Marcia Westkott, *Mothers and Daughters*.

7: *Toward a New* ... Jean Baker Miller, *Toward a New Psychology of Women*.

7: a recent spate ... Louise Bernikow, *Among Women* (New York: Harper and Row, 1981); Judith Briles, *Woman to Woman: From Sabotage to Support* (Far Hills, N.J.: New Horizon Press, 1987); Paula J. Caplan, *Between Women: Lowering the Barriers* (Toronto: Personal Library, 1981); Paula J. Caplan and Ian Hall-McCorquodale, "Mother-Blaming in Major Clinical Journals," *American Journal of Orthopsychiatry* 55 (1985): 345–353; Paula J. Caplan and Ian Hall-McCorquodale, "The Scapegoating of Mothers: A Call for Change," *American Journal of Orthopsychiatry* 55 (1985): 610–613; Faith Conlon, Rachel daSilva, and Barbara Wilson, eds., *The Things that Divide Us* (Seattle: Seal Press, 1985); Andrea Dworkin, *Woman Hating* (New York: E. P. Dutton, 1974); Luise Eichenbaum and Susie Orbach, *Between Women* (New York: Viking, 1988); Lucy Rose Fischer, *Linked Lives: Adult Daughters and Their Mothers* (New York: Harper and Row, 1987); Karen Fite and Nikola Trumbo, "Betrayals among Women: Barriers to a Common Longing, *Lesbian Ethics* 1 (1984); Jane Flax, "The Conflict between Nurturance and Autonomy in Mother-Daughter Relationships and within Feminism," *Feminist Studies* 4 (1978): 171–189; Audre Lorde, *Sister Outsider* (Trumansburg, N.Y.: The Crossing Press, 1984); Valerie Miner and Helen Longino, *Competition: A Feminist Taboo?* (New York: The Feminist Press, 1987); Letty Cottin Pogrebin, *Among Friends* (New York: McGraw-Hill, 1987); Janice Raymond, *A Passion for Friends: Toward a Philosophy of Female Affection* (Boston: Beacon Press, 1987); Alice Walker, *In Search of Our Mothers' Gardens: Womanist Prose* (San Diego, Ca.: Harcourt, Brace, Jovanovich, 1983).

11: In general, women ... Judith Arcana, *Every Mother's Son: The Role of Mothers in the Making of Men* (Seattle: The Seal Press, 1986), 257; and Janet Surrey, "The 'Self-in-Relation': A Theory of Women's Development" (Work in Progress Paper No. 13, Wellesley, Ma.: Wellesley College, The Stone Center, 1985); and Jean Baker Miller, *Toward a New Psychology of Women* (Boston: Beacon Press, 1976).

11: the real story ... According to a Plains Indian legend (Helen Carmichael Porter, personal communication, 14 June, 1988), in order for us to develop into fully realized people, we need to experience the entire spectrum of human feelings. This range is represented by positions on a wheel. And since all humans share the same potential for feelings, in terms of the legend, we need to occupy every position on that wheel. We can occupy some positions through direct experience and others through hearing stories. Empathic listening to someone else's description of a life very different from our own can teach us about feelings and events that were previously quite foreign to us. Thus, by learning our mother's story, we occupy her space on the wheel and learn how the world—and our relationship—looks from her vantage point. In telling our own stories, we may glimpse some order in what has seemed the chaos of our lives.

16: her own mother ... Harriet Goldhor Lerner, *The Dance of Anger* (New York: Harper and Row, 1985).

Chapter 2

21: shockingly rejecting ... Zenith Henkin Gross, *And You Thought It Was All Over! Mothers and Their Adult Children* (New York: St. Martin's Press, 1985), 174.

22: rare research studies ... Lorette K. Woolsey and Laura-Lynne McBain, "Issues of Power and Powerlessness in All-Woman Groups," *Women's Studies International Forum* 10 (1987), 579–588.

25: Anger ... Crucial works to read on women and anger include: Teresa Bernardez, "Gender-Based Countertransference of Female Therapists in the Psychotherapy of Women," in Marjorie Braude, ed., *Women, Power, and Therapy: Issues for Women* (New York: Haworth, 1987), 25–39; Teresa Bernardez, "Women and Anger: Cultural Prohibitions and the Feminine Ideal (Work in Progress Paper No. 31, Wellesley, Ma.: Wellesley College, The Stone Center, 1988; Harriet Goldhor Lerner, "Sugar and Spice: The Taboos against Female Anger," *Menninger Perspective* (Winter 1977), 5–11; and Harriet Goldhor Lerner, *The Dance of Anger* (New York: Harper and Row, 1985).

25: if you expect ... Jennifer Chambers, personal communication, January 20, 1988.

28: *Women and Self-esteem* ... Linda Tschirhart Sanford and Mary Ellen Donovan, *Women and Self-Esteem: Understanding and Improving the Way We Think and Feel about Ourselves* (New York: Penguin, 1984).

32: a positive similarity ... Fischer, *Linked Lives*, 88.

36: I believe that prior ... Ruth Minden, "Glancing Backward, Looking Forward: Insights into Mothering" (Unpublished paper, Ontario Institute for Studies in Education, 1986), 3.

37: "The Female World ..." Carroll Smith-Rosenberg, "The Female World of Love and Ritual: Relations between Women in Nineteenth-Century America," *Signs: Journal of Women in Culture and Society* 1 (1985): 1–29. Please note that I am not a historian, and historical review is not a major purpose of this book. For fascinating historical perspectives, see the article by Smith-Rosenberg and the works by Elisabeth Badinter, Gerda Lerner, Jessie Bernard, and others listed in the Bibliography.

37: emotional centrality ... Smith-Rosenberg, "The Female World," 13.

37: hostility and criticism ... Smith-Rosenberg, "The Female World," 14.

37: Women, who had little . . . Smith-Rosenberg, "The Female World," 14.

37: expressions of hostility . . . Smith-Rosenberg, "The Female World," 15.

Chapter 3

39: Zenith Henkin Gross . . . Gross, *And You Thought It Was All Over!*

40: skill level . . . Ann Crittenden Scott, "The Value of Housework—for Love or Money," *Ms* 1, July 1972, 56–59. Note that these were the ratings in 1970, when the women's movement was in the air; our mothers were raising us before that time, so the esteem in which they were held would appear to have been very low.

40: "in the garden . . ." Jessie Bernard, *The Future of Motherhood* (New York: The Dial Press, 1974), x.

41: our double load . . . Esther Greenglass, "A Social-Psychological View of Marriage for Women," *International Journal of Women's Studies* 8 (1985): 24–31.

42: Paradoxically, motherhood . . . Chambers, personal communication, January 20, 1988.

42: Philip Wylie . . . Philip Wylie, *Generation of Vipers* (New York: Rinehart and Co., Inc., 1946).

42: razzmatazz . . . Wylie, *Generation of Vipers*, 185–186.

43: "momism . . ." The definition of "momism" as referring to mothers' "excessive domination" of their families comes from *New Webster's Dictionary of the English Language*, Deluxe Encyclopedic Edition, 1981.

43: How To Be a Jewish Mother . . . Dan Greenburg, *How To Be a Jewish Mother* (Los Angeles: Price Stern Sloan, 1965).

43: *Portnoy's Complaint* . . . Philip Roth, *Portnoy's Complaint* (New York: Random House, 1969).

44: Our everyday language . . . For excellent readings on these issues, see Ethel Strainchamps, "Our Sexist Language," in Vivian Gornick and Barbara K. Moran, eds., *Women in Sexist Society* (New York: Basic Books, 1971), 347–361; Letty Cottin Pogrebin, *Growing Up Free: Raising Your Kids in the 80s* (New York: McGraw-Hill, 1980); Casey Miller and Kate Swift, *Words and Women* (Garden City, N.Y.: Anchor Books, 1977); Dale Spender, *Man Made Language* (New York: Routledge Chapman Hall, 1985).

45: *The Myth of Women's* . . . Caplan, *The Myth of Women's Masochism*.

46: I was Anne's mother . . . Nancy Mairs, *Plaintext: Deciphering a Woman's Life* (New York: Harper and Row, 1987), 72.

47: Two articles . . . Caplan and Hall-McCorquodale, "Mother-Blaming in Major Clinical Journals," 345–353, and Caplan and Hall-McCorquodale, "The Scapegoating of Mothers," 610–613.

48: writing about their . . . Marcel Kinsbourne and Paula J. Caplan, *Children's Learning and Attention Problems* (Boston: Little, Brown, 1979).

48: As sociologists . . . Alison I. Griffith and Dorothy E. Smith, "Contributing Cultural Knowledge: Mothering as Discourse," in J. Gaskell and A. McLaren, eds., *Women and Education* (Calgary: Detselig Press, 1987), 87–

103; Alison I. Griffith and Dorothy E. Smith, "Coordinating the Uncoordinated: How Mothers Manage the School Day," *Perspectives in Social Problems*, in press; Dorothy E. Smith and Alison I. Griffith, "Mothering for Schooling," *Perspectives in Social Problems*, in press.

49: mothers spend far . . . Joseph Pleck, "Employment and Fatherhood: Issues and Innovative Policies," in Michael E. Lamb, ed., *The Father's Role: Applied Perspectives* (New York: John Wiley, 1986), 385–412.

49: fathers in studies . . . Paula J. Caplan, Jessie Watters, Georgina White, Ruth Parry, and Robert Bates, "Toronto Multi-Agency Child Abuse Research Project: The Abused and the Abuser," *Child Abuse and Neglect: The International Journal* 8 (1984): 343–351.

49: serious distortion . . . Caplan et al., "Toronto Multi-Agency Child Abuse" for discussion of this problem.

49: "Study of Family . . ." Press release titled: "Study of Family Interaction Leads to New Understanding of Abusive Parents" (University of Toronto Research Highlights. Simcoe Hall, University of Toronto, Public and Community Relations, October 1987), 1.

50: Harsh/intrusive . . . "Study of Family Interaction."

50: In a pamphlet . . . Helen Thomas, *Child Abuse, Neglect, and Deprivation: A Handbook for Ontario Nurses* (Toronto: Registered Nurses Association of Ontario, 1983), 21.

50: Dr. Kathleen . . . Kathleen Coulbourn Faller, "Decision-Making in Cases of Intrafamilial Child Sexual Abuse," *American Journal of Orthopsychiatry* 58 (1988): 121–128.

51: men are like alcoholics . . . Carolyn Cole, personal communication, May 1986.

51: "never to mention it . . ." Carolyn Cole, personal communication, September 25, 1987.

52: Mahler advised . . . Margaret S. Mahler, Fred Pine, and Anni Bergman, *The Psychological Birth of the Human Infant: Symbiosis and Individuation* (New York: Basic Books, Inc., 1975).

53: The irony is . . . Caplan et al. "Toronto Multi-Agency Child Abuse."

53: Suzanne Somers . . . Suzanne Somers, on "Donahue" (television show on alcoholism), February 2, 1988.

54: prisoners-of-war . . . J. Sigal, "Effects of Paternal Exposure to Prolonged Stress on the Mental Health of the Spouse and Children," *Canadian Psychiatric Association Journal* 21 (1976): 169–172.

55: Aphrodite Matsakis . . . Aphrodite Matsakis, *Viet Nam Wife: The Other Forgotten Warrior* (Kensington, Md.: Woodbine Press, 1988).

55: "It began . . ." Fred A. Bernstein, *The Jewish Mothers' Hall of Fame* (Garden City, N.Y.: Doubleday and Co., 1986), 112.

57: Phyllis Chesler . . . Phyllis Chesler, *Mothers on Trial: The Battle for Children and Custody* (New York: McGraw-Hill, 1986).

57: Good mothers . . . Chesler, *Mothers on Trial*, and Matsakis, *Viet Nam Wife*. I have also seen this in my own clinical experience.

59: Disrespect for mothers . . . See Daniel Sonkin, ed., *Domestic Violence on Trial* (New York: Springer, 1987).

59: Dr. Jaffe explains . . . Paula J. Caplan and Mary Lou Fassel, "Women get Blame in Incest Cases," *Globe and Mail* (Toronto), 10 February 1987.

61: fear of the unknown . . . Caplan and Fassel, "Women get Blame."

61: to prove their manliness . . . Nancy Chodorow, *The Reproduction of Mothering: Psychoanalysis and the Sociology of Gender* (Berkeley: University of California Press, 1978); and Dorothy Dinnerstein, *The Mermaid and the Minotaur* (New York: Harper & Row, 1977).

63: "I simply found . . ." Zella Wolofsky, "Reconciliation of the Mother-Daughter Relationship: A Personal Odyssey (Unpublished paper, Ontario Institute for Studies in Education, 1986), 11.

64: "emotional comforts . . ." Gloria I. Joseph and Jill Lewis, *Common Differences: Conflicts in Black and White Feminist Perspectives* (New York: Anchor Books, 1981), 96.

Chapter 4

70: "Daughters feel anger . . ." Susan Koppelman, ed., *Between Mothers and Daughters: Stories Across a Generation* (New York: The Feminist Press, 1985), xxxiv.

77: "Woman needs to give . . ." Irene Claremont de Castillejo, *Knowing Woman* (New York: Harper and Row, 1973), 149–154.

77: "reflexive maternal . . ." Mairs, *Plaintext*, 74.

77: "Inspire her . . ." Lydia Howard Sigourney, *Letters to Mothers* (New York: Harper and Brothers, 1845), 124.

78: "How much help . . ." Edith Neisser, *Mothers and Daughters* (New York: Harper and Row, 1973), 98.

78: "Junior housekeepers . . ." Neisser, *Mothers and Daughters*.

78: Jungian theorist . . . de Castillejo, *Knowing Woman*, 15.

78: Toni Grant . . . Tony Grant, *Being a Woman: Fulfilling your Femininity and Finding Love* (New York: Random House, 1988).

78: "Women have been taught . . ." H. Lerner, "Sugar and Spice," 7.

78: "a monster, anomalous . . ." Dinnerstein, *The Mermaid and the Minotaur*, 112.

78: "Self-affirmation . . ." Sheila Rowbotham, *Woman's Consciousness, Man's World* (Harmondsworth, England: Penguin, 1973), 76.

79: Research shows . . . Fischer, *Linked Lives*, 116; and Anita Fochs Heller, *Health at Home: Women as Health Guardians* (Ottawa: Canadian Advisory Council on the Status of Women, 1986).

79: So resilient . . . Nancy Reeves, *Womankind: Beyond the Stereotype* (Chicago: Aldine and Atherton, 1971), 197.

79: "If you're *not* . . ." Mary O'Brien, "The Reproduction of Mothering." Presented at "Don't Blame Mother" Women and Therapy Conference, Toronto, 21 May 1987.

84: *Mother Love* . . . Elisabeth Badinter, *Mother Love: Myth and Reality* (New York: Macmillan, 1980).

84: compelling evidence . . . Beverly Birns, "The Mother-Infant Tie: Fifty Years of Theory, Science and Science Fiction" (Work in Progress Paper No. 21, Wellesley, Ma.: Wellesley College, The Stone Center, 1985).

85: "a handy gland . . ." Jain Sherrard, *Mother-Warrior-Pilgrim* (Kansas City, Mo.: Andrews and McMel, 1980), 24.

85: "22 hours of labour . . ." Isabel Shessel, "On Being a Mother: Thoughts and Reflections" (Unpublished paper, Ontario Institute for Studies in Education, 1986), 5.

88: In other words . . . Bernardez, "Gender-Based Countertransference," 25–39; Bernardez, "Women and Anger"; and H. Lerner, *The Dance of Anger.*

88: "Praise is more . . ." Friedrich Nietzsche, *The Portable Nietzsche,* trans. and ed. Walter Kaufman (New York: Viking, 1954).

91: recent research . . . Anne C. Petersen, "Those Gangly Years," *Psychology Today* (September 1987): 28–34.

91: teenaged daughters tend . . . Fischer, *Linked Lives,* 116.

94: legitimate reasons . . . Bernardez, "Women and Anger"; Lerner, *The Dance of Anger.*

Chapter 5

97: victims are assumed . . . Nicole Walton-Allen, "Laypeople's Perceptions of Family Violence: An Examination of Stereotyped Learning (Unpublished M.A. thesis, Ontario Institute for Studies in Education, 1984); Caplan, *The Myth of Women's Masochism.*

98: a sense of your own . . . Florynce Kennedy, *Color Me Flo: My Hard Life and Good Times* (Englewood Cliffs, N.J.: Prentice-Hall, 1976), 87.

99: Thomas Babe's . . . Thomas Babe, *A Prayer for My Daughter* (New York: Samuel French, 1977).

99: she is troublesome . . . Elena Gianini Belotti, *Little Girls* (London: Writers and Readers Publishing Cooperative, 1975).

99: behavior may deviate . . . Arcana, *Every Mother's Son,* 98.

101: "penis envy . . ." Sigmund Freud, "Femininity," in "New Introductory Lectures in Psychoanalysis," 1932, *The Standard Edition of the Complete Psychological Works of Sigmund Freud,* vol. 22, trans. James Strachey (London: The Hogarth Press and the Institute of Psychoanalysis, 1964).

101: "I despise . . ." Freud, "Femininity," 124.

102: preferential treatment . . . Karen Horney, *New Ways in Psychoanalysis* (New York: W. W. Norton, 1939).

102: "When the daughter . . ." Kim Chernin, *Reinventing Eve: Modern Woman in Search of Herself* (New York: Harper and Row, 1988), 123.

102: "this tiny bit . . ." Simone de Beauvoir, *The Second Sex* (New York: Vintage, 1974), 307.

104: Brazelton . . . T. Berry Brazelton, *Infants and Mothers: Differences in Development* (New York: Delacorte, 1983); T. Berry Brazelton, *Toddlers and Parents* (New York: Dell, 1986).

104: cerebral palsy . . . Chesler, *Mothers on Trial.*

106: Children *are* harmed . . . Caplan, *The Myth of Women's Masochism.*

107: their "insatiable" . . . Freud, "Femininity," 122.

107: "immoderate" needs . . . Freud, "Femininity," 123.

109: Betty Friedan . . . Betty Friedan, *The Feminine Mystique* (New York: Dell, 1963).

110: "Everything is fine . . ." Belotti, *Little Girls*, 40.

115: the belief that mothers . . . For instance, see Signe Hammer, *Daughters and Mothers: Mothers and Daughters* (New York: Signet, 1976), 14–15; Mahler et al., *The Psychological Birth of the Human Infant;* Margaret Mahler, "On Childhood Psychoses and Schizophrenia: Autistic and Symbiotic Infantile Psychosis," in R. Eissler et al., eds., *The Psychoanalytic Study of the Child* (New York: International Universities Press, 1952); Eichenbaum and Orbach, *Understanding Women.*

115: *The Good Mother* . . . Sue Miller, *The Good Mother* (New York: Dell, 1986), 126.

115: mothers never achieve . . . Hammer, *Daughters and Mothers;* Eichenbaum and Orbach, *Understanding Women;* Chodorow, *The Reproduction of Mothering.*

116: When professionals . . . A great deal of literature about psychotherapy is liberally sprinkled with these buzz words, including Mahler et al., *The Psychological Birth of the Human Infant;* Mahler, "On Childhood Psychoses and Schizophrenia"; Eichenbaum and Orbach, *Understanding Women;* and most of the current writings about family therapy.

116: But to be able . . . Paula J. Caplan, *Between Women;* 184–185.

116: Wellesley College . . . See all books and papers by Judith Jordan, Alexandra Kaplan, Jean Baker Miller, Irene Stiver, and Janet Surrey in Bibliography of this book. They, with the work by Rachel Josefowitz Siegel, constitute a great deal of the most important work currently being written about personality theory, interpersonal relationships, and women.

116: Rachel Josefowitz Siegel . . . See all articles by Rachel Josefowitz Siegel listed in Bibliography of this book (see also above note).

116: "relational ability . . ." Surrey, "The 'Self-in-Relation'."

116: "women do not want . . ." Christina Robb, "A Theory of Empathy: The Quiet Revolution in Psychiatry," *The Boston Globe Magazine*, 16 October 1988, p. 56.

117: "a model of growth . . ." Surrey, "The 'Self-in-Relation'."

118: "I was five years old . . ." Wolofsky, "Reconciliation of the Mother-Daughter Relationship, 1.

119: "Yes, yes, of course . . ." Colette, *In My Mother's House* and *Sido*, trans., Una Vincenzo Troubridge and Enid McLeod, (London: Secker and Warburg, 1969), 125.

119: women have so much . . . Dinnerstein, *The Mermaid and the Minotaur.*

119: reality that marriage . . . quoted by Lucy Freeman, "Family Theme Highlights Spirited Annual Meeting," *Ortho Newsletter* (Summer 1987), 26.

Chapter 6

135: Dr. Albert Ellis . . . Albert Ellis and Windy Dryden, eds., *The Practice of Rational–Emotive Therapy* (New York: Springer, 1987); Albert Ellis and Russell Grieger, eds., *Handbook of Rational–Emotive Therapy*, vol. 1 (New York: Springer, 1977); and Albert Ellis and Russell Grieger, eds., *Handbook of Rational–Emotive Therapy*, vol. 2 (New York: Springer, 1986).

144: "expressive training . . ." The principles and techniques of expressive training as described here and in Appendix A are in the form taught to me by psychologist Dr. Paul Kirwin at the Veterans Administration Hospital in Durham, North Carolina, in 1970, and were further developed and expanded by Dr. Kirwin in his work with psychologist Dr. Jacqueline Damgaard. See: Paul Kirwin, "Affect expression training in psychiatric patients: The verbalization of feeling–cause relationships" (unpublished manuscript, Durham, N.C., Veterans Administration Hospital, 1970); Jacqueline Damgaard, "Structured versus unstructured procedures for training groups in the expression of feeling–cause relationships" (doctoral dissertation, Duke University, 1973).

Chapter 7

147: "the more you love . . ." Marilyn French, *Her Mother's Daughter* (New York: Ballantyne, 1988), 72.

148: "Could a greater . . ." Henry David Thoreau, *Walden* and *Civil Disobedience* (combined edition) (Harmondsworth, Middlesex, England: Penguin Books, Ltd., 1985), 53.

151: "My friends speak . . ." Anna Quindlen, *Living Out Loud: Home Thoughts from the Front Lines of Life* (New York: Random House, 1988), 104.

151: Karen Glasser Howe . . . Karen G. Howe, "Telling Our Mother's Story," in Rhoda K. Unger, ed., *Representations: Social Constructions of Gender* (Amityville, N.Y.: Baywood, 1989), 49.

162: Nikki Gerrard . . . Nikki Gerrard, "Feminist Therapy and Oppression within Mental Health Systems: Contradictions, Struggles, Alliances, and Change" (Presented to National Women's Studies Association convention, Minneapolis, June 1988).

164: Freda Paltiel . . . Freda Paltiel, personal communication, September 18, 1988.

165: "I've transformed . . ." Rebecca Goldstein, *The Mind-Body Problem* (New York: Laurel, 1983), 189.

174: "after six years . . ." Wolofsky, "Reconciliation of the Mother-Daughter Relationship," 13.

Chapter 8

177: My six-year-old . . . Nikki Gerrard, "Women and the Psychological Development of Self: A Theoretical and Subjective Journey through Object Relations and Self-in-Relation Theories" (Presented to Institute of Section on Women and Psychology, Canadian Psychological Association, Montreal, June 1988).

190: Betty Friedan . . . Friedan, *The Feminine Mystique.*

193: maternal responsibility . . . Fischer, *Linked Lives.*

193: "We Are Not Your Mothers . . ." Rachel Josefowitz Siegel, "We Are Not Your Mothers" (Presented at Association for Women in Psychiatry Convention, Denver, 1987).

197: Nikki Gerrard . . . Nikki Gerrard, "A Critical Analysis of Guilt in Relation to Women with a Focus on Mothers and Daughters" (Presented to Feminist Therapists Association First Annual Meeting, Toronto, May 1987).

199: "She does have power . . ." Robin Morgan, *Dry your Smile* (Garden City, N.Y.: Doubleday, 1987), 279.

199: matrophobia . . . Rich, *Of Woman Born.*

200: Martha Robbins . . . Martha A. Robbins, "Our Mothers' Legacies: Mourning the Myth of Motherhood" (Presented at Woman-Defined Motherhood: A Conference for Therapists, Goddard College, Plainfield, Vermont, 18 September 1988).

Chapter 9

205: Emotionally healthy . . . Janet Surrey, "Mother-Blame and Mother-Hate" (Presented at Woman-Defined Motherhood: A Conference for Therapists, Goddard College, Plainfield, Vermont, 17 September 1988).

205: step outside . . . Mairs, *Plaintext*, 69.

205: "We are together . . ." Walker, *In Search of Our Mothers' Gardens: Womanist Prose.*

206: "One day . . ." Arcana, *Our Mothers' Daughters*, 33–34.

209: You set out walking . . . David A. Friendly, personal communication, June 15, 1988.

209: Barbara and Robin Miller . . . Barbara Miller and Robin Miller, "Confronting Racial Dichotomization: Mothering the Black-White Child" (Presented at Woman-Defined Motherhood: A Conference for Therapists, Goddard College, Plainfield, Vermont, 17 September 1988).

209: Karen Howe . . . Karen G. Howe, "Telling our Mother's Story," in Rhoda Unger, ed., *Representations: Social Constructions of Gender* (New York: Baywood, 1989), 44–59.

210: Adrienne Rich's . . . Rich, *Of Woman Born.*

211: "Prospective Immigrants . . ." Adrienne Rich, "Prospective Immigrants Please Note," *Snapshots of a Daughter-In-Law: Poems 1954–1962* (New York: W. W. Norton, 1967), 59.

213: "I remember my fury . . ." Susan Griffin, "Forum: On Wanting To Be the Mother I Wanted," *Ms* (January 1977), 100.

🍂 Bibliography

ALCOTT, LOUISA MAY. *Little Women*. New York: Grossett and Dunlap, 1947.

ALTA. *Momma: A Start on All the Untold Stories*. Albion, Ca.: Times Change Press, 1974.

ANDERSEN, MARGARET. *Mother Was Not a Person*. Montreal: Black Rose Books, 1972.

ARCANA, JUDITH. *Every Mother's Son: The Role of Mothers in the Making of Men*. Seattle: The Seal Press, 1986.

ARCANA, JUDITH. *Our Mothers' Daughters*. Berkeley: Shameless Hussy Press, 1979.

ASCHER, CAROL; DE SALVO, LOUISE; AND RUDDICK, SARA. *Between Women*. Boston: Beacon Press, 1984.

ATWOOD, MARGARET. "Significant Moments in the Life of My Mother." In *Close Company: Stories of Mothers and Daughters*, edited by Christine Park and Caroline Heaton, 5–20. London: Virago, 1987.

BABE, THOMAS. *A Prayer for My Daughter*. New York: Samuel French, 1977.

BADINTER, ELISABETH. *Mother Love: Myth and Reality*. New York: Macmillan, 1980.

BART, PAULINE. Review of Chodorow's "The Reproduction of Mothering." In *Mothering: Essays in Feminist Theory*, edited by Joyce Trebilcot, 147–152. Totowa, N.J.: Rowman and Allanheld, 1983.

BARUCH, GRACE; BARNETT, ROSALIND; AND RIVERS, CARYL. *Lifeprints: New Patterns of Love and Work for Today's Women*. New York: McGraw-Hill, 1983.

BASS, ELLEN, AND DAVIS, LAURA. *The Courage to Heal: A Guide for Woman Survivors of Child Sexual Abuse*. New York: Harper & Row, 1988. (See especially p. 125, section on "Working through Mother Blame".)

BASSOFF, EVELYN. *Mothers and Daughters: Loving and Letting Go*. New York: New American Library, 1988.

BAUM, CHARLOTTE; HYMAN, PAULA; AND MICHEL, SONYA. *The Jewish Woman in America*. New York: New American Library, 1976.

BELL-SCOTT, PATRICIA. "A Critical Overview of Sex Roles Research of Black Families." *Women Studies Abstracts* 5 (Spring 1976): 1–9.

BELOTTI, ELENA GIANINI. *Little Girls*. London: Writers and Readers Publishing Cooperative, 1975.

BERNARD, JESSIE. *The Future of Motherhood*. New York: The Dial Press, 1974.

BERNARDEZ, TERESA. "Gender-Based Countertransference of Female Therapists in the Psychotherapy of Women." In *Women, Power, and Therapy: Issues for Women*, edited by Marjorie Braude, 25–39. New York: The Haworth Press, 1987.

BERNARDEZ, TERESA. "Women and Anger: Cultural Prohibitions and the Feminine Ideal." *Work in Progress Paper No. 31*. Wellesley, Ma.: Wellesley College, The Stone Center, 1988.

BERNIKOW, LOUISE. *Among Women*. New York: Harper & Row, 1981.

BERNSTEIN, FRED A. *The Jewish Mothers' Hall of Fame*. Garden City, N.Y.: Doubleday and Co., 1986.

BETTELHEIM, BRUNO. *A Good Enough Parent*. New York: Alfred A. Knopf, 1987.

BIRNS, BEVERLY. "The Mother-Infant Tie: Fifty Years of Theory, Science and Science Fiction." *Work in Progress Paper No. 21*. Wellesley, Ma.: Wellesley College, The Stone Center, 1985.

BLAXTER, MILDRED, AND PATERSON, ELIZABETH. *Mothers and Daughters: A Three-Dimensional Study of Health Attitudes and Behavior*. Brookfield, Vt.: Gower, 1982.

BOWE, CLAUDIA. "The Urgent Crisis in Day Care." *Cosmopolitan* (November 1986): 298–302, 360–361.

BOYLAN, CLARE. *Last Resorts*. London: Hamish Hamilton, 1984.

BRANS, JO. *Mother, I Have Something to Tell You*. Research by Margaret Taylor Smith. Garden City, N.Y.: Doubleday and Co., 1987.

BRAUDE, MARJORIE, ED. *Women, Power, and Therapy: Issues for Women*. New York: The Haworth Press, 1987.

BRAZELTON, T. BERRY. *Infants and Mothers: Differences in Development*. New York: Delacorte, 1983.

BRAZELTON, T. BERRY. *Toddlers and Parents*. New York: Dell, 1986.

BRETT, MARY ANN. "Let's Hear from Disabled Mothers." *The Toronto Star*, 14 September 1987, C9.

BRILES, JUDITH. *Woman to Woman: From Sabotage to Support*. Far Hills, N.J.: New Horizon Press, 1987.

BRODY, ELAINE. "Women-in-the-Middle: The Mental Health Effects of Parent Care." *Women's Mental Health Occasional Paper Series* (National Institute of Mental Health), 1987.

BURCK, FRANCES WELLS. *Mothers Talking: Sharing the Secret*. New York: St. Martin's Press, 1986.

BUTLER, SANDRA. *Conspiracy of Silence: The Trauma of Incest*. San Francisco: Volcano Press, 1985.

CAINE, LYNN. *What Did I Do Wrong?*. Toronto: Paper jacks, 1986.

CAPLAN, PAULA. *Between Women: Lowering the Barriers*. Toronto: Personal Library, 1981.

CAPLAN, PAULA J. "Making Mother-Blaming Visible: The Emperor's New Clothes." Presentation at panel on "Mother-Blaming and Mother-Hate: What Electra Did to Clytemnestra." Presented at *Woman-Defined Motherhood: A Conference for Therapists*, Goddard College, Plainfield, Vermont, September 17, 1988.

CAPLAN, PAULA. *The Myth of Women's Masochism*. New York: E. P. Dutton, 1985; New York: Signet, 1987, North American Paperback Edition (includes new chapter).

CAPLAN, PAULA J., AND FASSEL, MARY LOU. "Women Get Blame in Incest Cases. *Globe and Mail* (Toronto), 10 February 1987.

CAPLAN, PAULA J., AND HALL-MCCORQUODALE, IAN. "Mother-Blaming in Major Clinical Journals." *American Journal of Orthopsychiatry* 55 (1985): 345–353.

CAPLAN, PAULA J., AND HALL-MCCORQUODALE, IAN. "The Scapegoating of Mothers: A Call for Change." *American Journal of Orthopsychiatry* 55 (1985): 610–613.

CAPLAN, PAULA J.; WATTERS, JESSIE; WHITE, GEORGINA; PARRY, RUTH; AND BATES, ROBERT. "Toronto Multi-Agency Child Abuse Research Project: The Abused and the Abuser." *Child Abuse and Neglect: The International Journal* 8 (1984) 343–351.

CHAMBERS, JENNIFER. Personal communication, 20 January 1988.

CHAPIAN, MARIE. *Mothers and Daughters*. Minneapolis: Bethany House, 1988.

CHERNIN, KIM. *In My Mother's House: A Daughter's Story*. New York: Harper & Row, 1983.

CHERNIN, KIM. *Reinventing Eve: Modern Woman in Search of Herself*. New York: Harper & Row, 1988.

CHESLER, PHYLLIS. *Mothers on Trial: The Battle for Children and Custody*. New York: McGraw-Hill, 1986.

CHESLER, PHYLLIS. *Sacred Bond: The Legacy of Baby M*. New York: Times Books, 1988.

CHESLER, PHYLLIS. *With Child: A Diary of Motherhood*. New York: Berkeley Books, 1981.

CHESLER, PHYLLIS. *Women and Madness*. New York: Avon Books, 1973.

CHESS, STELLA. "The 'Blame the Mother' Ideology." *International Journal of Mental Health* 11 (1982): 95–107.

CHESS, STELLA, AND WHITBREAD, JANE. *Daughters: From Infancy to Independence*. Garden City, N.Y.: Doubleday and Co., 1978.

CHODOROW, NANCY. *The Reproduction of Mothering: Psychoanalysis and the Sociology of Gender*. Berkeley: University of California Press, 1978.

CHODOROW, NANCY, AND CONTRATTO, SUSAN. "The Fantasy of the Perfect Mother." In *Rethinking the Family: Some Feminist Questions*, edited by Barrie Thorne and Marilyn Yalom, 54–75. New York: Longman, 1982.

CLAREMONT DE CASTILLEJO, IRENE. *Knowing Woman*. New York: Harper & Row, 1973.

CLIFTON, LUCILLE. *An Ordinary Woman*. New York: Random House, 1974.

COHLER, BERTRAM, AND GRUNEBAUM, HENRY. *Mothers, Grandmothers, and*

Daughters: Personality and Childcare in Three-generation Families. New York: John Wiley and Sons, 1981.

COLE, CAROLYN. Personal communication, May 1986.

COLE, CAROLYN. Personal communication, 25 September 1987.

COLE, CAROLYN, AND BARNEY, ELAINE E. "Safeguards and the Therapeutic Window: A Group Treatment Strategy for Adult Incest Suvivors." *American Journal of Orthopsychiatry* 57 (1987): 601–609.

COLETTE. *In My Mother's House* and *Sido.* Translated by Una Vincenzo Troubridge and Enid McLeod. London: Secker and Warburg, 1969.

CONLON, FAITH; daSILVA, RACHEL; AND WILSON, BARBARA, EDS. *The Things that Divide Us.* Seattle: The Seal Press, 1985.

CONROY, PAT. *The Prince of Tides.* Boston: Houghton Mifflin, 1986.

COONS, PHYLLIS, "New Alliances." *Radcliffe Quarterly* (December 1984): 31–32.

CREAN, SUSAN. *In the Name of the Fathers: The Story Behind Child Custody.* Toronto: Amanita, 1988.

CUNNINGHAM, TERRY. *An Exploratory View: Attitudes of Black Teenage Females toward Familial Relationships.* Atlanta: Atlanta University School of Social Work, 1980.

DALLY, ANN. *Inventing Motherhood: The Consequences of an Ideal.* New York: Schocken Books, 1982.

DAMGAARD, JACQUELINE. "Structured Versus Unstructured Procedures for Training Groups in the Expression of Feeling–Cause Relationships." Ph.D. diss., Duke University, 1973.

DAVIDSON, CATHY N. "Mothers and Daughters in the Fiction of the New Republic." In *The Lost Tradition: Mothers and Daughters in Literature,* edited by Cathy N. Davidson and E. M. Broner, 115–127. New York: Frederick Ungar, 1980.

DAVIDSON, CATHY N., AND BRONER, E. M., EDS. *The Lost Tradition: Mothers and Daughters in Literature.* New York: Frederick Ungar, 1980.

DAY, INGEBORG. "Daughters and Mothers." *Ms.* (June 1975): 49–53, 78–83.

deBEAUVOIR, SIMONE. *The Second Sex.* New York: Vintage, 1974.

DINNERSTEIN, DOROTHY. *The Mermaid and the Minotaur.* New York: Harper & Row, 1977.

"DONAHUE" Television Show on Alcoholism. 2 February 1988.

DUNCAN, ERIKA. "The Hungry Jewish Mother." In *The Lost Tradition: Mothers and Daughters in Literature,* edited by Cathy N. Davidson and E. M. Broner, 231–241. New York: Frederick Ungar, 1980.

DWORKIN, ANDREA. *Woman Hating.* New York: E. P. Dutton, 1974.

EHRENREICH, BARBARA, AND ENGLISH, DEIRDRE. *For Her Own Good: 150 Years of the Experts' Advice to Women.* Garden City, N.Y.: Anchor, 1979.

EICHENBAUM, LUISE, AND ORBACH, SUSIE. *Understanding Women: A Feminist Psychoanalytic Approach.* New York: Basic Books, 1983.

EICHENBAUM, LUISE, AND ORBACH, SUSIE. *Between Women.* New York: Viking Press, 1988.

ELLIS, ALBERT, AND DRYDEN, WINDY, EDS. *The Practice of Rational–Emotive Therapy.* New York: Springer, 1987.

ELLIS, ALBERT, AND GRIEGER, RUSSELL, eds. *Handbook of Rational–Emotive Therapy*. Vol. 1. New York: Springer, 1977.

ELLIS, ALBERT, AND GRIEGER, RUSSELL, eds. *Handbook of Rational–Emotive Therapy*. Vol. 2. New York: Springer, 1986.

ENGEL, BARBARA A. *Mothers and Daughters: Women of the Intelligentsia in Nineteenth-Century Russia*. New York: Cambridge University Press, 1983.

FALLER, KATHLEEN COULBOURN. "Decision-Making in Cases of Intrafamilial Child Sexual Abuse." *American Journal of Orthopsychiatry* 58 (1988): 121–128.

FELLMAN, ANITA CLAIR. " 'Don't Expect to Depend on Anybody': The Mother-Daughter Relationship of Laura Ingalls Wilder and Rose Wilder Lane." Presented to Institute of Section on Women and Psychology, Canadian Psychological Association, Vancouver, 1987.

FIRMAN, JULIE, AND FIRMAN, DOROTHY. *Mothers and Daughters: Healing the Relationship*. New York: Crossroad Publishing Co., 1989.

FISCHER, LUCY ROSE. *Linked Lives: Adult Daughters and Their Mothers*. New York: Harper & Row, 1987.

FITE, KAREN, AND TRUMBO, NIKOLA. "Betrayals among Women: Barriers to a Common Longing." *Lesbian Ethics* 1 (1984).

FLAX, JANE. "The Conflict Between Nurturance and Autonomy in Mother-Daughter Relationships and within Feminism." *Feminist Studies* 4 (1978): 171–189.

FODOR, RENEE. "The Impact of the Nazi Occupation of Poland on the Jewish Mother-Child Relationship." *YIVO Annual of Jewish Social Science* 11 (1956–7): 270–285.

FRASER, SYLVIA. *My Father's House: A Memoir of Incest and Healing*. Toronto: Doubleday Canada Limited, 1987.

FREEMAN, LUCY. "Family Theme Highlights Spirited Annual Meeting." *Ortho Newsletter* (Summer 1987): 1 and 17–39.

FRENCH, MARILYN. *Her Mother's Daughter*. New York: Ballantyne, 1988.

FREUD, SIGMUND. "Femininity." In "New Introductory Lectures in Psychoanalysis," [1932] *The Standard Edition of the Complete Psychological Works of Sigmund Freud*. Vol. 22. Translated by James Strachey. London: The Hogarth Press and The Institute of Psychoanalysis, 1964.

FRIDAY, NANCY. *My Mother/My Self*. New York: Delacorte Press, 1977.

FRIEDAN, BETTY. *The Feminine Mystique*. New York: Dell, 1963.

FRIENDLY, DAVID A. Personal communication, 15 June 1988.

FROST, BETH. "My Mother's Friend." *Radcliffe Quarterly* (December 1984): 26–28.

GEE, ELLEN M., AND KIMBALL, MEREDITH M. *Women and Aging*. Toronto: Butterworths, 1987.

GENEVIE, LOIS, AND MARGOLIES, EVA. *Motherhood Report: How Women Feel about Being Mothers*. New York: McGraw-Hill, 1988.

GERRARD, NIKKI. "A Critical Analysis of Guilt in Relation to Women with a Focus on Mothers and Daughters." Paper presented to Feminist Therapists' Association First Annual Meeting, Toronto, May 1987.

GERRARD, NIKKI. "Feminist Therapy and Oppression within Mental Health Systems: Contradictions, Struggles, Alliances, and Change." Paper presented to National Women's Studies Association Convention, Minneapolis, June 1988.

GERRARD, NIKKI. "Women and the Psychological Development of Self: A Theoretical and Subjective Journey through Object Relations and Self-in-Relation Theories." Paper presented to Institute of Section on Women and Psychology, Canadian Psychological Association, Montreal, June 1988.

GERRARD, NIKKI. "Undoing Crazymaking: Feminist Therapy—A Stitch in Time Saves Nine." *Popular Feminism Lecture Series, Paper No. 7*, Centre for Women's Studies in Education, Ontario Institute for Studies in Education, Toronto, 11 January 1988.

GILLIGAN, CAROL. *In a Different Voice: Psychological Theory and Women's Development*. Cambridge, Ma.: Harvard University Press, 1982.

GOLDSTEIN, REBECCA. *The Mind-Body Problem*. New York: Laurel, 1983.

GORDON, LINDA. *Heroes of Their Own Lives: The Politics and History of Family Violence, Boston 1880–1960*. New York: Viking Press, 1988.

GORNICK, VIVIAN. *Fierce Attachments*. New York: Farrar, Straus, and Giroux, 1987.

GRANT, TONI. *Being a Woman: Fulfilling Your Femininity and Finding Love*. New York: Random House, 1988.

GREENBERG, JOANNE. "Hunting Season." In *Motherlove: Stories by Women about Motherhood*, edited by Stephanie Spinner, 111–119. New York: Dell, 1978.

GREENBURG, DAN. *How To Be a Jewish Mother*. Los Angeles: Price Stern Sloan, 1965.

GREENGLASS, ESTHER. "A Social–Psychological View of Marriage for Women." *International Journal of Women's Studies* 8 (1985): 24–31.

GRIFFIN, SUSAN. "Forum: On Wanting To Be the Mother I Wanted." *Ms.* (January 1977): 98–105.

GRIFFITH, ALISON I., AND SMITH, DOROTHY E. "Constructing Cultural Knowledge: Mothering as Discourse." In *Women and Education*, edited by J. Gaskell and A. McLaren, 87–103. Calgary: Detselig Press, 1987.

GRIFFITH, ALISON I., AND SMITH DOROTHY E. "Coordinating the Uncoordinated: How Mothers Manage the School Day." *Perspectives in Social Problems*. In press.

GRINNELL, GRETCHEN. "Women, Depression and the Global Folie: A New Framework for Therapists." In *Women, Power, and Therapy: Issues for Woman*, edited by Marjorie Braude, 41–58. New York: The Haworth Press, 1987.

GROSS, ZENITH HENKIN. *And You Thought It Was All Over! Mothers and Their Adult Children*. New York: St. Martin's Press, 1985.

GUNDLACH, JULIE KETTE. *My Mother Before Me*. Seacaucus, N.J.: Lyle Stuart, 1986.

GUY-SHEFTALL, BEVERLY. "Mothers and Daughters: A Black Perspective." *Spelman Messenger* 98 (1982): 4–5.

HAMMER, SIGNE. *Daughters and Mothers: Mothers and Daughters*. New York: Signet, 1976.

HANSCOMBE, GILLIAN, AND FORSTER, JACKIE. *Rocking the Cradle: Lesbian Mothers, a Challenge in Family Living*. Boston: Alyson, 1982.

HARE-MUSTIN, RACHEL T., AND BRODERICK, PATRICIA C. "The Myth of Motherhood: A Study of Attitudes toward Motherhood." *Psychology of Women Quarterly* 4 (1979): 114–128.

HEFFNER, ELAINE. *Mothering: The Emotional Experience of Motherhood after Freud and Feminism*. Garden City, N.Y.: Doubleday, 1978.

HELD, VIRGINIA. "The Obligations of Mothers and Fathers." In *Mothering: Essays in Feminist Theory*, edited by Joyce Trebilcot, 7–20. Totowa, N.J.: Rowman and Allanheld, 1983.

HELLER, ANITA FOCHS. *Health and Home: Women as Health Guardians*. Ottawa: Canadian Advisory Council on the Status of Women, 1986.

HIRSCH, MARIANNE. "Mothers and Daughters." *Signs* 7 (Autumn 1981): 200–222.

HOOKS, BELL. *Feminist Theory from Margin to Center*. Boston: South End Press, 1984.

HORNEY, KAREN. *New Ways in Psychoanalysis*. New York: W. W. Norton, 1939.

HOWE, KAREN G. "Women and Work: Defining and Changing Students' Perceptions in a Women's Studies Course." Paper presented at Third Annual Women and Work Symposium, Women and Work Research and Resource Center, Graduate School of Social Work, University of Texas, Arlington, Texas, 1–2 May 1986.

HOWE, KAREN G. "Telling Our Mother's Story." In *Representations: Social Constructions of Gender*, edited by Rhoda Unger. New York: Baywood, 1989.

HURLEY, DAN. "A Sound Mind in an Unsound Body." *Psychology Today* (August 1987): 34–43.

HURSTON, ZORA NEALE. *Their Eyes Were Watching God*. Urbana: University of Illinois Press, 1987.

IRIGARAY, LUCE. "And the One Doesn't Stir without the Other." Translated by Helene Vivienne Wenzel. *Signs* 7 (1981): 60–67.

JOHNSON, MIRIAM M. *Strong Mothers, Weak Wives: The Search for Gender Equality*. Berkeley: University of California Press, 1988.

JORDAN, JUDITH V. "Empathy and Self Boundaries." *Work in Progress Paper No. 16*. Wellesley, Ma.: Wellesley College, The Stone Center, 1988.

JORDAN, JUDITH V. "The Meaning of Mutuality." *Work in Progress Paper No. 23*. Wellesley, Ma.: Wellesley College, The Stone Center, 1986.

JORDAN, JUDITH V.; SURREY, JANET; AND KAPLAN, ALEXANDRA. "Women and Empathy." *Work in Progress Paper No. 2*. Wellesley, Ma.: Wellesley College, The Stone Center, 1982.

JOSEPH, GLORIA I., AND LEWIS, JILL. *Common Differences: Conflicts in Black and White Feminist Perspectives*. New York: Anchor Books, 1981.

KAGAN, JEROME. *The Nature of the Child*. New York: Basic Books, 1984.

KALERGIS, MARY MOTTEY. *Mother: A Collective Portrait*. New York: E.P. Dutton, 1987.

KAPLAN, ALEXANDRA. "Reflections on Gender and Psychotherapy." In *Women, Power, and Therapy: Issues for Women,* edited by Marjorie Braude, 11–24. New York: The Haworth Press, 1987.

KAPLAN, ALEXANDRA. "The 'Self-in-relation': Implications for Depression in Women." *Work in Progress Paper No. 14.* Wellesley, Ma.: Wellesley College, The Stone Center, 1984.

KAUFMAN, MICHAEL, ED. *Beyond Patriarchy: Essays by Men on Pleasure, Power, and Change.* Toronto: Oxford University Press, 1987.

KAUFMAN, MICHAEL. "The Construction of Masculinity and the Triad of Men's Violence." In *Beyond Patriarchy: Essays by Men on Pleasure, Power and Change,* edited by Michael Kaufman, 1–29. Toronto: Oxford University Press, 1987.

KELLERMAN, DANA F., GENERAL SUPERVISOR. *New Webster's Dictionary of the English Language.* Delair Publishing Co., 1981.

KENNEDY, FLORYNCE. *Color Me Flo: My Hard Life and Good Times.* Englewood Cliffs, N.J.: Prentice-Hall, 1976.

KILEY, DAN. *The Wendy Dilemma: When Women Stop Mothering Their Men.* New York: Arbor House, 1984.

KINGSOLVER, BARBARA. *The Bean Trees.* New York: Harper & Row, 1988.

KINSBOURNE, MARCEL, AND CAPLAN, PAULA J. *Children's Learning and Attention Problems.* Boston: Little, Brown, 1979.

KIRWIN, PAUL. "Affect Expression Training in Psychiatric Patients: The Verbalization of Feeling–Cause Relationships." Durham, N.C.: Veterans Administration Hospital, 1970. Unpublished manuscript.

KITZINGER, SHEILA. *Women as Mothers.* New York: Random House, 1979.

KOHN, ALFIE. "Girl Talk, Guy Talk." *Psychology Today* (February 1988): 65–66.

KOME, PENNEY. *Somebody Has To Do It: Whose Work Is Housework?* Toronto: McClelland, 1982.

KOPPELMAN, SUSAN, ED. *Between Mothers and Daughters: Stories Across a Generation.* New York: The Feminist Press, 1985.

KONSTANTAREAS, MARY, AND HOMATIDIS, SOULA. "Mothers of Autistic Children: Are They the 'Unacknowledged Victims'?" Paper presented to the Institute of the Section on Women and Psychology, Canadian Psychological Association Convention, Winnipeg, 1983.

KRAMARAE, CHERIS, AND TREICHLER, PAULA A. *A Feminist Dictionary.* Boston: Pandora Press, 1985. (Sections on "Mother" and "Motherhood".)

LADNER, JOYCE. *Tomorrow's Tomorrow: The Black Woman.* Garden City, N.Y.: Anchor Books, 1972.

LAMB, MICHAEL E., ED. *The Father's Role: Applied Perspectives.* New York: John Wiley and Sons, 1986.

LANDERS, ANN. "It's Never Too Late for Forgiveness." *Toronto Star,* 12 September 1985: C5

LANDERS, ANN. "Too Few Phone Calls from Son Leave Mother Feeling Lonely." *The Toronto Star,* 22 May 1986: D3

LANDSBERG, MICHELE. *Women and Children First: A Provocative Look at Mod-*

ern Canadian Women at Work and at Home. Toronto: Macmillan of Canada, 1982.

LAURENCE, MARGARET. *The Diviners.* Toronto: Bantam-Seal Books, 1976.

LAWS, JANICE, AND STRICKLAND, JOYCE. "Black Mothers and Daughters: A Clarification of the Relationship as an Impetus for Black Power." *Black Books Bulletin* 6 (1980): 26–29, 33.

LAZARRE, JANE. *The Mother Knot.* New York: Dell, 1976.

LEIFER, MYRA. *The Psychological Effects of Motherhood: Study of First Pregnancy.* New York: Praeger, 1980.

LeMASTERS, E. "Parenthood as Crisis." *Marriage and Family Living* 19 (1957): 352–355.

LERNER, GERDA. *The Female Experience: An American Documentary.* Indianapolis: The Bobbs-Merrill Company, 1977.

LERNER, HARRIET GOLDHOR. *The Dance of Anger.* New York: Harper & Row, 1985. (Especially chapter on "Anger at our Impossible Mothers," 67–87.)

LERNER, HARRIET GOLDHOR. *The Dance of Intimacy.* New York: Harper & Row, 1989.

LERNER, HARRIET GOLDHOR. "Sugar and Spice: The Taboos against Female Anger." *Menninger Perspective* (Winter 1977): 5–11.

LERNER, HARRIET GOLDHOR. *Women and Therapy.* Northvale, N.J.: Jason Aronson, 1988.

LEVENE, JUDI, AND KONSTANTAREAS, MARY. "Mothers of Disturbed Children." Presentation in panel at *Don't Blame Mother Conference*, Toronto, 22 May 1987.

LEVINE, HELEN. "The Power Politics of Motherhood." In *Perspectives on Women in the 1980s,* edited by Joan Turner and Lois Emery, 28–40. Winnipeg: University of Manitoba Press, 1983.

LEWIS, JANE. "Introduction: Reconstructing Women's Experience of Home and Family." In *Labour and Love: Women's Experience of Home and Family, 1850–1940,* edited by Jane Lewis, 1–24. Oxford: Basil Blackwell, 1986.

LIUTKUS, JOANNE. Review of "To a Safer Place." *Healthsharing* (Winter 1987): 33.

LOEWENSTEIN, S. "An Overview of the Concept of Narcissism." *Social Casework* 58 (1977): 136–142.

LORDE, AUDRE. *From a Land Where Other People Live.* Detroit: Broadside, 1973.

LORDE, AUDRE. *Zami: A New Spelling of My Name.* Trumansburg, N.Y.: The Crossing Press, 1982.

LORDE, AUDRE. *Sister Outsider.* Trumansburg, N.Y.: The Crossing Press, 1984.

LOW, NATALIE. "Mother-Daughter Relationships: The Lasting Ties." *Radcliffe Quarterly* (December 1984): 1–4.

LOWELL, M. C., AND FIORINO, D. L. "Combatting Myths: A Conceptual Framework for Analyzing the Stress of Motherhood." In *Advances in Nursing Science,* vol. I, 75–84.

LUXTON, MEG. *More than a Labour of Love: Three Generations of Women's Work in the Home.* Toronto: The Women's Press, 1980.

LUXTON, MEG, AND ROSENBERG, HARRIET. *Through the Kitchen Window: The Politics of Home and Family.* Toronto: Garamond, 1986.

MAHLER, MARGARET S. "On Childhood Psychoses and Schizophrenia: Autistic and Symbiotic Infantile Psychosis." In *The Psychoanalytic Study of the Child*, edited by R. Eissler et al. New York: International Universities Press, 1952.

MAHLER, MARGARET S. *On Human Symbiosis and the Vicissitudes of Individuation*. New York: International Universities Press, 1968.

MAHLER, MARGARET S.; PINE, FRED; AND BERGMAN, ANNI. *The Psychological Birth of the Human Infant: Symbiosis and Individuation*. New York: Basic Books, 1975.

MAIRS, NANCY. *Plaintext: Deciphering a Woman's life*. New York: Harper & Row, 1987.

MARGOLIS, MAXINE. *Mothers and Such: Views of American Women and Why They Changed*. Berkeley: University of California Press, 1984.

MATSAKIS, APHRODITE. *Viet Nam Wife: The Other Forgotten Warrior*. Kensington, Md.: Woodbine Press, 1988.

MAYNARD, FREDELLE BRUSER. "A Mother and Two Daughters." *Lilith* (Summer 1988): 29–31.

MAYNARD, RONA. "Let's Stop Blaming Mum." *Homemaker's Magazine* (May 1983): 8–26.

McBRIDE, A. B. *The Growth and Development of Mothers*. New York: Harper & Row, 1973.

McGINLEY, PHYLLIS. "Girl's-Eye View of Female Relatives," poem in *Times Three*. New York: Viking Press, 1960.

McMILLAN, TERRY. *Mama*. New York: Washington Square Press, 1987.

MERCER, RAMONA. *First-Time Motherhood*. New York: Springer, 1986.

MERKIN, DAPHNE. *Enchantment*. New York: Fawcett Crest, 1984.

MILLER, BARBARA, AND MILLER, ROBIN. "Confronting Racial Dichotomization: Mothering the Black-White Child." Paper presented at Woman-Defined Motherhood: A Conference for Therapists. Goddard College, Plainfield, Vermont, 17 September 1988.

MILLER, CASEY, AND SWIFT, KATE. *Words and Women*. Garden City, N.Y.: Anchor Books, 1977.

MILLER, JEAN BAKER. "Connections, Disconnections and Violations." *Work in Progress Paper No. 33*. Wellesley, Ma.: Wellesley College, The Stone Center, 1988.

MILLER, JEAN BAKER. "The Construction of Anger in Women and Men." *Work in Progress Paper No. 4*. Wellesley, Ma.: Wellesley College, The Stone Center, 1983.

MILLER, JEAN BAKER. "The Development of Women's Sense of Self." *Work in Progress Paper No. 12*. Wellesley, Ma.: Wellesley College, The Stone Center, 1984.

MILLER, JEAN BAKER. *Toward a New Psychology of Women*. Boston: Beacon Press, 1976.

MILLER, JEAN BAKER. "What Do We Mean by Relationships?" *Work in Progress Paper No. 22*. Wellesley, Ma.: Wellesley College, The Stone Center, 1986.

MILLER, JEAN BAKER. "Women and Power: Some Psychological Dimensions."

Work in Progress Paper No. 1. Wellesley, Ma.: Wellesley College, The Stone Center, 1982.

MILLER, JEAN BAKER. "Women and Power." In *Women, Power, and Therapy: Issues for Women*, edited by Marjorie Braude, 1–10. New York: The Haworth Press, 1987.

MILLER, SUE. *The Good Mother.* New York: Dell, 1986.

MINDEN, RUTH. "Glancing Backward, Looking Forward: Insights into Mothering." Unpublished paper. Ontario Institute for Studies in Education, 1986.

MINER, VALERIE, AND LONGINO, HELEN. *Competition: A Feminist Taboo?* New York: The Feminist Press, 1987.

MORAGA, CHERRIE. *Loving in the War Years.* Boston: South End Press, 1983.

MORGAN, KATHRYN. "The Perils and Paradoxes of Feminist Pedagogy." *Resources for Feminist Research* 16 (1987): 49–51.

MORGAN, KATHRYN. "Women and Moral Madness." In *Feminist Perspectives: Philosophical Method and Morals*, edited by S. Mullet, L. Code, and C. Overall, 146–167. Toronto: University of Toronto Press, 1988.

MORGAN, ROBIN. *Dry Your Smile.* Garden City, N.Y.: Doubleday, 1987.

MORRISON, TONI. *Beloved.* New York: New American Library, 1987.

MORRISON, TONI. "SEEMOTHERMOTHERISVERY NICE." In *Black-eyed Susans*, edited by Mary Helen Washington, 99. New York: Anchor Press, 1975.

MORRISON, TONI. *Sula.* New York: Knopf, 1974.

NEISSER, EDITH. *Mothers and Daughters.* New York: Harper & Row, 1973.

NIETZSCHE, FRIEDRICH. *The Portable Nietzsche.* Edited and translated by Walter Kaufman. New York: Viking, 1954.

NIMAN, HAROLD. "The Price of Custody." Presented in "Domestic Law: A Colloquium on the Law and Practice of Custody." Annual Institute on Continuing Legal Education, Family Law for the Specialist, Toronto, 1987.

NORMAN, MARSHA. *The Fortune Teller.* New York: Random House, 1987.

NORMAN, MARSHA. *'Night, Mother.* New York: Hill and Wang, 1983.

O'BRIEN, MARY. *The Politics of Reproduction.* Boston: Routledge and Kegan Paul, 1981.

O'BRIEN, MARY. "The Reproduction of Mothering." Presented at "Don't Blame Mother" Women and Therapy Conference, Toronto, 21 May 1987.

OLSEN, TILLIE. "I Stand Here Ironing." In *Between Mothers and Daughters: Stories Across a Generation*, edited by Susan Koppelman, 177–187. New York: The Feminist Press, 1985.

OLSEN, TILLIE, ET AL. *Mothers and Daughters: That Special Quality, an Exploration in Photographs.* New York: Aperture, 1987.

OLSEN, TILLIE. *Mother to Daughter, Daughter to Mother: A Daybook and Reader.* New York: Feminist Press at the City University of New York, 1984.

OLSEN, TILLIE. *Tell Me a Riddle.* New York: Dell, 1986.

ONTARIO ADVISORY COUNCIL ON WOMEN'S ISSUES. *Sole Support M.O.M. (Mothers on the Move): Brief to the Ontario Government on Sole Support Mothers.* November 1987.

OSBORN, JUDITH. "Mothers and Daughters in Ancient Near Eastern Literature." In *The Lost Tradition: Mothers and Daughters in Literature*, edited by Cathy N. Davidson and E. M. Broner, 5–14. New York: Frederick Ungar, 1980.

PALTIEL, FREDA. Personal communication, 18 September, 1988.

PARKER, G. "Re-Searching the Schizophrenogenic Mother." *Journal of Nervous and Mental Disorders* 170 (1982): 452–462.

PAYNE, KAREN, ED. *Between Ourselves: Letters Between Mothers and Daughters, 1750–1982.* Boston: Houghton Mifflin, 1983.

PEARCE, DIANA, AND MCADOO, HARIETTE. *Women and Children: Alone and in Poverty.* Washington, D.C.: National Advisory Council on Economic Opportunity, 1981.

PEARSON, JESSICA. "Mothers and Daughters: Measuring Occupational Inheritance." *Sociology and Social Research* 67 (January 1983): 204–217.

PETERSEN, ANNE C. "Those Gangly Years." *Psychology Today* (September 1987): 28–34.

PLECK, ELIZABETH. *Domestic Tyranny: The Making of American Social Policy Against Family Violence from Colonial Times to the Present.* New York: Oxford University Press, 1987.

PLECK, JOSEPH. "Employment and Fatherhood: Issues and Innovative Policies." In *The Father's Role: Applied Perspectives*, edited by Michael E. Lamb, 385–412. New York: John Wiley and Sons, 1986.

POGREBIN, LETTY COTTIN. *Among Friends.* New York: McGraw-Hill, 1987.

POGREBIN, LETTY COTTIN. *Growing Up Free: Raising Your Kids in the 80s.* New York: McGraw-Hill, 1980.

POLLACK, SANDRA, AND VAUGHN, JEANNE, ED. *Politics of the Heart: A Lesbian Parenting Anthology.* Ithaca, NY: Firebrand Books, 1987.

PORTER, HELEN CARMICHAEL. Personal communication, 14 June, 1988.

POWELL, GLORIA. "Growing up Black and Female." In *Becoming Female: Perspectives on Development*, edited by C. Kopp. New York: Plenum, 1979.

PRESS, AIDA K. "Consider Naomi: In Defense of Mothers-in-Law." *Radcliffe Quarterly* (December 1984): 12–14.

PRICE, JANE. *Motherhood: What It Does to Your Mind.* London: Pandora Press, 1988.

PROZAN, CHARLOTTE KRAUSE. "An Integration of Feminist and Psychoanalytic Theory." In *Women, Power, and Therapy: Issues for Women*, edited by Marjorie Braude, 59–71. New York: The Haworth Press, 1987.

QUINDLEN, ANNA. *Living Out Loud: Home Thoughts from the Front Lines of Life.* New York: Random House, 1988.

RABUZZI, KATHRYN ALLEN. *Motherself: A Myth Analysis of Motherhood.* Bloomington, In.: Indiana University Press, 1988.

RAFKIN, LOUISE, ED. *Different Daughters: A Book by Mothers of Lesbians.* Pittsburgh/San Francisco: Cleis Press, 1987.

RAPHAEL, BETTY-JANE. "Mothers and Daughters." *Ladies Home Journal* (September 1978).

RAYMOND, JANICE. *A Passion for Friends: Toward a Philosophy of Female Affection.* Boston: Beacon Press, 1987.

REEVES, NANCY. *Womankind: Beyond the Stereotype.* Chicago: Aldine and Atherton, 1971.

REID, PAMELA T. "Socialization of Black Female Children." In *Women: A Developmental Perspective,* edited by Phyllis W. Berman and Estelle R. Ramey. Bethesda, Md.: National Institutes of Health, 1982.

RENVOIZE, JEAN. *Going Solo: Single Mothers by Choice.* London: Routledge and Kegan Paul, 1985.

RICH, ADRIENNE. " 'Disloyal to Civilization': Feminism, Racism, and Gynephobia." *Chrysalis* 7 (1977): 9–27.

RICH, ADRIENNE. *Of Woman Born: Motherhood as Experience and Institution.* New York: W.W. Norton and Co., 1976.

RICH, ADRIENNE. *Snapshots of a Daughter-in-Law: Poems 1954–1962.* New York: W. W. Norton and Co., 1967.

RIDDINGTON, JILLIAN. "Single Parenting in a Wheelchair: What Do You Do with a Sick Kid when You Can't Afford an Ambulance and You Can't Walk?" *Resources for Feminist Research/Documentation sur la Recherche Feministe* 14 (March 1985): 34–37.

RILEY, JOAN. *Waiting in the Twilight.* London: The Women's Press, 1987.

ROBB, CHRISTINA. "A Theory of Empathy: The Quiet Revolution in Psychiatry." *The Boston Globe Magazine* (16 October 1988): 10–56.

ROBBINS, MARTHA A. "Our Mothers' Legacies: Mourning the Myth of Motherhood." Presented at Woman-Defined Motherhood: A Conference for Therapists, Goddard College, Plainfield, Vermont, 17 September, 1988.

ROBINSON, LILLIAN S. "Poverty, Purpose, Pride." (Review of *Dignity: Lower Income Women Tell of Their Lives and Struggles.* Oral histories compiled by Fran Leeper Buss.) Ann Arbor, Mi.: University of Michigan Press, 1985. *Women's Review of Books* 3 (December 1985): 1 and 3–4.

RODGERS, CAROLYN M. *IT IS DEEP, How I got Ovah.* New York: Doubleday and Co., 1969.

RODGERS-ROSE, LA FRANCES, ED. *The Black Woman.* Beverly Hills: Sage Publications, 1980.

ROGERSON, CAROL. "Winning the Battle; Losing the War—The Plight of the Custodial Mother after Judgement." Presented in "Domestic Law: A Colloquium on the Law and Practice of Custody." Annual Institute on Continuing Legal Education, Family Law for the Specialist, Toronto, 1987.

ROSENFELD, ANNE H. "Knowing When to Call the Doctor." *Psychology Today* (October 1987): 12.

ROSINSKY, NATALIE M. "Mothers and Daughters: Another Minority Group." In *The Lost Tradition: Mothers and Daughters in Literature,* edited by Cathy N. Davidson and E. M. Broner, 280–290. New York: Frederick Ungar, 1980. (This chapter is about minority group mothers and daughters.)

ROSSI, ALICE. "Transition to Parenthood." *Journal of Marriage and the Family* 30 (1968): 26–39.

ROSSITER, AMY B. "In Private: An Inquiry into the Construction of Women's Experience of Early Motherhood." Unpublished doctoral dissertation. University of Toronto, 1986.

ROTH, PHILIP. *Portnoy's Complaint.* New York: Random House, 1969.

ROTHMAN, BARBARA KATZ. *The Tentative Pregnancy: Prenatal Diagnosis and the Future of Motherhood.* New York: Viking Press, 1986.

ROTUNDO, E. ANTHONY. "Patriarchs and Participants: A Historical Perspective on Fatherhood." In *Beyond Patriarchy: Essays by Men on Pleasure, Power, and Change,* edited by Michael Kaufman, 65–80. Toronto: Oxford University Press, 1987.

ROWBOTHAM, SHEILA. *Woman's Consciousness, Man's World.* Harmondsworth, England: Penguin, 1973.

RUBIN, NANCY. *The Mother Mirror.* New York: G.P. Putnam's Sons, 1984.

RUDDICK, SARA. "Maternal Thinking." *Feminist Studies* 6 (1980): 354–380.

RUDDICK, SARA. "Maternal Thinking." In *Mothering: Essays in Feminist Theory,* edited by Joyce Trebilcot, 213–230. Totowa, N.J.: Rowman and Allanheld, 1983.

RYAN, MARY P. *Womanhood in America: From Colonial Times to the Present.* New York: New Viewpoints, 1975.

SAGE: A Scholarly Journal on Black Women 1 (Fall 1984). Special issue on Blacks' mother-daughter relationships.

SANFORD, LINDA TSCHIRHART, AND DONOVAN, MARY ELLEN. *Women and Self-Esteem: Understanding and Improving the Way We Think and Feel about Ourselves.* New York: Penguin, 1984.

SANUA, VICTOR D. "Sociocultural Factors in Families of Schizophrenics: A Review of the Literature." *Psychiatry: Journal for the Study of Interpersonal Processes* 24 (1961): 246–265.

SARTON, MAY. "The Muse as Medusa." *Collected Poems.* Guilford, Ct.: Norton, 1974.

SCARR, SANDRA. *Mother Care-Other Care.* New York: Basic Books, 1984.

SCHNEIDER, SUSAN WEIDMAN. *Jewish and Female: A Guide and Sourcebook for Today's Jewish Woman.* New York: Simon and Schuster, 1985. (See especially the section called "Mothers and Daughters from a Feminist Perspective," 268–281.)

SCOTT, ANN CRITTENDEN. "The Value of Housework—for Love or Money." *Ms.* 1 (July 1972): 56–59.

SEIDMAN, THEODORE R. (M.D.), AND ALBERT, MARVIN H. *Becoming a Mother.* Greenwich, Ct.: Fawcett Publications, Inc., 1956.

SEXTON, ANNE. *The Book of Folly.* San Jose, Ca.: Gousha, 1972.

SEXTON, ANNE. "The Double Image." *To Bedlam and Part Way Back.* San Jose, Ca.: Gousha, 1960.

SHAPIRO, SUSAN. "Between Love and Ambition: A Daughter and Mother Find Each Other." *Cosmopolitan* (November 1986): 64.

SHEN, JEROME T. Y. "Sexual Abuse of Adolescents." *Postgraduate Medicine* 71 (1982): 213–219.

SHERRARD, JAIN. *Mother-Warrior-Pilgrim.* Kansas City, Mo.: Andrews and McMel, 1980.

SHESSEL, ISABEL. "On Being a Mother: Thoughts and Reflections." Unpublished paper. Ontario Institute for Studies in Education, 1986.

SHREVE, ANITA, AND HELD, JULIUS. *Remaking Motherhood.* New York: Viking Press, 1987.

SIEGEL, RACHEL JOSEFOWITZ. "Antisemitism and Sexism in Stereotypes of Jewish Women." In *A Guide to Dynamics of Feminist Therapy,* edited by Doris Howard, 249–257. New York: Harrington Park Press, 1986.

SIEGEL, RACHEL JOSEFOWITZ. "Old Women as Mother Figures." Presented at Woman-Defined Motherhood: A Conference for Therapists, Goddard College, Plainfield, Vermont, 17 September, 1988.

SIEGEL, RACHEL JOSEFOWITZ. "We Are Not Your Mothers." Presented at Association for Women in Psychology Convention, Denver, 1987.

SIEGEL, RACHEL JOSEFOWITZ. "Women's 'Dependency' in a Male-Centered Value System: Gender-Based Values Regarding Dependency and Independence." *Women and Therapy* 7 (1988): 113–123.

SIGAL, J. "Effects of Paternal Exposure to Prolonged Stress on the Mental Health of the Spouse and Children." *Canadian Psychiatric Association Journal* 21 (1976): 169–172.

SIGOURNEY, LYDIA HOWARD. *Letters to Mothers.* New York: Harper and Bros., 1845.

SLUCKIN, WLADYSLAW; HERBERT, MARIN; AND SLUCKIN, ALICE. *Maternal Bonding.* Oxford: Basil Blackwell, 1983.

SMITH, BETTY. *A Tree Grows in Brooklyn.* New York: Harper & Row, 1947.

SMITH, DOROTHY E., AND GRIFFITH, ALISON I. "Mothering for Schooling." *Perspectives in Social Problems,* in press.

SMITH, LIZ. *The Mother Book: A Compendium of Trivia and Grandeur Concerning Mothers, Motherhood and Maternity.* New York: Crown, 1984.

SMITH-ROSENBERG, CARROLL. "The Female World of Love and Ritual: Relations between Women in Nineteenth-Century America." *Signs: Journal of Women in Culture and Society* 1 (1985): 1–29.

SNOWDEN, GAIL. "Mirror Images." *Radcliffe Quarterly* (December 1984): 29–30.

SONKIN, DANIEL, ED. *Domestic Violence on Trial.* New York: Springer, 1987.

SPENDER, DALE. *Man Made Language.* New York: Routledge, Chapman & Hall, 1985.

SPINNER, STEPHANIE, ED. *Motherlove: Stories by Women about Motherhood.* New York: Dell, 1978.

STACK, CAROL. *All Our Kin: Strategies for Survival in a Black Community.* New York: Harper & Row, 1974.

STARKMAN, E. "Hold the Blessing, Diaries." In *Women and Aging: An Anthology by Women,* edited by Jo Alexander, Debi Berrow, Lisa Domitrovich, Margarita Donnelly, and Cheryl McLean, 134–136. Corvallis, Or.: Calyx, 1986.

STEINEM, GLORIA. "Ruth's Song: Because She Could Not Sing It Herself." In *Outrageous Acts and Everyday Rebellions,* 129–146. New York: Holt, Rinehart, and Winston, 1983.

STIVER, IRENE. "Beyond the Oedipus Complex: Mothers and Daughters." *Work in Progress Paper No. 26*. Wellesley, Ma.: Wellesley College, The Stone Center, 1986.

STIVER, IRENE. "The Meaning of Care: Reframing Treatment Models." *Work in Progress Paper No. 20*. Wellesley, Ma.: Wellesley College, The Stone Center, 1985.

STIVER, IRENE. "The Meanings of 'Dependency' in Female-Male Relationships." *Work in Progress Paper No. 11*. Wellesley, Ma.: Wellesley College, The Stone Center, 1984.

STRAAYER, AMY CHRISTINE. "High Heels." In *Between Mothers and Daughters: Stories Across a Generation*, edited by Susan Koppelman, 279–284. New York: The Feminist Press, 1985.

STRAINCHAMPS, ETHEL. "Our Sexist Language." In *Women in Sexist Society*, edited by Vivian Gornick and Barbara K. Moran, 347–361. New York: Basic Books, 1971.

STRECKERT, WILLIAM. *Their Mothers' Sons*. Philadelphia: Lippincott, 1956.

STROM, KAY, AND STROM, LISA. *Mothers and Daughters Together*. Grand Rapids, Mi.: Baker Book House, 1988.

"Study of Family Interaction Leads to New Understanding of Abusive Parents." *University of Toronto Research Highlights*. Simcoe Hall, University of Toronto, Public and Community Relations, October 1987.

SUNSHINE, ILANA. "Mother-Blaming by Mental Health Professionals: Update." Assisted by Maureen Gans. Toronto: Unpublished paper, 1987.

SURREY, JANET. "Mother-Hatred, Mother-Blaming." Presentation in panel on "Mother-Blaming and Mother-Hate: What Electra Did to Clytemnestra." Presented at Woman-Defined Motherhood: A Conference for Therapists, Goddard College, Plainfield, Vermont, 17 September, 1988.

SURREY, JANET. "Relationship and Empowerment." *Work in Progress Paper No. 30*. Wellesley, Ma.: Wellesley College, The Stone Center, 1987.

SURREY, JANET. Personal communication, 25 January, 1988.

SURREY, JANET. "The 'Self-in-Relation': A Theory of Women's Development." *Work in Progress Paper No. 13*. Wellesley, Ma.: Wellesley College, The Stone Center, 1985.

THOMAS, HELEN. *Child Abuse, Neglect and Deprivation: A Handbook for Ontario Nurses*. Toronto: Registered Nurses Association of Ontario, 1983.

THOMPSON, DANIEL. *Sociology of the Black Experience*. Westport, Ct.: Greenwood Press, 1974.

THOREAU, HENRY DAVID. *Walden* and *Civil Disobedience* (combined edition). Harmondsworth, Middlesex, England: Penguin Books, Ltd., 1985.

THORNE, BARRIE. "Feminist Rethinking of the Family: An Overview." In *Rethinking the Family: Some Feminist Questions*, edited by Barrie Thorne and Marilyn Yalom, 1–24. New York: Longman, 1982.

TREBILCOT, JOYCE, ED. *Mothering: Essays in Feminist Theory*. Totowa, N.Y.: Rowman and Allanheld, 1983.

VALERIO, ANITA. "It's in My Blood, My Face—My Mother's Voice, the Way I Sweat." In *This Bridge Called My Back: Writings by Radical Women of Color*, edited by Cherrie Moraga and Gloria Anzaldua, 41–45. New York: Kitchen Table, 1983.

VINCENT, CLARK. "An Open Letter to the 'Caught Generation'." *Family Coordinator* 21 (April 1972): 148.

WADE-GAYLES, GLORIA. *No Crystal Stair: Visions of Race and Sex in Black Women's Fiction*. New York: The Pilgrim Press, 1984.

WADE-GAYLES, GLORIA. "The Truths of Our Mothers' Lives: Mother-Daughter Relationships in Black Women's Fiction." *SAGE: A Scholarly Journal on Black Women* 1 (Fall 1984): 8–12.

WALKER, ALICE. *In Search of Our Mothers' Gardens: Womanist Prose*. San Diego, Ca.: Harcourt, Brace, Jovanovich, 1983.

WALKER, ALICE. Quoted in "Author Alice Walker Discusses 'The Color Purple'." *The Wall Street Journal*, 19 December 1985: 26.

WALTERS, MARIANNE; CARTER, BETTY; PAPP, PEGGY; AND SILVERSTEIN, OLGA. *The Invisible Web: Gender Patterns in Family Relationships*. New York: Guilford, 1988.

WALTON-ALLEN, NICOLE. "Laypeople's Perceptions of Family Violence: An Examination of Stereotyped Learning." Unpublished M.A. thesis. Ontario Institute for Studies in Education, 1984.

WEISSMAN, MICHAELE. "At Home with Tira." *Ms.* (September 1987): 36–43.

WEITZMAN, LENORE. *The Divorce Revolution: The Unexpected Social and Economic Consequences for Women and Children in America*. New York: The Free Press, 1985.

WESTKOTT, MARCIA. "Mothers and Daughters in the World of the Father." *Frontiers* 3 (1978): 16–21.

WINE, JERI DAWN; MOSES, BARBARA; AND SMYE, MARTI DIANE. "Female Superiority in Sex Difference Competence Comparisons: A Review of the Literature." In *Sex Roles: Origins, Influences, and Implications for Women*, edited by Cannie Stark-Adamec, 148–163. Montreal: Eden Press Women's Publications, 1980.

WINE, JERI DAWN; SMYE, MARTI DIANE; AND MOSES, BARBARA. "Assertiveness: Sex Differences in Relationships Between Self-Report and Behavioral Measures." In *Sex Roles: Origins, Influences, and Implications for Women*, edited by Cannie Stark-Adamec, 176–186. Montreal: Eden Press Women's Publications, 1980.

WOLLSTONECRAFT, MARY. *Vindication of the Rights of Woman*. Harmondsworth, Middlesex, England: Penguin Books Ltd., 1982. (First published 1792).

WOLOFSKY, ZELLA. "Reconciliation of the Mother-Daughter Relationship: A Personal Odyssey." Unpublished paper. Ontario Institute for Studies in Education, 1986.

WOO, MERLE. "Letter to Ma." In *This Bridge Called My Back: Writings by Radical Women of Color*, edited by Cherrie Moraga and Gloria Anzaldua, 140–147. New York: Kitchen Table: 1983.

WOOLSEY, LORETTE K., AND MCBAIN, LAURA-LYNNE. "Issues of Power and Powerlessness in All-Woman Groups." *Women's Studies International Forum* 10 (1987): 579–588.

WYLIE, PHILIP. *Generation of Vipers.* New York: Rinehart and Co., Inc., 1946.

YALOM, MARILYN. *Maternity, Mortality and the Literature of Madness.* University Park, Penn.: Pennsylvania State University Press, 1985.

YEATS, WILLIAM BUTLER. "A Prayer for My Daughter," *Selected Poems and Plays of William Butler Yeats,* edited by M. L. Rosenthal. New York: Collier, 1962.

YEZIERSKA, ANZIA. *Bread Givers.* New York: George Braziller, 1925.

ZAMIR, AVIVA, AND COHEN, CINDY. *Mothers and Daughters: Interviews with Kibbutz Women.* Norwood, Penn.: Norwood Editions, 1986.

♥ Index

About the Author

Paula J. Caplan, Ph.D., is a clinical and research psychologist, Professor of Applied Psychology at the Ontario Institute for Studies in Education and Assistant Professor of Psychiatry and Lecturer in Women's Studies at the University of Toronto, and a frequent lecturer and workshop leader. Her work has been featured widely in both scholarly and popular publications. As an expert on mother–daughter relationships, she has appeared on many national television and radio programs, including "Phil Donahue" and "The Today Show." She is author of *The Myth of Women's Masochism*. Dr. Caplan was born and raised in Springfield, Missouri, and now lives in Toronto with her family.